BENGAL DISTRICT GAZETTEERS
BHAGALPUR

BENGAL DISTRICT GAZETTEERS
BHAGALPUR

BY

J. BYRNE

GYAN

ISBN : 978-81-212-1836-8 (HB)

First Published, 1911

Published, 2018

Published by

Gyan Publishing House
5, Ansari Road
Daryaganj, New Delhi-110002
Phone: 011-47034999, 9811692060
www.gyanbooks.com
E-mail: books@gyanbooks.com

Printed at: G. Print Process, Delhi.

PREFACE.

This volume follows the plan of the various volumes of District Gazetteers compiled by Mr. O'Malley.

I desire to express my sincere acknowledgments for assistance rendered to me by Messrs. Hammond (I.C.S., Collector of Bhagalpur): and Hubback (I.C.S., Assistant Settlement Officer, Bihar): also to Captain Barnardo, I.M.S., Civil Surgeon of Bhagalpur, and to Mr. G. E. Fawcus of the Indian Educational Service, for the revision of Chapters IV and XIII, respectively. Babu Nilmoni Dey, Asisstant Settlement Officer, has also helped me very much.

Kurseong, 1910.

J. BYRNE.

PLAN OF CONTENTS.

TABLE OF CONTENTS.

CHAPTER I.

PHYSICAL ASPECTS.

CHAPTER II.

HISTORY.

CHAPTER III.

THE PEOPLE.

CHAPTER IV.

PUBLIC HEALTH.

CHAPTER V.

AGRICULTURE.

PAGES.

CHAPTER VI.

NATURAL CALAMITIES.

CHAPTER VII.

RENTS, WAGES AND PRICES.

CHAPTER VIII.

PAGES.

OCCUPATIONS, MANUFACTURES AND TRADES.

CHAPTER IX.

MEANS OF COMMUNICATION.

CHAPTER X.

LAND REVENUE ADMINISTRATION.

CHAPTER XI.

GENERAL ADMINISTRATION.

CHAPTER XII.

LOCAL SELF-GOVERNMENT.

CHAPTER XIII.

EDUCATION.

CHAPTER XIV.

PAGES.

GAZETTEER.

GAZETTEER

OF THE

BHAGALPUR DISTRICT.

CHAPTER I.

PHYSICAL ASPECTS.

General description. THIS District, the chief and central district of the Division that bears the same name, is situated between 24° 33′ and 26° 34′ N., and between 86° 19′ and 87° 31′ E. Its length is about 140 miles and its breadth varies from 14 to 45 miles. It extends over 4,226 square miles, and its population was, in 1901, 2,088,953.

Boundaries. It is bounded on the north by the independent State of Nepāl; on the east, north of the Ganges, by the District of Purnea; on the south and east, south of the Ganges, by the Sonthāl Parganās, and on the west by the Districts of Darbhangā and Monghyr. The administrative head-quarters are at Bhāgalpur town, situated on the Ganges, which crosses the district from west to east and divides it into two parts of approximately equal area.

Formation of the district. The District as it at present exists is the outcome of many changes. In 1765 A.D., when the East India Company was invested with the Diwani, Bhāgalpur District was a huge tract in the east of Sarkar Mungir, Subah Behar, lying altogether to the south of the Ganges except the parganā of Chai. The boundaries were rather indeterminate on the south and west. The area of the district was 8,225 square miles at the time of Buchanan-Hamilton's survey (circa 1812 A.D.) including, as it did then, most of the modern districts of Monghyr and the Sonthāl Parganās south of the Ganges. Since then the southern portion has been greatly restricted in area, and the northern portion has been greatly extended.

The first great reduction in the area of the southern portion was made in 1832 when a separate Deputy Collectorship was established at Monghyr, where there had been a Joint-Magistrate since 1812, subordinate to the Magistrate of Bhāgalpur

A great addition, however, soon followed in 1838, when the three extensive *parganās* of Nāredigar, Malhani Gopal, and Nīsankpur Kurha, north of the Ganges, were transferred from Tirhut to this District; the Revenue and Sessions Court jurisdiction of Kabkhand and Uttarkhand being, at the same time, removed from Tirhut to Bhāgalpur, and their Magisterial and Fiscal jurisdiction to Monghyr. This increase of area was more than counterbalanced by the operation of Act XXXVII of 1855, by which the Sonthāl Parganās were erected into a separate Non-Regulation district; and the Damin-i-Koh, *parganās* Tilīagarhī, Jamūnī, Chītaulīya, Kānkjol, Bahādurpur, Akbarnagar, Ināyatnagar, Makrāin, Sūltānganj, Umbar, Sūltānābād, Godda, Umlū-Motīya, Passay, Hendwah, together with *tāppās* Muniāri, Belpattā, and a portion of *parganās* Bhāgalpur and Sathiāri, were detached from Bhāgalpur. In 1864 Bhāgalpur still further lost the character of a south Ganges district which it had possessed in the eighteenth century, by the addition of seven hundred square miles of country on the north of the river. *Parganās* Kabkhand and Uttarkhand were entirely transferred from Monghyr, and *parganās* Dhaphar and Nāthpur from Purnea. Several petty changes of jurisdiction have since taken place, such as the transfer of Kharakpur to Monghyr in 1874, but these have not affected the District as a whole. The Revenue, Magisterial, and Sessional jurisdictions of Bhāgalpur are now conterminous.

GENERAL ASPECT OF THE DISTRICT. The District is divided into two nearly equal portions by the river Ganges. The northern division forms an eastward continuation of the great alluvial plain of Tirhut as far as the limit of the Kosī floods, where the physical characteristics of the country assume the aspects of the sandy flats of Purnea. A large part is subject to annual inundation by many rivers, whose sources lie in the southern ranges of the Himālayas, as well as by the overflow of the Ganges over its northern bank. These rivers are inter-connected by numerous channels of considerable depth and width, called *dhārs*, so that, except in years of unusually scanty rainfall, the region is well supplied with the means of irrigation. There is very little high land in this part of Bhāgalpur, the principal elevated tracts being narrow ridges of land on the banks of the larger rivers from which the land slopes gradually inwards, often meeting a similar incline from some other river; and marshes or chains of marshes, frequently of great extent, are formed in the interlying plains. There is also a run of high land, forming a very marked feature of the scenery, in the south-east corner of the Súpūl subdivision. It is about twenty miles long, varying in breadth from one to six miles, and is in places covered with thick *sāl* forest. The two north-eastern *parganās* which, at the beginning of this century, constituted one of the most fertile portions of the Sub-Tarāi rice tract, and supported the great grain mart of Nāthpur have lost a considerable portion of their cultivable area in consequence of changes in the course of the Kosī river. Similar devastation has taken place along the whole western bank of this river down to its confluence with the Ganges and large tracts of once fertile land have been laid under a deep layer of sand, which destroys the productive power of the soil. At the same time, the fear of further movements of the river has driven back cultivation, and its place has been taken by a grass jungle, which, where not too high, affords pasturage to numerous herds of cattle during the hot months before the rains begin. At the present time, it seems that the Kosī is gradually working its way back eastwards again.

The southern division of the District is bounded along its northern face by the river Ganges, and has a generally level surface, except near the southern frontier. It is traversed by several streams, having their sources in the hills of the Santāl Parganās, the most important of which is the Chāndan. This river enters the District a broad and impetuous torrent, but as it approaches the low land, it spreads over the country in about fifteen different channels, only three of which ever reach the Ganges. One of these streams retains the name of Chāndan; but it is a mere water-course which, flowing through a hard soil of nodular limestone, pours its waters into the Ganges at Champanagar, two miles west of the town of Bhāgalpur. A broad and well-raised belt of limestone on which the town of Bhāgalpur is situated, extends along the southern bank of the Ganges, and forms a natural and effectual barrier against incursions of the river. This remarkable formation, about two miles broad, runs almost continuously beside the river from near Monghyr to Colgong, a distance of sixty miles; it is densely wooded with mangoes, jacks, fan-leaf palms, and date-trees. On leaving the belt of woodland, the country is found to be very low and almost treeless to the south. Fine rice-lands exist south of Sultanganj, Bhāgalpur, Sabour and Ghogha. South from the line between Sultanganj and Nathnagar the country is subject to inundations from both the Chāndan and the Ganges, and is not much cultivated, except in the winter and spring when it yields rich crops of wheat and pulses. Still further south, the country rises a few feet, and rice is extensively cultivated. Wheat, sugar-cane, poppy, mustard, *arhar*, and garden products are also seen, bespeaking the richness of the soil, which is here of a light-greyish colour. Mango-groves and palm-trees, acacias, banian and *pīpal* trees are abundant; and whenever a small stream affords facilities, the lands in its immediate vicinity are watered from it.

About thirty miles south of the town of Bhāgalpur, the country begins to wear a different aspect, as the land rises by an easy ascent, and the hilly tract commences. The soil being less deep than to the northward, and lying upon rocks of primitive formation, the water is nearer the surface and the trees attain a growth exceeding anything that is ever found on the deep alluvial plains of the Ganges. The *mahuā* (Bassia latifolia) now becomes common, but palms almost cease to be seen. The mango-trees are no longer found in planted groves, but are scattered about in small groups; the cotton-tree attains a great size, measuring sixty or seventy feet in circumference, and patches of *dhāk* jungle appear. The better kinds of upland yield Indian-corn in the rains and wheat or mustard seed in the cold weather; the poorer are sown with millet (*kūrthī*) in the autumn, whilst there is still sufficient moisture in the soil. The sides of the low rolling hills are terraced for the cultivation of rice, which is irrigated by means of a careful system of reservoirs and embankments. A full account of the systems of irrigation in vogue in the south of the district is given in Chapter V*—Agriculture, further on.

River System.

THE RIVER SYSTEM of Bhāgalpur District consists of a reach of the Ganges about sixty miles in length, with numerous Himālayan affluents on the north bank; and on the south a few hill-streams, which, during the greater part of the year, are sandy water-courses, but in the rainy season become rivers of considerable size, unnavigable, however, from their rapidity and the uncertainty of their floods. The northern rivers have mostly a direction from north to south, with a slight inclination eastwards. The larger of these rise amongst the Nepāl foot hills and fall, after a more or less tortuous course, into the Ghagrī, which itself joins the Kosī, the great river that is the natural boundary between this district and Purnea, about six miles from its confluence with the Ganges. The principal of these northern rivers are, (1) the Tiljūgā, (2) the Bātī, (3) the Dhimrā, (4) the Talabā, (5) the Parwān, (6) the Dhúsan, (7) the Chalaunī, (8) the Loran, (9) the Katnā, (10) the Dāūs, and (11) the Ghagrī. The Chāndan alone amongst the southern streams is deserving of notice. The following is a brief account of each of the above rivers, their courses and the more remarkable of the drainage channels, or *dhārs* that fall into them.

---

* See page 78 below.

The GANGES first touches Bhāgalpur District at Tūlsīpur, and for about ten miles forms the boundary between *parganās* Jahāngīrā in Bhāgalpur and Pharkiyā in Monghyr; it then regularly enters the District opposite the village of Sultānganj, where a great mass of granite rises out of its bed. Thence the vast river flows with two great bends, the first northward round the town of Bhāgalpur, and the second southward to Colgong, where it meets a low range of hills, by which its course is again diverted in an almost northerly direction for eight miles until it reaches Patharghāt. At that point it receives the united waters of the Kosī and all the northern rivers of the District. The Ganges throughout this part of its course is navigable during the whole year for the largest native boats and for river steamers of very considerable tonnage. The average width of its bed is three miles, but during the hot weather the waterway has a width of only half a mile, the rest being a dazzling plain of white sand. During the rainy season the whole of the deep bed is filled, and a margin of from five to ten miles on the northern bank and from one to two miles on some parts of the southern bank are inundated. Ganges.

The TILJUGA rises in the hills of the Sub-Tarāi of Nepāl, and enters Bhāgalpur at the most northern point of *parganā* Nāredigar; after which it forms the western boundary between Bhāgalpur and Darbhanga down to the south-west corner of *parganā* Malhani Gopāl, from which it passes into *parganā* Kabkhand as far as the village of Tilkeswar. Here it bends south-east across the great Monghyr *parganā* of Pharkiyā, and again entering Bhāgalpur near Balhar, crosses *parganā* Chhāī in a due easterly direction and falls into the Kosī a little to the south-west of Saurā Gadi. At Rawāl in *parganā* Nāredigar, fifteen miles from Nepāl, it sends off a number of channels or *dhārs*, which irrigate and drain the greater part of this *parganā* and of the north of Malhanī Gopāl. It receives its first affluent, the Bālan, from Tirhut at Rasiārī, where it also formerly bifurcated, the two branches uniting again four miles south-east of Bhajā. The western branch was then the larger of the two, but of late years it has gradually silted up, and is now only navigable in the rains for boats of five hundred *maunds* up to Bagtā, beyond which it is only a shallow drainage channel and soon completely disappears. Near Tilkeswar the Dhimrā falls into the Tiljūgā, bringing a great quantity of water. Before it re-enters Bhāgalpur from Pharkiyā, it receives through the Katnā the united waters of the Talabā, Parwān, Dhūsan and Loran. The Tiljūgā is navigable for boats of two thousand *maunds* or seventy tons burthen up Tiljūgā.

to Tilkeswar, and beyond that for boats of a quarter of that tonnage up to Dīghīā within ten miles of the Nepāl frontier. This river forms the main water communication of the north-west of the District. Mr. Wickes reported in 1874 that, as a rule, a number of embankments are annually constructed across the Tiljūgā for irrigation purposes from Rasiārī upwards, and that they greatly interfere with the value of the river as a navigable channel; for although the first heavy flood breaches them, it only partially removes them, and boats, particularly those travelling up stream, have great difficulty in passing. In some cases the flood bursts through the embankment near either bank leaving an island in the middle of the stream with a narrow dangerous passage on each side of it; in other places the centre of the embankment gives way and a narrow channel is formed in the middle of the stream with the ends of the broken *bandh* projecting into the river like a spur on each side causing an almost impossible rapid; and, again, in a few instances, the whole of the upper portion of the *bandh* is carried away, leaving the foundation which bars the river as a sunken weir right across its whole width.

The BATI was described by the Revenue Surveyor* as being nothing more than an arm of the Tiljūgā, and frequently called by its name. He says it formerly separated from the parent stream at the village of Belā on the north-western boundary; but this channel has long since been dried up, and, in many places, can scarcely be discerned, so that it could never have been very deep. The river, however, seems to have had a separate source in the north of *parganā* Nāredigar, the old bed referred to being only one of those cross channels, which join most of the rivers of this part of the country, at various points in their course. It falls into the Tiljūgā at Gopālpur by the Ladūa *khāl*.

The DHIMRA is an insignificant stream when it enters this District, rapid during the rains, but in the hot weather in many places dry, the intermediate patches of water being stagnant. It rises in Nepāl, and for the first ten miles of its course in Bhāgalpur divides the *parganās* of Dhaphar and Nāredigar. After flowing south through the latter *parganā* and then through Malhani Gopāl and Uttarkhand, it empties itself into the Tiljūgā at Tilkeswar. It is very liable to freshets from the hills, and most of the channel is protected by embankments, which along its lower reaches have been allowed of recent years to fall into decay through the neglect and apathy of the riparian landowners. For the last twelve miles of its course, it has a remarkably wide

* Report published in 1869.

bed, through the middle of which a meagre stream flows when there is no flood.

The TALABA seems to have formerly occupied a much more important place in the river system of the District than it now does. Its old bed, which is still clearly discernible from bank to bank, measures from fifteen to twenty chains across. Judging by the direction of its larger *dhārs* (branches), it is probable that it once received the waters now carried by the lower Tiljūgā. Its upper course quickly dries up after the cessation of the rains and the bed is annually cultivated, the land producing rich crops with very little tillage. It forms the western boundary of *parganā* Nīsankpur Kūrhā. After its union with the Parwân and Loran it loses its name to form, with them, the Katnā. Talaba.

The PARWAN AND DHUSAN RIVERS both take their rise in the south-eastern corner of *parganā* Nāredigar, the former from a *dhār* of the old Talabâ river, and the latter from a spring near the village of Belārhatā. They pursue different courses about two and a half or three miles apart, until their waters mingle at Singeswarsthān, where there is a temple of Siva Mahādeo. Their point of confluence is considered a place of much sanctity and several thousands of devout Hindus resort to the shrine in February to pay their devotions, bringing with them small quantities of Ganges water, which they throw over the image of the god. At this place the Dhūsan loses its own name; and the mingled waters, under the name of the Parwān, flow on towards the south. This river, after a tortuous course of nearly thirty miles, forms the Sahsāl swamp, the outlet from which under the name of the Katnā (an appellation which indicates an artificial origin) flows into *parganā* Pharkiyā, a mile and a quarter below the point where that *parganā* meets *parganās* Chhāī and Nisankpur Kūrhā. The Parwān is alone navigable. Parwan. Dhusan.

The CHALAUNI rises from a marsh in *parganā* Harāwat, enters *parganā* Nāredigar at the village of Thalla Garhī, and, flowing close to the common boundary of both *parganās* for five miles, suddenly swerves off to the right, and then runs very tortuously towards the south, throwing out many channels, and finally falling into the Loran at the village of Panduā. It is principally used for irrigation. A few small boats ply on it for two or three months in the year, but they are only fishing and passenger skiffs. Chalauni.

The LORAN rises in a swamp on the eastern boundary of *parganā* Nīsankpur Kūrhā, near the Purnea boundary and, after a course of twelve miles, is joined by the Chalaunī. It then Loran.

runs to the southern limit of the *parganā*, touches on the Sahsāl swamp, and mingling with the Parwān, forms the Katnā.

Katnā. The KATNA, as already mentioned, is formed by the united waters of the Talabā, Parwān, and Loran. It is a considerable river, bounding the Chhāī *parganā* for about four miles on its north-eastern extremity, and then running into *parganā* Pharkiyā of Monghyr. It joins the Tiljūgā eight miles from the western frontier of Bhāgalpur; and the two streams combine to form the great river Ghagrī. The Katnā is navigable for boats of four hundred *maunds* (or fourteen and a half tons) throughout its whole course, which is only about twelve miles.

Dāūs. The DAUS is described in the following passage by the Revenue Surveyor, Mr. Pemberton:—"Tradition states that it rises in the Murang of Nepāl, and runs parallel with the Bir *bándh*, or embankment, of *parganā* Dhaphar into Haráwat; but I must confess when I surveyed *parganā* Dhaphar I could find no trace of a river at the place described. I found a small dry channel close to the *bándh*, but this appeared to have been formed by clay having been dug out at different times to repair it. My own opinion is that the Dáús is nothing more than a small arm of the Herun or Kúsí: it is impossible to say which, as these rivers have been united since 1847; and that it is fed by *dhárs* from them. It enters *parganá* Dhaphar from Nisankpur Kúrhá, and runs in a very narrow channel near its eastern boundary for about seven miles, when it spreads out into a swamp varying from twenty to sixty or sixty-five chains wide, and maintains this width until it empties itself into the Ghagrí river. A great part of the swamp dries up during the cold and hot weather, and is cultivated with indigo, yielding an exceedingly fine crop; but the produce cannot at all times be depended on, as the river is subject to inundations from the Kosí. When these occur, the planters are severe sufferers." The tradition concerning the source of this river is, however, supported by the evidence of Dr. Buchanan-Hamilton, who describes the Bir Bándh as commencing from the source of the Dáús. The indigo cultivation has disappeared with the ruin of the old factories, and rice is now largely grown in its place.

Ghagri. The GHAGRI is usually described as consisting only of the lower reaches of the Tiljúgá; but as the new name is assumed after the influx of the Katná, which brings with it the drainage of half of the northern portion of the District, it seems more fit to regard it as a distinct river. It enters this District from *parganá* Pharkiyā, and passes due east through Chhái to join the Kosī.

The CHANDAN is the largest of the hill streams in the south of the District. It rises near Deogarh, in the Santál Párganás, and is fed by numerous minor streams. It passes under the sub-divisional head-quarters of Bánká, and falls into the Ganges by several mouths. A more detailed description* of this river is given under the heading "Embankments," in connection with the works carried out by the neighbouring landholders to restrain its floods, which sometimes inundate the country for miles round, and cause great injury to the autumn crops. Chāndan

The KOSI, although touching Bhāgalpur, is the great river of Purnea, and a full description of it will be found in the Gazetteer of that District. Kosi.

CHANGES IN THE RIVER COURSES.—Important changes have taken place in the main course of the Ganges immediately north of the Civil Station. About 1864 the stream lay directly below the town of Bhāgalpur, and steamers anchored close under the houses of the residents. During the few years previous to that date, the Ganges ran equally near to the northern bank formed by *parganā* Chhái. At the presentday it flows midway between those two courses, being separated from either bank by great island-like accretions of sandy alluvium, sometimes many square miles in extent. In Dr. Buchanan-Hamilton's time (1807-13), as shown by his map, the bed of the river had worked its way up to the most northern point which it has reached within the past century. Major Rennell's map shows it in 1781 as passing a little south of Dr. Buchanan-Hamilton's course. In 1850 Major Sherwell represents it as washing the southern limestone bank, to which it seems for many years after to have, more or less, clung, except for a short period about 1860. The old southern bed, locally known as the Jamunia, is still a large channel in the rains.

The changes in the upper waters of the Kosī, where that river belongs to Bhāgalpur District, are even more remarkable. The steady westerly movement, which seems to have been going on for hundreds of years, is here conspicuous, and has been very strongly marked during the last half century. The large commercial centre of Nāthpur, which in 1850 lay some miles to the west of the river, has now not only been swept away, but its site has been left many miles to the eastward. This river is now gradually going back eastwards.

The changes in the minor rivers are not so easy to follow; but there has apparently been a great diversion of the north-western drainage from the Talabá to the Tiljūgā.

THE BANKS of the rivers vary in abruptness, very much in proportion to the firmness or friability of the soil through which River channels.

* See pages 88, 106 below.

they flow. The southern bank of the Ganges is mostly formed of a hard red soil rich in nodular limestone, and, except where sandy accretions have been built out from it, abrupt. On the opposite side, a large part of the northern bank declines gently. In places where the current of the river has come into direct contact with the new land, and partly broken it away, the fracture is almost perpendicular, and in the dry weather when the river is low, the bank rises sheer from the water like a wall twenty or thirty feet high. The banks of the Dhimra are in places abrupt, but for the most part slope with a long incline and are therefore liable to inundation. The banks of the Ghúgrí and Tiljūgā are also usually sloping, and are cultivated in the cold weather down to the water's edge.

LAKES AND MARSHES.—There is no body of water in Bhāgalpur of sufficient size or depth to be called a lake. Shallow marshes are numerous, occurring principally in the Madhipura subdivision on either side of the river Loran. These are excellent shooting grounds in the cold season. They also stretch across west and east, in a chain, from the present source of the Talabá to the west bank of the Daleswarí. Considerable tracts of land on the south of the Ganges are inundated every year, but as they dry up and are cultivated in the cold weather, they cannot be called marshes. Indeed, they form one of the most fertile parts of the District, the cold weather crops being remarkably luxuriant.

Forests—Botany. There is no tract of woodland in Bhāgalpur District which deserves the name of a forest, but there is much low jungle interspersed with trees of large size in the south of *parganās* Bhāgalpur and Dánrá Sakhwārā, and in *parganās* Nisankpur Kúrhá and Haráwat, north of the Ganges. Along the southern hills there are two distinct tracts, one stretching from near the Umarpur Police Station to the Belhár outpost of Katúriyá, including *tappá* Chāndan. The second begins near Chāndan, and runs by Jáipur along the whole Santāl Parganās boundary to Lakshmípur. The former covers an area of above forty square miles and the latter about thirty. The northern forest tracts are *táluk* Thála Gariyá, in *parganā* Nāredigar, with an area of about 1,700 acres; Bhagwánpur, with an area of 3,400 acres; Srípur, with an area of 2,500 acres; Visnupur, with an area of 1,500 acres; Garhajhar, Káhá, Maurá, Gidá and Parsá, with an area of 5,600 acres; Chariyá, with an area of 1,150 acres, in *parganā* Nisankpur Kúrhá; and *táluk* Chalauni, with an area of 1,700 acres in *parganā* Haráwat.

The following are the trees most frequently met with in these woods, with some of the products derived from them. The first place must be given to the (1) *sál* or *sakuá* (Shorea robusta), which is very plentiful in the southern hills and in the neighbourhood of the Nepál frontier. Few large trees are now to be seen, as they are regularly cut down when the trunks have grown to a height of fifteen feet, to be used to support the roofs of huts. If larger, they are considered unwieldy, as the art of sawing is not practised by the hill-men. The extraction of the resin, which is always followed by the death of the tree, prevents its growing to a large size; but some immense specimens of *sáls* are still to be met with in the north of the district. (2). The *abnús*, or Indian ebony-tree (Diospyros melanoxylon) is a valuable tree, its black heart-wood being largely used by cabinet and ornamental furniture makers. The outer wood is white and soft, and is usually eaten away by insects. The ripe fruit is used in curries and is very astringent in flavour.

The terminalias are very important trees in Bhāgalpur. The (3) *ásan* (T. tomentosa) is the principal of them, and it is on the leaves of this tree that the *tasar* silk-worm (Antheræa paphia) is fed. This valuable insect is reared now only on *ásan* trees in the jungle of thana Katauria. With a view, perhaps, to confining the employment to themselves, the rearers have established certain rules of purity which they allege are absolutely necessary, and any infringement of which would totally destroy the success of their operations. Women, who would seem to be best fitted for such work, are entirely excluded, even their wives not being permitted to approach the workers. The low castes are excluded, as their appetites are defiled by the gross impurity of animal food. The workers eat sparingly, once a day, of rice cleaned without boiling (*aluá dhán*) and seasoned only with vegetables. They are not permitted to employ the washerman or the barber. The best cocoons are produced in the forests, whence they are brought by the wandering tribes. From these cocoons three successive broods are obtained, but those reared from the wild cocoons, *dhaba*, are said to be the best; the others, *sarihán*, *járhan*, and *langa*, gradually degenerate. The cocoons for breeding are placed in a large flat basket. When the moths cut their way out, they immediately pair. In from fifteen to twenty hours afterwards, the males die, and are thrown away, and from twenty to twenty-five impregnated females are placed in a cylindrical basket with a narrow mouth, which is covered with leaves. Some leaves are also laid on the bottom of the basket. On the latter leaves, in the course of the day, the females deposit their eggs about 150 to 350 a-piece, and are then thrown away. The eggs are placed in small baskets made of the leaves of the *bel* tree. On the ninth day the eggs are hatched; and the baskets on which they are lying are put upon a tree, over the leaves of which the young insects immediately spread. When they have consumed all the leaves of one tree, they are removed to other trees, and in thirty-six days from the time of their being hatched begin to spin. In fifteen days this operation is completed, and the cocoons are collected. The yield of a cocoon, that is, the tissue wound from it, gives usually about 10·2 grains troy of silk. From 700 to 1,000 cocoons are required for the production of a piece of silk from four to five yards long, and 1¼ yard wide, which sells at from eight to ten rupees. The only operation attended with any trouble is the removing the worms from one tree to another. The worms, however, must be watched, as crows and other birds, and hornets are apt to destroy them. Cocoons intended for sale are killed by being put in boiling water, and then dried in the sun. All the large branches of the *âsan* tree are lopped near the stem, and young shoots, which produce large succulent leaves, are permitted to grow. The worms are only applied to the same tree once in two years, a whole year's rest being necessary before new branches begin to appear. The old die after being denuded of their leaves. The local supply of cocoons is insufficient to meet the local demand, and cocoons are largely imported from Gaya (Nawada subdivision), the Sonthal Parganas, Birbhum and Hazaribagh (Giridih subdivision). None come from Malda or Murshidabad.

Some experiments made formerly in Bombay led to the belief that the *tasar* worm might be domesticated, but it seemed doubtful whether this operation would not be more expensive than in the case of the common silk-worm (Bombayx mori). In India there are special difficulties. The plaster or cement exuded by the worm with the filaments is peculiarly tenacious, and cannot be dissolved in water of a lower temperature than 200° Fahr.—a heat that can be kept up in the reeling basins only by the use of steam. The silk is also said to be difficult to dye in the finer shades of colour. Another obstacle is presented by an inherent defect in the filaments themselves. The thread of the *tasar* silk-worm is spun from a double spinnaret, and the filaments do not lie parallel, although close side by side; they are spirals, touching each other only at the exterior points of their curves, and united by the natural gum in, and with which, they are exuded. It is on its spiral texture that the well-known elasticity of the silk depends. In reeling the silk, it is necessary that the spirals should be worked well into each other, so as to form an even round thread; but it is doubtful whether the filaments can be brought to bear the amount of *croissure* necessary to produce the round thread, and till this can be effected, it will be impossible to provide an article of export which will be acceptable in the European market. Such being the conditions of successful manufacture, there does not appear to be any prospect of reviving the reeling of *tasar* silk as a village industry. If an effective system of reeling be devised, it can only be carried out under skilled supervision in large filatures. A full account of the local silk-weaving industry is given in Chapter VIII below.*

(4) The *kawá* (Terminalia Arjuna) is an immense tree, and is held sacred by the hill people. The kernels of the fruit of the (5) *buhirá* (T. belerica) are eaten by the natives, and are said to taste like filberts. The tree is a large one yielding a white wood, durable though soft. Its gum, which much resembles gum Arabic, is abundant, and dissolves readily in water. (6) The *badám* (T. Catappa) is also a timber tree. (7) The *hará* (T. chebula) produces the myrobalams of trade. The tender leaves are punctured by an insect in order to deposit its eggs. The wound enlarges through the extravasation of sap, into a hollow gall, from which good ink is derived. It also yields to the cotton-dyeing caste of Chhipis a most durable yellow. (8) The *kadam* (Nauclea cadamba) is a large tree with thick foliage. (9) The *amaltas* (Cassia fistula) is remarkable for its pendant racemes of bright yellow flowers. (10) The *mahuá* is a most useful tree. A description of it is given lower down under the heading "Fruit Trees." (11) *Bijasár*, the *paisar* of the women and the *pitsál* of Bengal, is a large timber-tree. It yields a red juice, which hardens in the air into a dark red, very brittle, gummy resin, and has a strong astringent taste. (12) The *sitsál* (Dalbergia latifolia) is not common, and its wood—black, with branching light-coloured veins—is not much used. (13) The *sissú* (D. sissoo) yields to boat-builders their crooked timbers and knees. It and the *sitsál* grow to a large size. (14) The *palás* (Butea frondosa) grows to a large size in Bhāgalpur, and yields a ruby-coloured astringent gum. There are several species of Acacia. The best known are—(15) A. Arabica (*bábal*); (16) A. farnesiana; (17) A. sirissa (*sirish*) and (18) A. tomentosa (*sáin bábál*). (19) Entada pursœtha (*gilla*), which, like the Acacias, was formerly included in the genus Mimosa, is remarkable for the size of its nuts, and the hardness of the interior albumen, which is used by washermen for crimping linen. From (20) Acacia catechu is obtained the native drug called *kath*, which is eaten along with *pán*. It is prepared either from the chopped up heart-wood of the tree, or from the exuded gum yielded by cutting through the

* Page 124-126.

bark. All acacias, particularly the two first-mentioned and a related species (21) Albizzia stipulata (*simlaki*), produce gum, having much of the appearance and qualities of gum Arabic. (22) The *sálái* (Boswellia thurifera) yields frankincense, and is a large conspicuous tree. The resin, although plentiful, is not much collected. (23) The *píyár* (Buchanania latifolia) is a timber tree, the kernels of whose fruit take the place of almonds amongst natives. (24) The *karanji* (Sterculia urens) is remarkable for its white bark and usually leafless condition. (25) The *paprá* (Gardenia latifolia) is a small but very ornamental tree. (26) The *kachnár* (Bauhinia variegata) is a tall, elegant tree, little used but for firewood. (27) The *tentul* (Tamarindus Indicus) is not a common tree, but is met with occasionally of large size. (28) The *ijar* (Barringtonia acutangula) is the most common tree in the northern marshes. (29) The *kasmar* or *kasambar* (Schleichera trijuga) is a short, middling-sized tree, the pulpy subacid aril of whose fruit is edible. (30) The *katáil* and *ghúnt* (Zizyphus œnoplia and Z. xylopyra) are common shrubs in the jungle.

Fruit trees.

The Fruit trees indigenous to Bhāgalpur District are the following :—(1) The mango or *ám* (Mangifera Indica) is common all over the District, especially to the north of the Ganges. (2) The *mahuá* (Bassia latifolia), the most extensively grown tree in the southern hills. The ripe kernels are eaten like almonds, but are not wholesome. They also yield an oil, four pounds of kernel producing one pound of oil. After being dried in the sun for some days, they are broken in a mortar, and then put in a common oil mill and pressed. In the cold season the oil is thick, but in hot weather it becomes liquid. In most parts it is only used for lighting purposes, being unfit for food on account of its bitter, disagreeable flavour. The poor in the hill tracts, however, use it in cookery, and remove the bitter taste by boiling it in water. The most important produce of the tree is the flower, which expands in the evening and falls the following morning. It is succulent, resembles a round berry and is full of a thick sweet juice, which would not be disagreeable but for a strong narcotic smell. When collected the flowers are spread on mats, or on a piece of clear ground, and dried in the sun and are then fit for sale. A single tree yields from 10 to 60 lbs. of dried flowers; but it is alleged that were care taken to keep off deer and monkeys, double that quantity might be procured. In the eighteenth century the flowers sold on the tree for from 6 to 3 *maunds* ($4\frac{1}{2}$ to $2\frac{1}{4}$ cwt.) to the rupee (then worth about 2*s*.); and in the year 1810-11 at Bánká, close to the forests, according to Dr. Buchanan-Hamilton, only one and a quarter *maunds* ($102\frac{2}{3}$ lbs.) was obtained for this money. The present price varies from sixty to eighty pounds for the rupee. In the southern parts of the District, the poor are compelled to derive from this flower a portion of their ordinary nourishment, amounting, according to Dr. Buchanan-Hamilton's estimate, to five-twelfths of their entire food during five months of the year. *Mahuá* flowers are, however, most used for the distillation of country spirit. The process is a very simple one. The flowers, with from an equal to a double quantity of water, are put in large earthen vessels with narrow mouths and left to ferment. This is effected in from four to eight days, according to the heat of the weather. The whole fermented mass, flowers and water, is then put into a still, and the spirit is drawn slowly off. It is never rectified, and after distillation is always very much diluted with water, and consequently will not keep above fifteen days. If rectified, or even if kept undiluted, it could be preserved longer, but in that case customers would not have enough for their money. The still is a large earthen jar, inclining a little to one side, placed over a rude fire-place, confined by two walls of earth. The head of the still is a small earthen pot inverted on the mouth of the larger and smeared with clay. Three tubes of hollow bamboo pass from the head to an equal number of narrow-mouthed, unglazed earthen jars that serve as receptacles, and are placed in a shallow trough containing water.

(3) The jack fruit or *kánthál* (Artocarpus integrifolia) is also very common. (4) The plantain or *kelá* (Musa sapientum), found everywhere, is of an inferior description. (5) The *khajur* or date palm, and the *tál* tree (Borassus flabelliformis), are both common throughout the District, being cultivated for the intoxicating fermented juice, called *tári*, obtained from them. The *khajur* is fit for tapping when ten years old, and lives about twenty years more, during which time a notch is yearly made in the stem just under the new leaves that shoot from its summit, and on opposite sides of the stem in alternate years. The cut is triangular, and at its lower corner a leaf is placed to collect into a pot the juice that exudes. The season commences about the beginning of October, and lasts until the end of April. The cut bleeds for from two to seven days, and is kept open by means of scraping the surface or removing a very thin slice from it. The tree is allowed an equal number of days' rest before a new incision is made. The cuts are made in the afternoon, and the juice exuding during the night is collected in the morning, the yield being about four pounds weight from each tree. Its taste when fresh is sweet, with somewhat the flavour of the water contained in a young cocoa-nut,

but slightly bitter and astringent. Owing to the coolness of the season it does not readily ferment. It is, therefore, collected in large earthen jars, which have been first filled up to a sixteenth of their capacity with old fermented liquor, and exposed to the sun for about three hours when the fermentation is complete. The spirit is sold for about a halfpenny a quart; and two quarts, or one penny's worth, will produce intoxication. At the season when the supply of date-liquor begins to fail, the *tál* trees commence to yield a more abundant, stronger, and cheaper drink, which, however, lasts for a much shorter time. About the end of March the *tál* begins to blossom, and throws out numerous flowering stems or spadices. Towards the close of April the ends of these are cut three times a day, a thin slice being removed at each cutting, and jars are suspended under them to catch the juice. New spadices shoot in succession for two months and continue to yield till the end of June. In Bhāgalpur only the male flowers are cut, the female ones being left to mature their fruit. The juice ferments without being exposed to the sun and without the addition of old juice, a circumstance due probably to its being collected in the hot weather. During the height of the season it sells for half the price of date-spirit, that is, for a farthing a quart; and as it is also nearly twice as strong, it forms one of the cheapest intoxicating liquors in the world. Some trees bleed throughout the rainy season, and their juice is used instead of yeast for making bread. (7) The tamarind, *imlí* or *tentúl* (Tamarindus Indica), thrives in Bhāgalpur, and the fruit is exported. (8) The plums, *bair* and *kúl* (Zizyphus jujuba and Z. vulgaris), are very common fruits. Three kinds are enumerated by natives, the *narkúli*, the *pátnái*, and the *desí*; the last is wild; the first, which is the best, tastes like the English pear, and the *pátnái* like half-ripe plums. They all ripen between June and August. (9) The *jám* or *jámun* (Eugenia jambolana); (10) the *ban jám* (E. fruticosa); (11) the *jámrúl* (E. alba); and (12) the *guláb jám* (E. jambos), are all eaten, the best tasting like half-ripe plums, and the wild sorts being little better than sloes. They ripen between June and August. (13) The *tipárí* or gooseberry of Europeans and *phuktá* of natives (Sida Asiatica), is a palatable fruit. (14) The *amrá* (Spondias mangifera) is a large plum-like fruit, rather wanting in flavour, which ripens in the cold weather. (15) The *kámrangá* (Averrhoa carambola) is found under two varieties—one producing a sweet, the other a sour, fruit; both blossom during the rainy season, the fruit ripening during December and January. (16) The custard apple or *átá* (Anona squamosa). (17) The bull's heart or *nóná átá* (Anona reticulata). (18) The *amaltás* or *aurá*, the *ámluki* of Bengal

(Emblica officinalis). (19) The guava or *unjir* (Psidium pyriferum). (20) The pumelo or *batāvī nebu* (Citrus decumana). (21) The lime or *nebu* (Citrus limomum); there are several varieties of this fruit. (22) The *papītā* (Carica payaya). (23) The *gāb* (Diospyros embryopteris). (24) The fig or *dumār* (Ficus carica). (25) The pomegranate or *anār* (Punica granatum). (26) The grape (Vitis vinifera); a green variety has been brought to the district from Lahore; it thrives well, but the fruit is small. (27) The *wāmpī* (Cookia punctata), a rare fruit—the climate is not favourable to it. (28) The *sapotā* (Achras sapota), there are some fine trees with excellent fruit in this district. (29) The *karandā* (Carissa carandas), plentiful in all gardens. (30) The *bijātī* (Ehretia serrata), a native of Bhutān, a few are found in the north of the district, fruit good. (31) The *khīrnī* (Mimusops kanki), with a rather large oval berry, a handsome tree. (32) The *māinā* (Vangueria spinosa), with a yellow succulent fruit of the size of a cherry, not much eaten. (33) The *pīr-ālu* (Posoqueria uliginosa), a small thorny tree yielding an edible berry. (34) *Jalpāi* (Elæocarpus serratus), said to resemble olives in taste; used in curries. (35) The *paniyāla* (Flacourtia cataphracta), a favourite fruit. (36) The *bainchī* (Flacourtia sepida), little eaten in this district. (37) The *badām* (Amygdalus communis); many trees of this excellent nut are met with in the district, grown from imported seed.

The north of the district is purely alluvial. The deposits which cover the immense alluvial plain of the Ganges and the Brahmaputra and their tributaries belong in part to an older alluvial formation which is usually composed of massive argillaceous beds of a rather pale, reddish-brown hue, often weathering yellowish, disseminated throughout which occur *kankar* and pisolitic ferruginous concretions. Four principal formations occur in the district. Alluvium, new and old; the Rājmahāl Trappean formation; the Damuda series, the coal measures of India; and the Gneissic series. The last-named rocks occupy a considerable area in the south of the district, in the Chāndan, Kataurīa, and Dānrā Sakhwārā *parganās*, where they are continuous with those forming the plateau of Hazāribāgh, and thus indeed with the immense stretch of similar rocks along the whole east side of the peninsula down to Mysore. The classification of these highly metamorphic fundamental rocks is everywhere one of the most difficult problems in geology; and as yet, in India, attention has been chiefly turned to other formations of more immediate interest or importance. Even within the small area under notice, great variety is to be found in these rocks, from the massive homogeneous granitoid and GEOLOGICAL FORMATION.

porphyritic gneiss, weathering into great domes with concentric structure, of which Mandar Hill is a fine example, through many varieties of well foliated gneisses, quartzose, micaceous, and hornblendic, to fine mica schists and trappoid hornblende rock. No normal order of succession or of grouping has as yet been made out in this complex series.

There are several detached patches of gneiss in Bhāgalpur District, isolated in the alluvium as near Panyá and Kherhi, and in the Ganges at Colgong and Pathargháttа. It is probable that the whole alluvial area is underlaid by these rocks, and at no great depth. The Damuda rocks, to which the Indian coal measures belong, are seen only at one spot within the District. The white clays and sandstone, about 150 feet thick, forming Pathargháta Hill, are of this formation. They rest upon gneiss at a few feet above high flood level. Every portion of the group is well exposed on the steep sides of the little hill, without any appearance of a carbonaceous layer. Yet there is a deep shaft on the summit, which is said to have been sunk for coal. The Damuda clay furnishes the great bulk of the material for the pottery works at Pathargháta. A finer kind of kaolin is obtained by crushing and washing a decomposed pegmatitic rock, extracted from shallow pits in the gneiss. On the east side of Pathargháta Hill, the sandstone is overlaid by strong beds of dark green basaltic trap. The slope or dip of the beds being easterly, the whole east end of the ridge, as well as some other small hills in that direction, are formed entirely of this rock. The same rock is seen again at the end and south of Pírpaintí. These outcrops are all outliers of the great trappean formation, of which the Rájmahál hills are composed. From the fossil plants in the sedimentary beds, interstratified with the eruptive rock, it has been ascertained that the formation corresponds with the Lias horizon of the European series. There are no known outcrops of these intertrappean beds in Bhāgalpur.

The alluvial formation occupies the greater part of the District. Much of it is clearly composed of deposits from the present rivers, whether by annual overflow or in consequence of periodical changes in the channel. But there is frequently observed a stiff clay with *kankar*, and often ochre, very unlike the ordinary silt as freshly deposited. This formation is often found, too, in positions where inundation does not now reach. For these reasons it has been distinguished as the old alluvium, though the precise relation between the two formations has not been satisfactorily determined. Some observers have maintained that the old alluvium is of marine or estuarian origin As yet, however, no fossils have been discovered to confirm that opinion. It is, therefore, very desirable that any organic remains found in these deposits should be carefully collected and submitted to competent authority.

The principal mineral product of Bhāgalpur is galena, found in large quantities in *parganās* Sahrúi Chándan, Katauria, and Danrá Sukhwárá. Much of it is argentiferous. The following report by Dr. Oldham, Superintendent of the Geological Survey of India, on some specimens sent to Government by the Collector of Bhāgalpur, shows the value of this mineral:—"The ores sent are galená, the sulphide of lead, the most common and widely distributed of the ores of lead, consisting of about 14 per cent. of sulphur and 86 per cent. of lead. Galená generally contains also an admixture of silver in varying quantities, often to an amount which renders the ore very valuable." Sulphuret of antimony, or *súrmá*, is also found in the same localities Copper is met with in the southern hills, as native copper, copper pyrites, a sulphuret of copper and iron, and malachite or green carbonate of copper. Talc, chlorite, and jasper are found in the south-western *parganās*. Iron ore is distributed over the whole of the hilly country, very abundantly in places, but the difficulties in working it from want of fuel and a good flux prevent its being much used. MINERALS.

THE FERÆ NATURÆ of Bhāgalpur are very numerous, when compared with those of most Districts of Bengal and Bihar, a circumstance probably due to the variety of the physical characteristics of the District, and to the fact that it lies between and merges into a number of tracts, distinct in their climate and elevation. The Fauna of Central India is represented by a few members found in the southern hills, which are really outlying ranges of the great Vindhyan system. The animals of Rájmahál, which are specifically distinct, add their quota on the east. North of the Ganges most of the mammals found in the central plain of Bengal are to be met with; whilst further north not a few representatives of the Nepál and Himálayan families occur, together with some of those peculiar to the Tarái. ZOOLOGY.

Monkeys are numerous both north and south of the Ganges. The *hanumán* or *langúr* (Presbytis entellus) is found only on the south of the river. It is strange that it has never availed itself of an opportunity of crossing over, but such is the case, every authority since Buchanan-Hamilton having failed to obtain a specimen to the north of the Ganges. A long-tailed monkey has, however, been occasionally seen in the northern boundary of the District, probably the Himálayan *langúr* (Presbytis

Schistaceus). The short-tailed monkey or *bandar* (Inuus rhesus) is numerous everywhere, particularly so in the northern forests. The Macacus radiatus, the showman's monkey, has been seen, but such specimens were probably escaped menagerie animals. Bats of many kinds are also met with. The most numerous of the frugivorous tribe is the large fox-bat or *bādur* (Pteropus Edwardsi), well known for its inroads on garden fruit. The small fox-bat or *Chāmgudrī* (Cynopterus marginatus) takes up its residence in every house. The Vampire (Megaderma lyra) is common, particularly in the Supaul subdivision. Several species of leaf bats (Rhinolophus) are found, chiefly in the hills. The long-armed bat (Taphozous longimanus) frequents out-houses and ruins everywhere. The wrinkle-lipped bat (Nyctinomus plicatus) is mostly an inhabitant of trees. The yellow bat (Nycticepus luteus) is occasionally found. The Harlequin bat (Nycticepus ornatus) is seen but rarely.

The Insectivora are fairly represented, the most common member of the order being the shrew, the *chhachhundā* of natives and musk-rat of Europeans (Sorex cærulescens). The large mouse-coloured shrew (S. murinus) and the Nepāl wood shrew (S. nemorivagus) are also met with. The Himālayan water shrew is occasionally seen near the hill streams in the north of the district. Some hedgehogs are also found, probably Erinacei collares. The Tupaia Elliotti, or Madras tree shrew, is found in the southern hills. Two kinds of bears have been recognised, the common black Indian bear (Ursus labiatus) and the *bhāl bajrā* (U. Indicus). They are both harmless animals, except when attacked. They live on black ants, termites, beetles, fruits, particularly the seeds of the Cassia fistula, date fruit, and honey, but their favourite food consists of the succulent petals of the *mahuā*. Colonel Tickell's account of the power of suction in the bear, as well as of its faculty of propelling wind from its mouth, has been verified in this district. By these means it is enabled to procure its common food of white ants and larvæ with ease. On arriving at an ant-hill, the bear scrapes with his forefeet until he reaches the large combs at the bottom of the galleries. He then with violent puffs dissipates the dust and crumbled particles of the nest, and sucks out the inhabitants of the comb by such forcible inhalations as to be heard at "two hundred yards' distance or more." Large larvæ are in this way sucked out from great depths under the soil. These bears are confined to the southern hills, and are becoming scarce. The hog-badger or *bhāl-sur* is an inhabitant of the Tarāi. It has been observed that this animal can walk erect on its hind feet. Some specimens kept in captivity, preferred fruit, rejecting animal food, whilst others seemed to thrive on meat and fish alone. The badger or *bījā* (Mellivora Indica) keeps to hilly tracts, and rarely exceeds three feet in total length. The yellow bellied weasel (Mustela Kathiah), a most offensively smelling animal, a native of Nepāl, is said to be met with in the Sub-Tarāi country. The Indian otter or *uth* (Lutra nair) is sometimes found in muddy streams, and is trained for fishing purposes. Its success in killing and bringing up a fish, often five times its own size, is remarkable Just outside the district, at Rājmahāl, the fishing castes bestow much care on training otters.

The tiger (Felis tigris) is occasionally found amongst the high grass jungles of the Kosī, and in the hills in the south of the district.

The leopard (felis pardus) is also found, chiefly to the south of the Ganges. The large tiger-cat (F. viverrina) is found in thick jungles, and also along the edges of marshes in the north. It has been known to carry off very young children and calves. The leopard cat (F. bengalensis), which is similarly distributed, is not such a large or powerful animal. There are several species of wild cats, the *janglī-billī* (F. chaus) being the most common. The common hyæna (Hyæna striata) is occasionally seen. Civets are numerous in Supaul and are met with in the southern hills, both the larger (Viverra zibetha) and the smaller (V. malaccensis) being represented. Both are kept in confinement by natives for the sake of the drug derived from their subcaudal glands. They live on small birds, and animals, eggs, snakes, frogs, and insects, and are in their turn eaten by some low castes, such as Musāhars. The *khatās* or common tree-cat (Paradoxurus musanga), also called toddy cat by Europeans from its well-established habit of drinking the juice of the Palmyra palm, is found in the southern *parganās;* and the Tarāi tree-cat (P. bondar) in the northern forests.

The Bengal and gold-spotted mongoose (Herpestes malaccensis and H. nepalensis) are abundant, and are prized for their antipathy to snakes. Their alleged immunity from the deadly poison of the cobra is believed to be due, more to their activity in escaping the deadly bite than to any peculiar power of resistance to its influence in their constitution.

The Indian wolf (Canis pallipes) has been seen on both sides of the Ganges, but is now very rare. It is called *hūndār* by the natives of Bhāgalpur. The jackal, or *gīdar* (Canis aureus) is the most plentiful of this genus. Its peculiar cry is heard everywhere marking, according to native opinion, the various watches of the night.

The wild dog or *bankutá* (Cuon rutilans) is said to be met with; its existence in Bhágalpur is not beyond doubt, although many dogs of a deep rusty colour and marked vulpine aspect are found wild in the southern hills. The Indian fox (Vulpes bengalensis) or *lomrí* is seen everywhere; it is a pretty little animal.

The whale tribe is represented by the Gangetic porpoise or *súns* (Platanista gangetica). It feeds on small fishes and crustacea and may be seen in large shoals at the mouth of the Ghúgrí. Its ordinary length is from 6 to 7 feet. Its habitat is muddy water, in which good sight is of little use. Its eyes are small, and the optic nerves rudimentary. The porpoises are shot and speared when they venture into shallow water. The lower classes of fishermen eat their flesh, and their oil is collected as a specific for rheumatism.

The rodents include squirrels, rats, hares, and porcupines. The striped squirrel (Sciurus palmarum) is the most common of the tribe. Indeed, it is doubtful whether any other squirrel is found. The gerboa rat (Gerbellus Indicus) is said to be sometimes met with. The natives call it *harin-mús* or antelope rat. The bandicoot (Mus bandicoota), which derives its name from the Telinga word *pandikoku* or pig rat, is found in towns. The brown rat (M. decumanus) is found in most masonry buildings; and the Nepál rat (M. plurimammis) in the northern plains. The common mouse (M. urbanus) is also plentiful. The Indian porcupine (Hystric leucura) or *sáhi*, is becoming scarce, as it is eaten by the lower castes. It is usually obtained by being smoked out of its burrows. When attacked it usually runs a little, and then suddenly charges backwards with its spines erect. The smaller or Bengal porcupine is also found and hunted down. The common Indian hare (Lepus ruficaudatus) or *khargosh* is very abundantly found; it is eaten by all classes, being considered pure food.

There are no wild elephants now in Bhāgalpur, but down to the end of the eighteenth century they were found in large numbers both north and south of the Ganges. Even in Dr. Buchanan-Hamilton's time (1807-13) they did much mischief along the foot of the southern hills, from Rájmahál to Monghyr. He states that they had then, according to native tradition, been only thirty or forty years in this part of the country. Whence they were said to have come, he does not mention. He estimated them in 1810 at one hundred head. He also speaks of a colony of elephants frequenting the marshy parts of the north of the District. The

Indian wild boar (Sus Indicus) is found in all parts of the District, but chiefly in the part north of the Ganges. It does considerable damage to crops, and it is freely eaten by numerous low castes.

There are no true stags in the District, but smaller deer are numerous. The *bárasingha* or swamp deer (Rucervus Duvancellii) is sometimes met with as high as eleven hands. It was common near the Tarái, but scarce in the southern hills. The *sámbhar* stag (Rusa Aristotelis) was similarly distributed: it is a taller and heavier animal than the last. It is hardly ever heard of now. Its horns vary very much in size, being sometimes short and very thick, and sometimes long, thin and curved. The spotted deer and hog deer are common both north and south of the Ganges. The former (Axis maculatus) is rarely ten hands high, but is generally more than two hands higher than any specimen of the latter (A. porcinus) that I have seen. The spotted deer are very gregarious, whilst the hog deer is a solitary animal, both sexes being generally found alone. The barking deer (Cervulus aureus) is also met with, and supplies better venison than any of the foregoing. Like the mouse deer (Memimna Indica), a pretty little animal about ten inches high, it is common in the hilly country to the south. A few four-horned antelopes (Tetraceros quadricornis) stray in from the Tarái. The antelope or *kálsár* (Antilope Bezoartica) is common on open plains in the north of the district, and affords much sport. Wild buffaloes (Bubalus arni) are now becoming very scarce, but may occasionally be seen in the north of the district. They were common formerly in the Kosi *diara* area.

The scaly ant-eater (Manis pentadactyla), the *bagar-kit* of some of the natives, and *ban rohit* or forest carp of others, is met with on the banks of streams in the north. A ring, made of its scales and worn on the left hand, is considered a charm against fever. Its flesh is also valued as an aphrodisiac.

The birds and reptiles of Bhāgalpur are almost identical with those of the adjoining district of Monghyr, which have been described in the Gazetteer of that district. The most plentiful small game are wild geese, wild duck, teal, green and rock pigeons, snipe, quail, ortolan, black, painted, grey, and double spurred partridges. There are also the *chandel*, or crested lark, the crane in all its varieties, peacocks, parakeets, parrots, hawks, doves of various kinds, the *bulbul*, spoonbill, *sarus*, *teru*, fishing eagle, vulture, kite, crow, jackdaw, owls, large and small, kingfishers, wood-peckers, jays, plovers, curlews, paddy-birds, *koel*, golden oriels, and common sparrows. Of reptiles, there are the black and brown cobra, the *dhemna*, the *koráit*, the green snake, the *mahil* tree-snake, and several kinds of water snakes, the *gosāmp*, blood-sucker, *bishkopra*, scorpion, centipede, and various kinds of lizards, the man-eating crocodile and the fish-eating gavial are both found especially in the north of the district.

Climate. Bhāgalpur being inland at some distance from the sea is subject to greater extremes of climate than districts in the south and east of the Province. The mean temperature varies from 62° in January to 86° in May. The highest average maximum temperature is 97° in April. Owing to the dry westerly winds that prevail during March and April, the humidity is much lower than at other times, averaging 52°. With the approach of the monsoon season the air becomes gradually more charged with moisture. The degree of humidity remains steady at 87° throughout July and August. In September when periods of fine weather alternate with the cloud and rain of the monsoon, the humidity is lower, and with the breaks of increasing length it falls to 76° in November, after which there is a slight increase, due partly to the unsettled weather caused by the cold season disturbances. From October until May the prevailing wind comes from the west. A very marked change takes place with the commencement of the monsoon, generally caused by the first cyclonic storm which enters Bengal from the bay. The moist winds from the bay flow northwards over the eastern districts of lower Bengal in the first place; afterwards they flow westwards owing to the influence of the Himālayan range; so that in Bihar, after the passage of the cyclonic storms, easterly winds set in and continue with but little interruption until the middle of September when the westerly winds become more common. Rainfall is only a fraction of an inch from November to April. In May 2·8 inches fall on an average, and the heaviest falls are 12·2 and 11·3 inches in July and August, respectively. The average annual fall is 49·5 inches. In the year 1899 73·94 inches fell: in 1908, 26·78. These are the highest and lowest recorded falls.

As the beginning of the rainy season occurs when a storm from the bay passes over Bihar, the commencement of the monsoon may be as early as the last week of May and as late as the first or second week of July. An important matter in connection with the monsoon in Bihar is its strength in September. If the westerly winds are stronger than usual in that month, storms from the bay recurve eastward and the rainfall is in consequence deficient. A short rainfall during September and an early cessation of the rains generally means at least a partial failure of the winter rice crop.

The effect of seasonal changes on the health of the inhabitants will be discussed later on.* The subjoined table gives the most important meteorological averages:—

	Temperature.			Humidity.	Rainfall.		
	Mean.	Mean maximum.	Mean minimum.	Mean	Inches.	Rainy days.	Barometric mean.
January ...	62	74	50	78	0·6	1	29·91
February .	66	78	53	69	0·7	2	·85
March ...	77	90	64	52	0·4	1	·74
April ...	85	97	73	57	0·9	1	·62
May ...	86	96	76	70	2 8	4	·55
June ...	86	93	78	81	8·3	10	·42
July ...	85	90	79	87	12·2	15	·40
August ...	84	89	79	87	11 3	13	·47
September	84	89	78	85	8·5	9	·58
October ...	80	88	71	78	3·5	3	·74
November ...	70	81	59	76	0·1	0	·86
December ...	63	75	51	77	0·1	0	·93
Year ...	77	87	68	75	49 5	59	29·67

The following table shows the annual rainfall of stations in the Bhāgalpur district from 1901 to 1908 and the averages for the district and for each station during that time:—

Stations.	1901.	1902.	1903.	1904.	1905.	1906.	1907.	1908.	Average local.
1	2	3	4	5	6	7	8	9	10
	In.	In.	In.	In.	In.	In.	In.	In.	In.
Madhipura ...	38·69	58·90	49·49	45·39	69·47	61·80	36·98	21·99	47·84
Bangaon (Syfabad)	32·07	43·52	32·32	41·68	66·03	No return.	40·78	No return.	42·73
Supaul	33·42	63·42	50 79	70·47	82·35	58·03	42 75	24·01	53 15
Pratapganj ...	28·71	66·66	55·02	46·23	73 08	72·07	52·87	25·61	52·53
Bhagalpur ...	32 97	41·92	30·88	43·01	55·35	39·45	50·84	18·13	30·06
Banká	40·80	38·42	35·42	72·49	58·50	38·66	47·85	33·60	45·71
Colgong	37·35	48·65	33·04	46 06	67·54	44·97	47·15	24·38	43·64
Bausi	40·49	39·38	38·03	49·73	59·24	49·94	43·51	39·78	45·01
District average (annual).	35·56	50·10	40·62	51·88	66·44	45 61	45 34	26·78†	...

* Chapter IV, page 58.

† The abnormally small rainfall in 1908 led to very severe scarcity in 1908-09, which will be more fully alluded to in Chapter VI—Natural Calamities, page 104.

CHAPTER II.

HISTORY.

Ancient History.

THE limits of the present District of Bhāgalpur being purely artificial, no connected account of the territory that now bears this name can be expected. Its history must be sought for in the history of the large areas of which it forms a part. It is known that of the portion south of the river some parts were comprised within the limits of the old Hindu kingdom of Anga, at the dawn of authentic history. The capital of that kingdom was Champa,[1] near the sight of the present town of Bhāgalpur. It may be farfetched to identify the sight of ancient Champa with modern Champanagar, but if this resemblance is merely a coincidence, it is at least a remarkable coincidence. Some authorities identify the plateau known as Karangarh with the site of the ancient capital. It is stated to have been built by a Rájá Varma, but nothing definite is known about him, as kings of this name are very numerous in the lists of kings of Magadha.[2] The name Bhāgalpur, as already stated, is interpreted to mean the 'city of good luck' or the 'city of refugees,' but no reliable clue has as yet been found to the origin of this name. It was attributed by Buchanan-Hamilton to later Moghul days.

In addition to the area formerly comprised in the kingdom of Anga, a large part of this district south of the river falls within the limits of the ancient kingdom of Magadha. Probably, too, the ancient kingdom of Gaur extended up to the east of this District, including perhaps the Sonthāl Parganās. North of the river the kingdom of Maithila lay, the old boundaries of which were, on the east, the Kosí river; on the west the Gandak; on the north the Himálayan range, and on the south the Ganges. It may be remarked here that the whole of this tract was assigned to Mohesh Thakur by the Emperor Akbar; the present Máhárájá of Darbhanga is directly descended from Mohesh Thakur, but his zamíndári is considerably smaller than the immense area once conferred on his ancestors. Formerly the name of

[1] See "Ancient Countries in Eastern India: Journal, Asiatic Society, Bengal, Vol. LXVI, Part I, No. 2, 1897, p. 85.

[2] Asiatic Researches, Vol. IX.

"Madhyadesh" was also applied to this area according to a very ancient cosmography.*

A list of kings of Magadha, reconstructed by Major Wilford, is given in Volume IX of "Asiatic Researches." As kings named Karna occur frequently in this list, at eras varying from thirteen or fourteen centuries B.C. to four or five centuries A.D., it is obviously impossible to determine from which of them the fort of Karangarh took its name.

Buchanan-Hamilton concluded that there were at least seven important kings named Karna who began to reign not long after the downfall of the Maurya dynasty founded by Chandragupta,† who rendered Magadha the leading province of India.

Gupta Kings.

Little that is accurate is known until some centuries after the Christian era. In the fourth century the Guptas, the 'Second Indian Empire,' became powerful—their capital also being at Patna—and were acknowledged supreme by the kings of the different countries now included in Bengal. The Chinese traveller, Hiuen Tsiang, after his term of years in the Buddhist monastery at Nalanda, travelled through South Bihar in the seventh century A.D. Champa under the rule of Khetauris, of Māl origin, was then a powerful kingdom, and included the parts of Bhāgalpur south of the river Ganges.

Pala and Sen Kings.

In the first half of the ninth century, the kings of the Pálá dynasty rose to power in the kingdom of Anga and extended their sway over Bihar and North Bengal. They were Buddhists, but were tolerant of Hinduism. The Sen kings gradually ousted them from Bengal and ultimately conquered Mithila, only to be vanquished by the Muhammadans under Muhammad-i-Bakhtyar, at the end of the twelfth century. About 1197 he conquered Bihar and about 1200 took possession of Gaur. He was the first Viceroy of Bihar and Bengal, under the Delhi emperors.

Muhammadan Invasion.

A succession of Muhammadan governors, in loose subjection to the Delhi emperors, gradually annexed most of Bengal. South Bihar was annexed to Delhi about 1330. About 1397 all Bihar was annexed to the kingdom of Jaunpur. A century later the Delhi emperors again got possession of Bihar. North Bihar was ruled from the middle of the fourteenth to the middle

---

* See Buchanan-Hamilton, Vol. II, pp. 19, 20, for fuller details.

† Chandragupta, grandfather of the more famous Asoka (reigned B.C. 272—231), was, it will be remembered, a refugee at the time of Alexander the Great's invasion of India (B.C. 327). The Greeks called him Sandrakottos. He captured Patna (B.C. 321) and became king of Magadha. He married the daughter of Seleucus, the Greek sovereign of Persia and Bactria, and received, at Patna Megasthenes, a Greek Ambassador, to whom posterity is indebted for the best account of Ancient India now extant.

The "First Indian Empire," *i. e.*, the Maurya Dynasty, came to an end about B. C. 185.

of the sixteenth century by Brāhman kings who were tributary to the Muhammadans.

When Baber's son, Humayun, tried to invade Bengal about 1540, he was blocked up by the Afghans under Shēr Shāh in the narrow defile between the Ganges and the Rajmāhal Hills. He must have traversed Bhagalpur on this expedition, which ended in his disastrous retreat and flight to Persia, where he remained in exile till 1555. He died in 1556 and Akbar succeeded him, and restored some sort of order, after two centuries of confusion. He finally broke the Afghan power and established the Moghul empire on a firm basis.

This district does not appear to have been in any way remarkable during all these troubled times. Monghyr was of great importance owing to its splendid position on the river and it overshadowed Bhagalpur. Sarkar Monghyr (*i.e.*, revenue division) was included in the Subah (or Province) of Bihar and Bhagalpur fell within the limits of Sarkar Monghyr.

Akbar's reign.

In 1580 the military revolt of Bengal against Akbar commenced, and Todar Mal, better known to history as Akbar's great finance minister and originator of a workable scheme for assessing land revenue, marched down to meet the rebels without encountering any serious opposition as far as Monghyr. The rebels with an army of about 30,000 cavalry were encamped at Bhagalpur. Todar Mal strengthened his position by entrenchments and, acting with a masterly inactivity, succeeded in prevailing on the local zamindārs to bring all available supplies to his camp. To avoid death by starvation the rebels had to separate, and this practically ended their invasion of Bihar which was restored to the Moghul Emperor.

For nearly two centuries Bihar was governed by Viceroys of the Delhi Emperor, but nothing distinctive has been recorded about any of them. Their seat of Government was established at Rajmāhal, a short distance from the eastern border of the present district of Bhagalpur, by Man Sing on his return from his Orissa campaign in 1592. A whole series of governors (*aumils*) of Bhagalpur are known but only by name. They do not appear to have ranked as high as the governors of Purnea, as few of them got the title of Nawab.

English rulers.

In 1769 this series of governors came to an end, and an Englishman, Mr. William Harwood, was appointed as "supervisor" with instructions to obtain a summary history of the provinces, the State produce and capacity of the lands, the amount of the revenues, the cesses and all demands whatsoever which are made on the cultivators, the manner of collecting them and the gradual rise of every new impost, the regulation of commerce and the administration of justice. The fiscal history of the district will be alluded to in Chapter X.

In 1777 and 1778 the hill tribes from the south, continuing the raids which, no doubt, they and their ancestors for centuries had continually made on Buddhist, Hindu, Afghan and Moghul alike, caused so much insecurity and alarm that an attempt to pacify them was made. With this policy of conciliation, which was entirely successful, the names of Mr. Augustus Cleveland, Collector of Bhagalpur, and of Captain James Browne of Rajmāhal are imperishably connected. The Cleveland memorial pyramid still exists, and a stone monument sent by the Court of Directors from England was erected in front of the house formerly occupied by Cleveland. The inscription on it runs as follows:— Cleveland.

To the Memory of Augustus Cleveland, Esq.,
LATE COLLECTOR OF THE DISTRICTS OF BHAUGULPORE AND RAJAMAHALL,
WHO, WITHOUT BLOODSHED OR THE TERROR OF AUTHORITY,
EMPLOYING ONLY THE MEANS OF CONCILIATION, CONFIDENCE, AND BENEVOLENCE,
ATTEMPTED AND ACCOMPLISHED
THE ENTIRE SUBJECTION OF THE LAWLESS AND SAVAGE INHABITANTS OF THE
JUNGLETERRY OF RAJAMAHALL,
WHO HAD LONG INFESTED THE NEIGHBOURING LANDS BY THEIR PREDATORY INCURSIONS,
INSPIRED THEM WITH A TASTE FOR THE ARTS OF CIVILISED LIFE,
AND ATTACHED THEM TO THE BRITISH GOVERNMENT BY A CONQUEST OVER THEIR MINDS—
THE MOST PERMANENT, AS THE MOST RATIONAL, MODE OF DOMINION,
THE GOVERNOR-GENERAL AND COUNCIL OF BENGAL,
IN HONOUR OF HIS CHARACTER, AND FOR AN EXAMPLE TO OTHERS,
HAVE ORDERED THIS MONUMENT TO BE ERECTED.
HE DEPARTED THIS LIFE ON THE 13TH OF JANUARY 1784, AGED 29.

About this time, grants of lands rent-free were made to numbers of old and invalid sepoys around Bhagalpur to induce them to settle there. This experiment was tried so as to have men on the spot capable of withstanding the inroads of marauding tribes. Along with Cleveland's "Hill Rangers"—an irregular levy raised about 1780 and disbanded about 1864—they succeeded in fulfilling their purpose and the inroads gradually ceased. But Cleveland's wise policy of pacification and conciliation no doubt had more to do with this immunity from raids than the reserve of trained men that was thus rendered available.

The subsequent history of the district is uneventful. The mutiny in 1857 seems to have left it quite untouched. When a panic began in Monghyr, on the rising of the troops at Dinapur, Mr. Yule, the then Commissioner of the Bhagalpur Division, stopped a detachment of 150 men of the Fifth Fusiliers who were on the Ganges, and posted one hundred of them at Bhagalpur. This maintained public tranquillity and kept Mutiny days.

the highway of the Ganges open for Outram's expedition up-country.

Formation of the District.

After the opening of a criminal court, about 1812, at Monghyr, it remained dependent on Bhágalpur, bearing to it the relation that a subdivisional charge bears now to a district, till about 1832 when an office for payment of revenue was opened at Monghyr.

In 1855-56, the Sonthál Parganás were formed into a separate district. In 1874 parganás Sakhrabadi, Durara, Singhaul, Kharagpur and Partabpara, with part of parganás Saboni and Lakhanpur and *tappas* Ladwah and Sewanwan—a total area of over 613 square miles—were transferred to Monghyr. Thus the huge tract covering over 8,000 square miles described by Buchanan-Hamilton as Bhágalpur lost a great part of its area. It gained on the north of the Ganges as it lost on the south, its greatest acquisition being that of parganás Naredigar, Malhani Gopal and Nisankpur Kurha from Tirhut in 1838. Again in 1864, parganás Kabkhand and Utarkhand were transferred to this district from Monghyr, and parganás Dhaphar and Nathpur from Purnea.

Madhipurá subdivision dates from 1845: Bánká from 1863 and Supaul from 1870.

Archæological Remains.

In this district there are still extant at several places remains of the highest interest to the antiquarian. A brief notice of the chief of them is here given. Fuller details must be sought for in General Cunningham's report on his Tour in Bihar and Bengal in 1879-80 (Volume XV of the reports of the Archæological Survey of India) and in Buchanan-Hamilton's account ("Eastern India," Vol. II, pages 19 to 61). The "List of Ancient Monuments in Bengal" revised up to 1895 (pages 421 to 430) is the most modern compilation dealing with this subject.

The oldest remains are probably those of the fort called Karangarh, which is believed to be of pre-Buddhist days. No systematic excavations have ever been made at its site, so its possibilities are unexplored at present.

Near the railway station at Sultanganj there are the remains of Buddhist monasteries. A colossal figure of Buddha, over seven feet high, made of copper, was found there, with several smaller images. Even the former name of this monastery is forgotten, the present name being demonstrably modern. Hiuen Tsiang describes the ruins of various monasteries near Bhágalpur, so this was probably in ruins then as no definite clue is given to it in his book. The inscriptions found here are in Gupta characters: hence it is safe to conclude that the monastery was flourishing about the third or fourth century of our era. In 1879, further excavations revealed a relic-chamber containing amongst other things a fragment of bone; the whole chamber was very like that just lately discovered near Peshawar, and contained the seven precious things of Buddhists, namely, gold, silver, crystal, sapphire, ruby, emerald and jacinth. Two coins were also found, one of Chandragupta II. These have enabled the date to be fixed at about 250 A.D In volume XXXIII of the Bengal Asiatic Society's Journal, a detailed account of the early excavations is given (pages 361, etc.).

Another mound close by is called Karangarh, but which Karna should be identified with this fort is not easy to decide.

Mandar-giri.

Among the Hindu remains, the most famous in legend is undoubtedly Mandar Hill or Mandargiri, near Bausi, in the Bánká Subdivision. The following description of it is reproduced from Hunter's Statistical Account.

Mandargiri is the name of a small mountain, upwards of seven hundred feet high, and of the greatest sanctity in Hindu mythology, situated near Bausi, about thirty miles south of the Headquarters Station. It is one great mass of granite, almost devoid of vegetation except near the summit and on one side, where it is, for the most part, overgrown with low jungle. Numerous small artificial tanks have been formed in the solid rock, at stages up its side, and the figure of a great serpent, cut in relief on its surface, has been made to coil round it. The ascent has been rendered easy by steps hewn in the rock, which run up about two-thirds of its height.

Mandar Hill is first mentioned in the account of the great deluge, when Vishnu floated on the waters in a profound slumber. The *Puránas* state that a giant of enormous stature then took birth from the secretions of his ears, and advanced to destroy Bráhma, Vishnu, and Siva—the Hindu Triad, who had been produced from other parts of his body. Vishnu gave him battle, and after a protracted struggle of ten thousand years' duration, succeeded in cutting off his head. As, however, the giant's headless trunk proved equally dangerous, Vishnu not only piled Mandar over it, but kept the hill pressed under his foot, that this monstrous being might not rise up again to destroy creation. Vishnu is, therefore, supposed to be always present in the hill under the name of Madhusúdan, so called from Madhukáitab—the name of the giant thus subdued. The hill is also believed to be the one that was used by the gods and Asurs in churning the ocean. This operation, as recorded in the Mahábhárata, was done partly to obtain the *amrita*, divine ichor, which confers immortality; and partly to recover the goddess of Fortune who, in obedience to the curse of a Munī, had forsaken heaven and descended into the depths of the sea. The great serpent, who supports the earth on his thousand heads, consented to act as a rope, whereby to work Mandar hill, which had been selected as the only churning-rod capable of withstanding the mighty movement. Vishnu himself in the form of a tortoise took the place of a socket on which to make the churning rod rotate. But the Hindus naturally hesitate to say that the Bhagalpur hill is identical with the gigantic Mandar of mythology, compared in their books with the fabulous Sumeru, which supports the heavens on its head, the earth on its navel, and the nether world on its base, and round whose sides the sun, moon, and stars roll in their orbits. The ignorant pilgrims, however, who annually flock to the hill, entertain no such doubt, especially when they behold with wonder and awe the coil of the serpent traced round its enormous girth. Having such memories associated with it, the great sanctity attached to the hill by the Hindus need not excite wonder.

Besides being a place of pilgrimage, the hill possesses great value in the eyes of the antiquarian, abounding, as it does, in interesting ruins as well as in natural and artificial curiosities. For a mile or two around its base are to be seen numerous tanks, several old buildings, some stone figures, and a few large wells—which attest the remains of a great city that has long since ceased to exist. This is the site of the modern village of Bausī, the former headquarters of the Bānkā subdivision. A common saying among the people of the neighbourhood is, that this city contained fifty-two *bāzārs* and fifty-three streets, besides four times twenty-two tanks. Near the foot of the hill there is a building, now in ruins, in the walls of which are an immense number of square holes, evidently intended to hold the small native lamps called *chirāghs.* The tradition runs, that on the night of the Dewālī festival, there were a hundred thousand lighted *chirāghs* placed in these holes by the inhabitants of the city—each householder being allowed to supply only one. About a hundred yards from the above structure there is a second large building of stone, which is generally ascribed to Rājā Cholā, who is said to have flourished twenty-two centuries ago. (The occurrence of the numbers twenty-two and fifty-two in the legends of Southern Bihar and Central Bengal is very noticeable, but has not been explained.) The walls of the building are of large stones fitting one upon another, no mortar having been used. The roof, which is composed of great slabs of marble-like hornstone, is supported upon stone beams eighteen inches wide by fifteen thick; and the verandah rests upon tapering blocks of the same material. There is a large hall in the centre, with an adjoining verandah in front, and six dark rooms on the side, lighted only through small windows which are of various devices. The rise of the city is no doubt due to the sanctity attached to the place, and the great veneration felt for Madhusūdan on the Mandar, which was not inferior to that inspired by Krishna at Mathurā, by Jagannāth at Purī or by Rāma at Nāsik. How or when the city fell into ruins it is difficult to say; but popular tradition ascribes its destruction as well as that of Madhusūdan's temple on the hill, to Kālā Pahār, who is charged, rightly or wrongly, with the demolition of every sacred relic of Hindu antiquity throughout Hindustān.

Not far from the building just mentioned, there is a triumphal arch built of stone, containing an inscription in Sanskrit which seems to show that the town was in existence in the Sākā year 1521 (A.D. 1597). It records the victory of one Chhatrapatī and the dedication of the arch to Madhusūdan. This victory evidently marks a series of struggles between the Hindus and Muhammadans, during which the city must have been gradually depopulated. After the destruction of the temple on the hill, the image of Madhusūdan was brought down to the plains and located in a new temple built near the arch. The present zamīndārs of Sabalpur, who claim to be descended from Chhatrapatī, assert that the image was removed to Bausī only when the city was wholly abandoned by the inhabitants. A custom now exists of carrying the image annually, on the Pous-Sankrāntī day, from Bausī to the foot of the hill, and swinging it on the triumphal arch built by Chhatrapatī. The removal of the idol to Bausī has lessened the sanctity of the hill in the estimation of Hindus; but, on the abovementioned day, there is an immense gathering of pilgrims ranging from thirty to forty thousand, who come from different parts of the country to bathe in a tank at the foot of the hill. The consequence is a large *melā* or fair which lasts for fifteen days. The origin of the fair is explained by the following legend:—A Rājā of Kānchipur called Cholā, probably the same as the chief before mentioned, was affected with leprosy, a disease which, according to the Hindus, visits only those who are specially accursed of heaven. In accordance with this belief he paid visits to all the sacred shrines in India, but could nowhere find relief. At last he came to the Mandar, and, happening to step into a pool of water at the foot of the hill, he was surprised to find his leprous ulcers vanish. He next washed his hands with the water, whereupon the disease disappeared from them also. He widened and deepened the spring, which was then called Manohar Kund, and named it Pāpharnī, or that which cleanses from sin. In commemoration of the event he instituted the *melā* or fair which takes place on the last day of Paush, because it was on that day that the Rājā used the water of the spring with such miraculous results. It is also believed that Brahma spent millions of years on the top of this hill, in contemplation and prayers to the Supreme Being. When he had at length concluded, he offered, according to custom, a betelnut and other things in a sacrificial fire. The betelnut rolled down the side of the hill and fell into the spring at its base, thus rendering its waters especially sacred, and giving them the virtue which cured Rājā Cholā of his leprosy. Dead bodies from the neighbourhood are burnt on its banks and the bones thrown into it, as if its waters were as holy as those of the Ganges. It is cleared at the time of the fair, but it is impossible to free the water from the stench arising from the putrefying and half burnt bodies that are seen floating on its surface throughout the rest of the year. In spite of this, the immense host of pilgrims, who assemble on the day of the fair, bathe in it, in the hope of obtaining salvation in a life to come; and women of the most respectable families come to perform their ablutions at night, that they may not be subject to the vulgar gaze.

After his miraculous cure, Rājā Cholā is said not only to have fixed his capital in the city near the famous spring, but to have spent his immense wealth in beautifying and adorning the hill with marble figures, stone temples, spacious tanks, and deep reservoirs. To him is also attributed the pious fraud of tracing the coil of the great serpent round its sides, so as to induce the belief that the hill was used by the gods in churning the ocean. This, as well as the steps hewn in the rock, must have cost enormous sums of money. An inscription at the side of the steps, which has lately been deciphered, seems to show that they were the work of a Buddhist king named Ugrabhairab. It is, however, probable that the inscription does not refer to the steps cut in the rock, but, as supposed by the decipherer, Bābu Rājendra Lāla Mitra, commemorates the dedication of a statue. Though there is at present no statue near the inscription, there are still many Buddhist and Hindu images to be seen lying here and there on the left side of the steps, which have evidently been transported from their original places, and mutilated and disfigured by Muhammadan bigotry. There is also a Buddhist temple near the summit of the hill which is still held in great veneration by the Jains. Even if the honour of cutting the steps in the rock really belongs to Ugrabhāirab, he could not, as a Buddhist, have traced the coil of the great serpent on the body of the hill in order to keep up the memory of a Hindu superstition. Sītākund, up to which the steps lead, is the name of an oblong tank about 100 feet long by 50 feet wide, excavated in the rock, nearly 500 feet above the surrounding plain. The pilgrims who visit it are persuaded to believe that it has derived its name from Sītā, who used to bathe in it during her stay in the hill with her husband, when banished from Oudh. On the northern bank of the Sītākund stood the first temple of Madhusūdan, said to have been built by Rājā Cholā, now entirely in ruins. It would appear to have been pulled down, the stones that formed it being hurled down the sides of the hill to the plain. According to the Brāhmans, Kālā Pahār could not destroy the image of Madhusūdan, for it leaped into the Sītākund on his approach, and opening a subterranean passage through the rock, proceeded to the large tank at Kajrāli near Bhāgalpur, where it remained concealed for many years. At length Madhusūdan appeared to a Pānde in a dream, and revealed to him the place of its concealment, whence it was conveyed back to the Mandar and located in a new temple at the foot of the hill. The zamīndārs of Sabalpur, by whose ancestors the new temple was built, affirm that the image of Madhusūdan after its plunge into the Sītākund, went direct to Pānchet, and then appeared to one of their ancestors in a dream; and that it was not till they had waited in vain upon the Rājā of that place for recovery of the image, that Madhusūdan condescended to appear in the tank at Kajrāli. A few feet above the Sītākund is another spring, which is called Sānkhkund, from a monster *sānkh* or shell, which is said to have rested beneath its waters. The *sānkh*, to judge of its size by the impression left on the bank—the only sign at the present day of its existence in the past—was about three feet long by a foot and a half wide. It is said to be the same shell that is designated Panchajanya in the Mahābharata, whose sound used to fill the ranks of the enemy with dismay. Further north is situated a spring named Akāshgangā, or the river of the sky. The only approach to it is by a wooden ladder about fifteen feet high. The water, which is contained in a cavity of the shape of a shallow cone cut in the rock, is only about three feet deep, and is very transparent. This cavity, to which no rain-water can find access, fills itself as often as it is emptied, being supplied from an unseen source—a fact noticed by Colonel

Franklin. On the left side of the Akāshgangā the colossal figure of Madhukāitab is traced on the rock. About fifteen feet below is a vaulted cave cut in a smaller ridge of rock. The chamber is about fifteen feet by ten, and gets higher as it recedes from the entrance owing to the inclination of the roof, on which there is an inscription in large letters, not yet deciphered. The only approach is by a small door which just enables a person to enter in a crouching posture; but does not admit sufficient light to show the interior. An ascetic residing on the hill, however, supplies visitors with lamps. The cave contains a most interesting group of sculpture portraying one of the incarnations of Vishnu. This stands in the middle of the cell, and its principal figure is a man-lion tearing to pieces the body of a Titan thrown over his thigh. A child stands underneath with half shut eyes, trembling at the fearful scene. There are other figures, such as those of Lakshmī, Saraswatī, Rāma, etc ; but the cave takes its name from the central image, to which it is principally dedicated. The legend to which the latter alludes is one of the most tragic of the purer and earlier myths of monotheistic Hinduism. There were two brother Asūrs or Titans, who by the favour of Siva, became so powerful that, expelling the gods, they usurped the thrones of heaven. In the pride of victory, the elder brother, named Hiranyakha, thought himself a match even for Vishnu in prowess, and sought him in the nether world to give him battle, but was killed in the encounter. In consequence of the death of his brother, the younger Titan, Hiranyakaship by name, hated Vishnu so intensely that he could not bear to hear his name pronounced in his presence. In course of time a son named Prahlād was born to him, who, forsaking the studies and pursuits suited to his age, began to pray to Vishnu night and day. The father, rendered furious at his son's behaviour, and finding it impossible to shake his constancy or induce him to forsake his devotion, ordered him to be put to death. Although successively hurled to the earth from the summit of a high hill, placed upon a flaming pile, thrown into the sea with weights fastened round his neck, and trampled under the feet of an elephant, Prahlād escaped uninjured. The monarch then asked his son how he had survived such fearful perils, to which he replied that Vishnu had preserved him. "But where is this Vishnu?" demanded the incensed father. "He is," replied the son, "present everywhere." "Is he present in that impervious and solid body?" asked Hiranyakaship, pointing with his finger to a large crystal globe that stood before him. "Yes, father," replied Prahlād, "he must be there, because he is omnipresent, and nothing can exist without him." Scarcely were these words uttered, when Hiranyakaship's scimitar shivered the crystal into a thousand pieces. At the same instant a terrific figure, with the head and foreclaws of a lion and underpart of a man, issued from amid the broken fragments, and throwing Hiranyakaship over his thigh, tore him to pieces. This fearful scene took place in the twilight; and the Titan perished thus, because, through the favour of Siva, it had been vouchsafed to him that he should die neither by the hands of god or demi-god, of man or beast, in the water or in the air, during the glare of day or the shades of night. This legend about Hiranyakaship is current in various other districts, as explanatory of local ruins.

Colonel Franklin, in the second volume of his Inquiry concerning the site of Pālibothrā, gives a detailed description of this mountain and its shrines. There are altogether twelve tanks on different sides of it, excavated in the rock. In the *Varāha Purāna* or Legend of the Fourth or Boar Incarnation of Vishnu, there occurs the following dialogue in which the sanctity of Mandar is set forth. Skanda, the son of Mahādeo, addresses Krishna, "O Bhagabān, thou hast spoken already of all things, of Tirthā and Hari Tirthā, of Benarasyā Tirthā, of Jagannāth, of Prayāg, and of Chākra Tirthā. I am now desirous to learn from thee the nature and situation of Mandar. Vouchsafe me its history, O chief of the *debatās*, for thou art worthy to relate it and spare not its details." The godhead Srī Maheswar replied, "My grateful child, by this inquiry thou shalt gratify thy heart. Know, then, that amongst the places of worship Mandar is the greatest in the world. It is the place of residence of holy men of pure disposition; of Lakshmi, with eyes like the lotus that entrance the heart. It also saw the destruction of the malignant demon Madhu, whose fall was celebrated with songs of joy in the holy Vedas by all the *debatās;* therefore no place of worship is superior in sanctity to Mandar Mandar covered with beautiful flowers the shrine where the *debatās* reverence the footstep of thee, O Vishnu, where Brahma himself was produced from the lotus, and where he paid worship and adoration at the feet of Mahādeo and Vishnu. There also dwells the goddess Devī, beautiful as the flower of the lotus, and delicate as the plant thereof." Bhagabān replied, "Know, O Rājā, that there is a place of worship which enchants the heart, where the wind blows with violence on all sides, a temple as yet hidden from the sight of men. It is Mandar, the greatest in the world. There Vishnu resides for ever, he who destroys the demon Madhu of malignant fame. It was Bhagabān who cast him under ground, and without difficulty placed the mountain Mandar on his head, an everlasting burden! Therefore, O Rājā, is Vishnu the sovereign of all the *debatās*. The sinner and the sin shall find equal absolution at Mandar. Whoever, O Rājā, shall in the future visit Mandar with due reverence, he shall be acceptable to the god, and be absolved from his sins by the grace of Vishnu." Kapila Mūnī then complains that he is old and infirm, that his strength is decaying, and his eye-sight weak, and asks how he may obtain relief from these infirmities. The god continues: "Mandar is conspicuous for a spacious lake situated at the foot of the mountain, wherein those who bathe shall become united to Vishnu. The water flows from the rock a stream of holy quality, glittering like the sunlight breaking in through surrounding darkness. O Rājā, that lake enchants the very soul. Sinners who bathe therein shall, together with their kindred and descendants, be absolved from sin and sickness. Fast, therefore, O Rājā! for one day, and then bathe, and be united to Vishnu. The act of ablution in this place is equivalent to the sacrifice of an Aswamedha-jajna (the Horse Sacrifice) at the place where Rāma mourned for his deceased father. There is half way up the mountain another lake whose waters glitter like gold. At sight of that water grief is dispelled from the heart. It flows from the mountains. Whenever thou visitest this mountain be thou abstemious in thy soul, O Rājā, and bathe therein in the presence of the great guardian of mankind, Jagat Gūrū, whose residence is on the southern summit. He who shall yield up his soul at this place shall be absolved from his sins, and he who shall voluntarily relinquish the pleasures of this world shall acquire a true knowledge of the divine being."

Colgong Rock Temple. The only rock-hewn temple in Bengal is to be found on an islet in the river at Colgong. On the summit of the same rock there was a large temple in Hiuen Tsiang's time, but it was long ago reduced to ruins. Both temples were probably desecrated at a very early date by the Muhammadan invaders. Colgong was considered a specially holy place by the Hindus, because the river takes a sudden bend north there. Such northern bends are believed to have been the scenes of amorous encounters of a god with a river-nymph.

Jahangira and Baiskaran. Not far from Sultanganj is situated Jahangira, which also derives its holy character from a northern bend (*uttara bahini*) of the Ganges which occurs here. Jahangira is a rocky islet and Baiskaran is a rocky promontory close to it on the mainland. The name has no connection with the Emperor Jehangir, but is derived from a hermit, Jahru Rishi, who formerly lived on the rock. From the sculptured figures on it, it seems that the place was originally esteemed holy by the Buddhists. As both Buddhist and Hindu carvings are found, it is safe to conclude that the Hindus appropriated this sacred place on the downfall of Buddhism.

On Baiskaran promontory there are also carvings in the rock, and inscriptions in Gupta characters which indicate that they were made about the third century A.D. Cunningham* inclines to the belief that both Jahangira and Baiskaran were always occupied by Brâhmans, not Buddhists, and explains the Buddhist carvings as due to the Brahmanical Avatara of Buddha. Three great *melas* and several smaller festivals are celebrated at Baiskaran every year. A mosque is now situated on the top of this promontory.

Eight miles north-east of Colgong is Patharghatta, where the road crosses the end of a long hill called *Chaurasi murti* or eighty-four images. There are numerous rock carvings and several caves at this place. The eighty-four images are carved on a rock facing the river and are believed to represent eighty-four sages (*muni*): or, according to Buchanan-Hamilton, the adventures of Rama and Krishna. The carvings are said to date prior to the eighth century A.D. **Patharghatta.**

There are caves at Barari from which have been recovered coins that were current in North India for several centuries before the Christian era. Hiuen Tsiang tells a legend about this place of days before the birth of Buddha (543 B.C.), somewhat as follows:—A herdsman tended his cattle near Champa. One day a bull strayed away and was thought to be lost, but he returned at evening all radiant with beauty. Even his lowing was wonderful. The other cattle, seized with fear, would not go near him. This went on for some time till at length the herdsman followed the bull one day through a cleft in the rocks and along a gallery for about four thousand feet. The gallery opened out and disclosed a charming wood filled with fruit trees and flowers, unknown to man. The leaves of the plants smelled sweet and the fruits on the trees were large and golden. The herdsman plucked one fruit, but was afraid to taste it. He then tried to carry it away, but it was snatched from him by a demon at the gate as he went out, behind the bull. **Barari.**

The herdsman returned at a later time and sought to secrete the glorious fruit in his clothes, but when half way through the gate on the demon's approach he was obliged to put it in his

* Archæological Survey Reports, Vol. XV, page 24. See also Asiatic Society's Journal (Bengal), 1864, Vol. XXXIII, page 360.

mouth and to swallow it whole. On this his stomach expanded till the man was wedged in the rocks unable to move. The king of the place came to see this marvel but could not break away the stones. The man gradually became petrified, still maintaining his human form. The rock was so hard that it was impossible to chisel it away. The remnants of the petrified man were shown to Hiuen Tsiang.

Remains north of the River.

On the north side of the river Ganges, the most important remains are those of the Bir Bandh—a long embankment that follows the course of the Dāūs river in parganas Dhaphar and Harwal. It is usually thought to be a fortification, but it has also been conjectured that this embankment was thrown up to prevent the river Kosi from going still further west.

The embankment seems to have formerly run down to above the point where the Dāūs falls into the Tiljūgā. Dr. Buchanan-Hamilton, in his description of it, gives the reasons commonly assigned for believing it to have been erected for military purposes. That it was made to restrain the river's overflow is, however, now the opinion of many. "There is," Dr. Buchanan-Hamilton writes, "a line of fortifications which extends due north from the source of the Dāūs river to the hills, and which is attributed by the best informed natives to a prince of the name of Bīr. This line has evidently been intended to form a frontier towards the west, has been abandoned in the process of building, and has probably been intended to reach to the Ganges along the Dāūs river, which is nowhere of a size sufficient to give any kind of security to a frontier. As the lines are said to extend to the hills, it is probable that the Bengālī province of Maithilá included the whole of the country called Murang. As the works were never completed, and have the appearance of having been suddenly deserted, it is probable that they were erected by Lakshman the Second, who, in the year 1207, was subdued and expelled from Nadiyā by the Musalmāns. Lakshman the First seems to have been a conqueror, and in order to check the progress of his arms, the king of Dehli is said to have erected a fort at Sarāigarh in Tirhut. It is curious to remark, that by the tradition on the spot, the works said to have been erected by Lakshman are not alleged to have been as a defence against the Muhammadans, but against a people called Oriswa. Now, in D'Anville's map of Asia, I find laid down exactly beyond these works a country called Odyssa, which no doubt must be the same. I am ignorant of the authority on which this learned geographer proceeded; nor can I pretend to ascertain whether the Oriswas were a people who had wrested part of Maithilá from the weak successor of Lakshman the First, or were the remains of tribes who had governed the country under the kings of the Pāl dynasty. Neither am I sure whether the Muhammadans suffered the Oriswas to remain undisturbed, or whether they swallowed up, at the same time, both them and their opponents in Bengal." Dr. Buchanan-Hamilton is incorrect in representing the embankment as commencing at the source of the Dāūs. Further on, he gives a more accurate account of it, thus :—The most remarkable antiquity is the line of fortifications running through the north-west corner of this district for about twenty miles. It is called *Mazūrni-kātā*, or "dug by hired men," although by far the greater part of the natives attribute its formation to a different cause. They differ, however, considerably in their accounts, some alleging that it was made by a god or *debatā*, while others give the honour to a devil or *rākshāsa*. It is only a few that support the opinion which I have adopted, of its being the work of man. I traced it from the boundary of Gurkhā [Nepāl] to that of Tirhut, at which it terminates; but all the natives agree that it reaches to the bank of the Tiljūgā, a river which comes from the west to join the Kūsī. They say that on a hill overhanging the river there was a fort of stone, from whence the works ran south. Where the Mazūrnikātā enters the Company's territories, it is a very high and broad rampart of earth with a ditch on its west side. The counter-scarp is wide, and at the distance of every bow-shot has been strengthened by square projections reaching the edge of the ditch. The whole runs in an irregular, zig-zag direction, for which it would be difficult to account. Further south, the width and dimensions of both rampart and ditch diminish, nor can any of the flanking projections be traced. For the last mile it consists merely of a few irregular heaps clustered together, apparently as if the workmen had suddenly deserted it when they had collected only a small part of the materials, by digging them from the ditch and throwing them from their baskets." The popular tradition referred to, is that in olden times there lived in the lower Nepāl hills a giant Asur or demon, who wooed Gangā, the goddess of the Ganges. She was unwilling to receive or refuse his advances at once, and therefore imposed on him a seemingly impossible task as the condition of her favour. He was to make a road from the bank of the Ganges to his home in the mountains, in a single night between sun-down and sun-rise. He commenced his task from the Nepāl end, and progressed with such rapidity that he had already before midnight completed the road to Gūriyahāt on the river Dāūs. At this the goddess became alarmed and applied to the cock in her difficulty. The cock crew, although the night was not half past, and the giant thinking that day was about to dawn, ceased from his work in despair, and retired to the mountains.

Old Forts. Ruins of old forts are found at Talbori, Barāntpur, Rājghāt, Madhūkarchak, Srīnagar, Patharghāt, Madanpur and Dhabaulī in Madhipura subdivision, and at Kapgarh and Bijalgarh in Supaul subdivision. There are also the remains of large houses at Sāhugarh and Khājuri, and of temples at Srīnagar, Barantpur, Rohtā, and Lohur. The fort at Barāntpur is identified by some with the fort and city of Birāt, mentioned in the Mahābhārat. Rājghāt seems to have been the residence and fortified town of some petty prince, of comparatively late times. Madhūkarchak fort is evidently a Musalmān ruin, from the peculiar small glazed tiles found in it. Srīnagar is known to have been erected by Srīdeo, a Bhar chieftain, probably three or four hundred years ago, at the same time that his brothers, Kāp and Bijal, built the forts called after their names. The forts at Dhabaulī, Madanpur, and Patharghāt were also built by three Bhar brothers for mutual protection; the ruins of the latter alone are clearly visible. It is not certain to whom the houses at Sāhugarh and Khājuri belonged, but it would seem probable that the former was in existence in the time of Sikandra Shāh, son of Ilyās Shāh, King of Bengal, as coins bearing the date of his reign have been found in the ruins. The shrine at Lohār has only a few stones standing, but is still a place of worship for the neighbouring villagers in times of epidemics and droughts. The temples at Barāntpur and Rhotā were built originally by Buddhists, probably about A.D. 1100, when the Pāl dynasty ruled in South Bīhar. An image of the goddess Maheswarī, or Chandī, has been found in the former; and also an inscription which states that it was endowed by "the conquering Sarbasinh Deo, who is adorned with every virtue, the blessed of Maheswarī, the joy-bestowing moon of the lotus-lineage of Budhesa." The Jalsīmā zamīndār has lately built a new temple on the ruins; and a yearly fair is held about the time of the Durgā-pūja holidays, when numerous buffaloes are offered up to Kālī, the goddess of destruction. Formerly, no doubt, Buddhist priests officiated; but at present a class of Goālās, called *debhars*, or "feeders on the idol," that is, who live on the offerings, are the attendant priests.

CHAPTER III.

THE PEOPLE.

THE first enumeration of the population of this district that has any claim to be considered scientifically accurate is that made in 1872. It showed a total population of 1,824,738. By 1881 the population had increased to 1,966,158. It is a commonplace that part of the general increase in population noticeable on comparing the figures of 1881 with those of 1872 is to be attributed to the greater care taken to secure accuracy in the returns in 1881. But that there was an absolute increase as well is beyond doubt. ACCURATE ENUMERATIONS.

In 1891 the total population was ascertained to be 2,032,696 and by 1901 it had risen to 2,088,953.

Elaborate actuarial calculations have established that an increase of 7 per cent. should be expected in any decennial period. The general average percentage increase, however, has proved to be only 4·7 in British territory in Bengal; and in this district it was only about 2·8 in the decade between 1891 and 1901. In the period between 1872 and 1881 the increase was by 7·7 per cent. and in the decade 1881 to 1891 it was 3·3 per cent. The marked decline in the rate of increase between 1881 and 1891 as compared with that in the period 1872 to 1881 must be attributed largely to the less accurate nature of the enumeration made in 1872.

The increase in population between 1891 and 1901 was far from being uniform throughout the district. It was greatest in the Supaul subdivision in which it amounted to 6·1 per cent. The bulk of this increase was in Pratabganj thāna, which was opened up by the railway in this interval. It is very interesting to note that between 1881 and 1891 the Supaul subdivision also showed the greatest increase. Next to it, the increase was greatest in the Sadar subdivision, in which it amounted to 6 per cent. The greater part of this increase was in Bhāgalpur and Colgong thānas, and it has been attributed to increased commercial activity in the two municipalities, which attracted more inhabitants into them.

In Bānkā subdivision the increase was 2·4 per cent., and in Madhipurā subdivision there was an absolute decrease of 2·8 per cent. Most of this was in thāna Kishanganj in which the decrease was 6·9 per cent. In Madhipurā thāna itself there was a decrease of 3 8 per cent. and in Bangaon alone of the three thānas of this subdivision there was an increase of 2 per cent. The causes of this falling off must be sought in the unhealthy nature of Kishanganj thāna. In the decade 1881 to 1891 its population showed a decrease of 7·5 per cent. The figur s for the decade 1891 to 1901 are not so disheartening. It is fair to conclude that the inhabitants are moving from that fever-stricken water-logged area to healthier areas further north, beyond the reach of the influence of the Kosī.

MIGRATORY MOVEMENTS.

It appears that in 1901 the total number of natives of this district, namely, 124,305 (comprising 66,491 males and 57,814 females) who had emigrated and were enumerated in other districts was in excess of the total number of immigrants, namely, 107,538 (comprising 58,006 males and 49,532 females) who were found in this district at the time the census was taken, but who were born elsewhere.

Thus it appears that the tendency to migration, so noticeable in Saran district, has spread to Bhāgalpur and that the losses by emigration substantially exceed the gains by immigration. In 1891 the balance was considerably the other way, the total number of immigrants then enumerated in this district being 154,564, and the total number of emigrants enumerated elsewhere being 125,127. It is of course quite impossible to distinguish temporary from permanent emigrants and immigrants. It may however be concluded that a large proportion of the emigration as well as of the immigration is only temporary as the male sex largely predominates, as shown above, in the figures both of emigrants and of immigrants, whereas in the district as a whole the females outnumber the males by over 33,000.

INTERMEDIATE CHANGES OF AREA.

The changes in the area of the district between 1872 and 1891 have of course vitiated to some extent the comparisons just made. Thus, in 1891, the population of the area which constituted the district in 1901 was 1,967,635 as against a total for the district as then constituted (1891) of 2,032,696.

Density of population.

The pressure of the population on the soil has gone on increasing steadily since 1872. In that year there were 432 persons per square mile in the district. In 1881 there were 465 persons. In 1891, there were 481 and in 1901 there were 494. This figure is considerably below that for the adjacent districts of Monghyr and Darbhanga with 527 and 873 persons per square mile, respectively; but it is considerably in excess of Purnea, which has only 375 per square mile.

Density by thanas.

The following thānas have a density per square mile not less than this average, 494:—

SADAR *Subdivision* (627)—

Bhāgalpur (1,050): Colgong (474): Sultanganj (576): Bihpur (549).

The high figure for Bhāgalpur is clearly due to the fact that it includes the municipal area in which the density per square mile is 9,470.

BANKA *Subdivision* (367)—

Amarpur (520).

MADHIPURA *Subdivision* (476)—

Madhipura (505): Bangaon (632).

SUPAUL *Subdivision* (547)—

Supaul (606).

In the following thānas the density is less than this average, 494—

SADAR *Subdivision* (627)—

Nil.

BANKA *Subdivision* (367)—

Banka (457): Katauria (223).

MADHIPURA *Subdivision* (476)—

Kishanganj (318).

SUPAUL *Subdivision* (547)—

Pratapganj (444).

Urban and rural population.

The total urban population is only 81,498. Bhāgalpur town accounts for 75,760 persons out of this total, and Colgong town for the remainder, namely, 5,738 persons. Thus only 4 per cent. of the population is urban and 96 per cent. is rural. Of the rural population 52 per cent. live in villages, the population of which varies from 500 to 2,000: 23 per cent. live in villages, the population of which varies from 2,000 to 5,000, and 20 per cent. in villages of which the population is 500 or less.

The town of Bhāgalpur alone of the large towns of Bihar shows a steady increase in population since 1872. From 1891 to 1901 the increase was by 9·6 per cent. This increase is attributed to great commercial activity consequent on the opening of new railway stations and the increased accommodation provided for goods. Still, with 96 per cent. of the district population purely rural, there cannot be said to be any indication of a considerable drain from the country to the towns.

Language.

The language prevalent in the district is the Maithili dialect of Bihari Hindi. Mithila, also called Tirhutia, was the country bounded on the north by the Himālayas, on the south by the Ganges, on the east by the Kosī and on the west by the Gandak, and it is famous as being the home of the Tirhutia Brāhmans. For a long time those of them who lived south of the Ganges were considered socially inferior to those who remained within the confines of Mithila, but this distinction seems to have passed away.

In the south of the district there is a dialect prevalent called "*chhikka-chhikki boli*," the most striking peculiarity of which is that those who speak it add a vowel sound (like "o" in "not") at the end of words. The Magahi dialect of Bihari Hindi has had some influence on the grammar and vocabulary of that part of the district lying south of the Ganges, but it has not ousted the Maithili dialect. The "*chhikka chhikki boli*" is so called from its frequent use of the syllable "*chhik*" in the conjugation of the verb substantive.*

Educated Muhammadans of course prefer to speak Urdu with more or less of a Persian admixture.

The character in most common use is the cursive Kaithi, an invention of the Kayasths who derived it obviously from the Devanagari character. In 1871 Sir George Campbell made the use of this character optional in all court transactions, in addition to the Persian character. In 1880 the further use of the Persian character was prohibited, and the exclusive use of Kaithi was prescribed. The use of this character has had the effect of gradually assimilating the language used in school books, petitions, etc., to that in common everyday use. Formerly a quite excessive number of Arabic and Persian words were used in the court languages current in Bihar.

The non-Aryan people in the south of the district speak their own languages, such as Sonthali, Uraon and Mundari. Most of those who speak these languages are found in Bāukā subdivision. There were 26,632 Sontals, 4,804 Uraons and 1,190 Mundas in the district at the time of the 1901 census.

Religions. The vast bulk of the population is Hindu. There were 1,875,309 Hindus, 209,311 Musalmāns, 775 Christians and 3,558 "others" in the district in 1901.

Between 1881 and 1891 there was a marked decline in the proportion of Hindus in the district. There was an increase from 1891 to 1901, the proportions per cent. to the total population being, in 1881, 89·73 : in 1891, 89·11 and in 1901, 89·77. The percentage in 1901 is thus only nominally in excess of that in 1881.

* Over 900,000 persons speak this dialect: see Grierson's Linguistic Survey, Vol. V, p. 95.

Among Musalmans, on the other hand, there has been a steady increase throughout this period. In 1881, the proportion of Musalmans to the total population was 9·44. In 1891, it was 9·62 and by 1901 it had risen to 10·02. This greater rapidity in growth among Musalmans is not peculiar to this district. In the province, as a whole, Musalmans are increasing at almost double the rate of increase observable among the Hindus. This is most probably due to greater reproductive power among the Musalmans. The growth by conversions to Islamism is practically *nil*, whereas there is a well-marked tendency on the part of animistic tribes to become assimilated to Hinduism. Again, a Muhammadan widow remarries more readily than a Hindu widow; and usually the disparity of age between husband and wife is less in the case of Musalmans than in the case of Hindus. Finally, it has been pointed out that when a Hindu widow becomes pregnant, as the result of an intrigue, her first instinctive impulse is towards procuring abortion. The Muhammadan widow, on the other hand under similar conditions, is said to welcome the appearance of pregnancy, and the probable advent of a child as circumstances calculated to induce her paramour to regularize her position by taking her into his zenana.

Christians. In all only 775 individuals were found in this district, who professed Christianity, in 1901. In 1891, the total was 536 and in 1881, 578. There has thus been an increase of about 33 per cent. since 1881. In 1901, the number of Native Christians was 514. There are several missionary bodies in the district. The chief foundation is probably that of the Roman Catholics at Latona near Supaul, in the north of the district It dates back its origin to the year 18[illegible]1. It has outlying branches at Dumurea and at Garhea, near Raghopur station Its congregation numbers nearly 400. There is a mission founded by the Church Missionary Society at Champanagar, a few miles from the town of Bhāgalpur. In the town itself there is a branch of the Church of England Zenana Missionary Society which displays much activity, inasmuch as the missionaries superintend a leper asylum, an orphanage and a high school. At Jaypur, in the south of the district, there is an independent mission.

Chief castes. According to numerical superiority, the following were the ten Hindu castes of most importance in this district in 1901:—

Abirs and Goalas	366,980
Dhanuks	102,680
Musahars	93,750
Chamars	90,390
Koiris	88,850

Tantis	...	...	...	80,200
Dosadhs	...	...	...	79,360
Brāhmans	...	...	...	76,530
Telis	...	...	...	72,130
Kewats	...	...	...	57,620

Among the Musalmans, 91,800 were classed as Shekhs, 30,450 as Kunjras and 29,290 as Jolahas.

Goalas. 366,980. The Ahirs and Goalas are grouped together and easily outnumber all other castes. They own cattle and have taken to agricultural pursuits in addition to their traditional pastoral profession.

They have a special caste godling named Bisu Raut who was torn to pieces by a Gourhi sorcerer (taking the form of a tiger) because milk was refused to him. His chief shrine is on the banks of the Gogri river.

It has been stated that the Goalas are too numerous to be of pure Aryan descent, and that it is probable that they are largely the descendants of aboriginals whose status was recognized as honourable owing to their profession as cattle-tenders. In addition to the godling just mentioned, they have another glorified hero whose adventures are well known all over Bihar in the ballad of Lūrik. The legend is here reproduced from Hunter's Statistical Account:—Lūrik was a native of Gaur and a favourite of the goddess Durgā. The story runs that one morning at daybreak, his wife, Mānjar, accidentally saw him dallying with Chānāin, the daughter of Sahadīp Māhāra, the Rājā of his native village, a bearer by caste. Being versed in astrology, she consults her books and finds therefrom that Lūrik was to run away with the Rājā's daughter on that very night. She tells her mother-in-law the misfortune that is to overtake the family, and requests her to defer the time for supper by pounding the rice again and again and to prolong the meal by preparing a large number of dishes. A considerable portion of the night is thus passed, and it is nearly daybreak when the family retire to rest, his wife binding Lūrik in her own clothes, and the mother spreading her bed so as to bar the only outlet from the cottage. The Rājā's daughter Chānāin, not finding Lūrik under the large tree where they had agreed to meet, marks it with five red spots, and advancing a few steps, calls on Durgā for aid. The goddess promises to bring Lūrik, and to prolong the night seven times, if it be necessary for the purpose, and finally opens a passage for him through the roof of his hut. The lovers having met at last, start for Hardī (in the present Madhipurā subdivision). On the way, the Rājā's daughter refuses to eat from Lūrik's plate unless he consents to make her his wife. After some hesitation, Lūrik places some *sindūr* on her forehead, and the marriage ceremony is performed by Durgā herself, assisted by her seven sisters.

One night whilst sleeping under a tree, Chānāin is stung by a serpent and dies. Lūrik, in his grief, erects a funeral pile, and, setting fire to it, sits on it with Chānāin in his arms. The fire is extinguished by some unknown power, to be again kindled and again extinguished. The universe trembles to the throne of the gods, and the gods sit discussing the extraordinary sight of a husband offering to die on his wife's funeral pile. A goddess is sent to earth. Assuming the shape of an old woman, she approaches the pile, and tells Lūrik to desist, but, finding him obstinate in his resolve, offers to revive the dead. The corpse is replaced on its bed, the serpent is summoned, and sucks its own poison from the wound; Chānāin is restored to life, and the serpent is killed. The lovers set out again on their travels. When near Rohinī, where Mahāpātiā, a goldsmith by caste, used to rule, they are surrounded by the Rājā's attendants, who invite Lūrik to a gambling match at the palace. The Rājā is a cheat, and by means of loaded dice wins everything from Lūrik including his beautiful wife, whom he covets more than anything else. Chānāin refuses to submit, and will only yield if she is herself vanquished in play. The game begins, Chánáin throws away the dice as unfair; takes new ones, and gains little by little everything the Rājā owns.

From Rohinī the travellers reach Hardī, the place of their destination. Here Lūrik is introduced to the Rājā, but the latter, incensed at his omission to bow before him, will not allow him a place in his capital unless he accepts the occupation of a cowherd. Lūrik indignantly replies that he will only turn cowherd, if the Rājā's daughter comes out herself to milk the cows. A battle ensues, which lasts for seven days and seven nights, and ends in the slaughter of the immense hosts of the Rājā, a result attributed to the goddess whose favour Chānāin obtains by offering to sacrifice her first-born. The Rājā now consents to give half his dominions to Lūrik, if he will bring him the head of his antagonist, the Rājā of Hanrwá. This he undertakes to do, and, on accomplishing the task, is proclaimed joint-king of Hardī, which position he holds for twelve years.

One night Lūrik happens to hear a woman weep near his place, and asks his mistress to enquire into the cause. As she goes out for the purpose, she is followed unseen by her lover. In reply to Chānāin's enquiries, the old woman says that her tears had been caused by the sight of the meals she has been accumulating for three days, in the vain expectation of her son, return from a journey. Fearing that this story will make Lūrik anxious to return home to his wife and mother, Chānāin advises the woman to complain falsely of some ill-treatment to account for her tears, if questioned by Lūrik on the subject. Lūrik, who has overheard everything, accuses her of falsehood, and says that if three days' absence of a son on duty can make a mother weep so much, his own mother and wife must have shed many tears during the twelve years of his self-imposed exile from home. This reflection works so powerfully on his mind, that he instantly departs for home, accompanied by his beautiful mistress whose residence he fixes in his neighbourhood.

This deification of a cowherd may of course be due to the need felt by the numerous cow-keepers of a special deity sprung from their own class, and is perhaps indicative of an attempt to rise in the social scale.

The legend of Jaydeb Dube, Bhay Haran.

It is convenient to insert in this place the best known legend from the south of the district. A Bārhām *bhut* is the ghost of a Brāhman who has died a violent death. They are found in various places always exercising a malignant influence. The best known is Jaydeb Dube, also known as Bhay Haran)fear dispeller) or Bhāiran. Banka is interesting as being the chief seat of the worship of this. The legend connected with his name is as follows, as derived from the translation of Bābu Rasbihāri Bose:—"Nowhere," the Bābu remarks, "as far as I know, does demon worship prevail in Bengal. But in Bhāgalpur District every village has its own demon, who is propitiated by offerings made at the foot of a tree, where he is supposed to reside. Belief in demons or ghosts is almost as prevalent in Bengal as it is in this District; but if annoyances are caused by them, the gods are invoked or exorcisms are practised to expel them, while in Bhāgalpur they are propitiated by presents, and their blessings asked in cases of difficulty or danger. Demon worship is not prevalent in all Behar, and its presence in the few Districts in which it exists, is probably owing to the close vicinity of the Kols." Dube Bhāiran, an astrologer of Upper India, was invited to the court of a Kshetaurī Rājā, named Birmā, to foretell future events. After consulting the stars, he built his dwelling on an auspicious spot near Birmā's palace at Dadrī, in Monghyr. The superstitious Rājā, being anxious to appropriate to himself the benefits that were inseparable from the lot of the man who owned the place, asked Bhāiran to give it up to him, but in vain. However, taking advantage of the seer's absence from home, he pulled down one of his cottages and built a wall at the place so as to enclose the ground within the limits of the palace. When Bhāiran returned he was deeply incensed against the Rājā; snatching a knife, he plunged it into his own body, and threw the flowing blood over the Rājā's palace, which instantly burst into flames and was reduced to ashes. Finding no place safe from the vengeance of the offended demon, Birmā threw himself on the mercy of Baidyanāth at Deogarh, but the demon appeared before the deity himself at his abode in Mount Kailās to demand the surrender of the prince. So terrible was the wrath of the Brāhman demon, that the mount began to tremble on the trident, on which the deity has fixed it, in order to make it more secure against earthquakes and other accidents to which the globe is subject. His wife, Parvatī, became alarmed, but the deity told her to appease the demon by treating him as her brother. She accordingly approached, like a hospitable Hindu lady, with a vessel of water in her hands and asked to be permitted to wash his feet. At this the demon became appeased, when the god assured him that he had not succoured Birmā in his temple, and that Bhāiran was welcome to deal with his victim in any way he pleased. At the same time the omnipresent deity told Birmā at Deogarh to go and seek for shelter at the hill of Mandar, the temple of Madhusūdan. The unfortunate Rājā went there in vain, and wandering thence to various sacred places, was at last killed on the top of Tīnpahār, crushed under the weight of a huge stone hurled at him by the ghost of Bhāiran's servant, Rājū Khawās. The ghost of Dube Bhāiran pursued the remaining Rājās of the Kshetaurī race and all that bore their name with unrelenting hatred, till not one of the ill-fated dynasty remained upon earth. There were fifty-two independent Kshetaurī Rājās holding sway in different parts of Behar just before the Muhammadan conquest of the country; but at the present time there are only four, those of Bārkop, Mahāganoyā, and Manihārī in Subdivision Goddá, and Hanruá in Subdivision Dūmkā in the Sonthāl Parganās, who claim to be descended from that race, and even these are not recognised as coming from the genuine stock.

In accordance with the above legend, Bhāiran is considered as only second to the great Baidyanāth at Deogarh. His servant, Rājū Khawās, who is said to have committed suicide on the death-bed of his master, is equally worshipped with him. The animal sacrifices, which Bhāiran, as a Brāhman, would not accept, are offered to his servant, while rice and sweetmeats are the share of the master. At Dadrí, the demon is supposed to take possession of the officiating priest, who speaks as one inspired. The legend has been given in full, as it takes as important a position in the south of the district as the ballad of Lūrik does in the north.

Dhanuks. 102,680. Next in number after the Goalas come the Dhanuks, who number 102,680. They are the caste that furnish most of the domestic servants at present. Their name is equivalent to "bowmen," and there is little doubt but that they are largely aboriginal by descent. They were probably recruited as soldiers by the Aryan invaders. Dhanuks are generally regarded as "clean" Sudras for whom high class Brāhmans will officiate and from whom other castes will take water, but often those who act as domestic servants are regarded as being lower in the social scale because they will eat the leavings of higher castes.

Musahars. 93,750. The Musahars are nearly all day-labourers. They lead a life very near the margin of subsistence and eat rats, snails, snakes or anything else that they can find. Probably they are the remnants of the original Dravidian inhabitants, who were reduced to slavery by the Aryan invaders. The vast majority of them are found in this district and in Monghyr. They worship their own caste deities, Hansaraj, Bansaraj and Dinabhadri.

Chamars. 90,390. The Chamars are fairly numerous, and fulfil extremely important functions in the social scheme. The Chamar works in leather, and is entitled by custom to the hides of all cattle that die. Consequently, when cattle do not die rapidly enough, the Chamar occasionally poisons them or is at least credited with hastening their death. He supplies shoes, whipthongs, drumheads, and any pieces of leather needed about a cart. The Chamain is the village midwife, and she attends professionally on the women of all castes during their confinement. Usually the Chamar and his wife are paid in grain by the village community.

Koiris. 38,850. The Koiris are the best agriculturists and can usually get more out of the soil than any other cultivators. Near big towns they act as market-gardeners and show considerable enterprise.

Tantis. 80,200. The Tantis were originally a purely "functional" caste, following the occupation of weavers. Now many of them have become petty agriculturists, with the decline of the indigenous weaving industry.

Dosadhs. 79,360. The Dosadhs are a very low caste—swineherds by traditional occupation. They also supply large numbers of labourers, and the post of village chowkidar is almost invariably held by a Dosadh. They were largely professional thieves and dacoits, but are reported to be giving up their predatory habits.

Brāhmans. 76,530. Though admittedly first in social position, the Brāhmans are not so strong numerically in this district as elsewhere.

Representatives of the Kananjia, Maithila, Gour and Sokaduipi divisions of Brāhmans are met with, and numerous subdivisions within these main divisions are found.

The Maithila Brāhmans are the most numerous and they still keep up their unique family records for the purpose of arranging marriages. They still merit the terse description attached to them by Rama Chandra when they refused to help him.* The keepers of the records are known as *panjiars* and they act along with *ghataks* or marriage-brokers. In this district, the annual meetings for arranging the marriages are held at Bangaon and Barari. The office of *panjiar* is now hereditary, but the permission of the Māharājā of Darbhanga must be taken before a *panjiar* can begin the exercise of his functions.

The main object aimed at by the maintenance of these genealogical records is the prevention of any marriage within the prohibited degrees of relationship. The institution of the system is attributed to Rājā Hara Singh Deva, one of whose ministers is said to have, through ignorance, married a lady within the prohibited degrees.

The traditional occupation of the Telis caste is oil-pressing and oil-selling, but, in addition, many of them have now acquired lands and follow agricultural pursuits. **Telis. 72,130.**

Kewats are traditionally boating and fishing castes, and are mostly found in the north of the district. Large numbers of them have abandoned their traditional occupation and have taken to agriculture. These are known as *grihastas* and are considered to hold higher social rank than the others. **Kewats. 57,620.**

It is hard to find any survivals of a genuine autonomous village community anywhere in Bhāgalpur. Most of the village officials named below are indistinguishable now from mere servants of the *zamindār* or other landlord. **The village community and officials.**

The *gomasta* is the landlord's chief agent and is responsible for rent collection, assessment of new holdings, resettlement of abandoned holdings and generally is supposed to watch the interests of his master in the local area committed to his charge. The *tahsildar* is a superior *gomasta*, with several villages under him. **GOMASTA. TAHSILDAR.**

The *patwari* was in theory a Government official appointed under Regulation XIII of 1817, to keep the village accounts. In fact, he is the landlord's servant, appointed by him at will. The history of the village *patwari* and of the various attempts **PATWARI.**

---

* *Grihe sura rahne bhitah, paraspara virodhinah: Kula bhimanini yuyam maithilyam bhavirshyatha.*

i. e., "Heroes at home; cowards in the battle-field; ever quarreling among yourselves and inordinately full of family pride shall you be in Maithila."

and suggestions made to rehabilitate him must be sought for elsewhere. Prior to the recent operations for the preparation of a record-of-rights under Chapter X of the Bengal Tenancy Act, both landlord and tenant were practically at the mercy of the *patwari* whenever rent cases came into court. In some places the *patwari* collects rents in addition to keeping the accounts. In addition to small fixed pay, he gets perquisities from all the servants. He also occasionally holds lands on favourable terms and not infrequently gets entire holdings into his hands and enjoys the fruits thereof while showing them as "unoccupied" or "abandoned" in the accounts.

Barahil Gorait.

The *barahil* and *gorait* are virtually peons who call the raiyats together, and attend on the *gomasta* or *tahsildar*.

Sonthal villages.

In the southern villages inhabited by Sonthāls, their own system of internal government by their own village headmen or *manjhis* is kept up.

Economic conditions.

The people of this district depend almost entirely on agriculture for their livelihood, and their prosperity or otherwise depends directly on the amount of the annual rainfall, and on its proper distribution. In Chapter VI full details of recent years of scarcity are given. In such years, the landless labourer is the first to suffer. But as now-a-days, the increased facilities for temporary emigration afforded by the improvement of communications tend to break down the old disinclination of the Indian peasant for quitting his native place, whatever may have been the pressure of want, the classes that first feel the pinch of want evince a spirit of enterprise that impels them to leave their homes in search of work. Thus in the late scarcity in 1907-08 there was a marked movement from the affected areas to those in which there were good crops to be harvested or other sources of employment to be found.

It is difficult to indicate precisely the exact extent to which the economic condition of any people improves, when the periods selected for comparison are not separated by a wide interval of time. Still, the following indications are worthy of consideration as they tend to show that there has been an increase in the demand for petty comforts and luxuries.

The increase in the prices of agricultural produce has given to the peasants more money to spend. This increase has not reacted unfavourably on the landless labourers, as they are usually paid in kind: moreover, there has been an all-round rise in wages which would more than counterbalance a rise in the price of food-grains, had the casual labourer to purchase his food-supplies. This increased prosperity is indicated in the increased revenue derived from the sale of exciseable articles. The casual labourer is a drinker in this district, and having more money to spend, he indulges his taste for liquor.

Again, trade, both export and import, has been brisk of late years The demand for imported luxuries, such as umbrellas, shoes, cigarettes, soap, piece-goods, and various articles of domestic use has increased.

Habits of thrift appear to be growing among the people. The figures for deposits in the post office savings banks have gone on steadily increasing for ten years past. In Chapter VII a note is given about the present state of the movement for the establishment of co-operative credit societies in this district. It is at present only in its infancy, but it has a good field for its future development in this district. In that same chapter will be found some further remarks on the material condition of the people.

Houses. The ordinary dwelling house is a poor erection of mud walls with a thatched roof. Bamboos and thatching grass make the roof, straw being too valuable as fodder for cattle to be used for thatch. In some places tiled roofs are found. In April and May when the hot west winds set in, fires that burn out a whole village are not infrequent. The few brass utensils needed for cooking and eating from constitute the only articles of any value in the house. A hand-mill or a pestle and mortar (*okri*) for husking rice completes the necessary equipment. There may or may not be found as well a *charpai* (string bedstead with bamboo frame) and a couple of heavy boxes with coarsely made native locks on them.

Dress. A loin cloth and head cloth for the men are all that is necessary. The women generally wear a bodice and a *sari*. The men may also wear a cotton *chadar* on their shoulders.

Food. Usually the coarsest and cheapest grains are used for food. *Bhadoi* or autumn rice is looked on as the crop that should furnish sustenance for the cultivator and his family for the year. The *aghani* or winter rice crop is generally sold to pay rent, pay a little to the *mahajan* (or repay in kind a loan of seed grain with very heavy interest) and purchase oil, salt, sugar, clothes and other things which the cultivator must buy.

Barley flour is largely eaten where this crop is grown as a *rabi* or spring crop. Maize and marua are grown as *bhadoi* crops and are much used as food-crops. Vegetables of various sorts are grown for home consumption, sweet potatoes being perhaps the most popular on account of the good yield.

Where *mahua* trees abound, its flowers enter very largely into the dietary of the people around In famine years it becomes invaluable as it appears to thrive when nothing else will grow. Among fruits, the mango, jack, guava, and plantain are in great demand.

Where fish can be had, they are very popular as articles of diet. Turtles, land-crabs and water-crabs are also eaten. Near Sonthal villages, it is difficult now-a-days to find any sort of game, or living thing. Even the birds are nearly all killed off by the youngsters in the village who bring them down with blunt-headed arrows, displaying considerable accuracy in the use of their bows and these rather clumsy-looking projectiles.

Political and social institutions. The existing social institutions seem all to be exotic and not of indigenous origin. The chief political association is the Bhāgalpur Landholders' Association. This is not a large body, but it exercises considerable activity. It is consulted at times by Government. It offers opinions on administrative measures and has earned unenviable notoriety by its frenzied opposition to the extension of Survey and Settlement proceedings under Chapter X of the Bengal Tenancy Act to the Bhāgalpur Division. In 1892, this body, with some kindred organizations, presented a memorial against these proceedings to the Governor-General in Council. In Sir Antony (now Lord) McDonnell's minute of September 20th, 1893, published in the Supplement to the *Calcutta Gazette* of 25th October 1893, the position taken up by the memorialists was demolished. In describing the benefits that the preparation of a record-of-rights would bring to both landlords and tenants he stated that they would—

. . . "tend to prevent disputes, facilitate the decision of disputes when they arise in the courts and secure the enjoyment to ten millions of people of their legitimate rights. These rights have been withheld for a century and the memorialists must excuse me if I do not take their word for it that the raiyats are now animated by a violent desire to forego these rights still longer."

It took nearly twelve years for these operations to reach Bhāgalpur district, the districts of Saran, Champaran, Muzaffarpur, Darbhanga and North Monghyr having been first dealt with. In 1904, this Association approached the Lieutenant-Governor, Sir Andrew Fraser, with another memorial traversing the methods of the Settlement Department in general and in particular its interpretation of section 29 of the Bengal Tenancy Act. However, an authoritative ruling * of the High Court proved the memorialists wrong and the Settlement Department absolutely right.

In Chapter VII some details about the relations between landlords and tenants will be found, which show that the

* *Bipin Bihari Mandal* v. *Krishnadan Ghose*, 32 Calcutta, 395.

Bhāgalpur landlords are not all above criticism in their dealings with their tenants.

There is a branch of the *Indian National Congress* at Bhāgalpur. Its outward activities were formerly confined to the election of delegates to the annual general meeting of the Congress, but of late it has become a centre for seditious agitation.

Social institutions.

A few sectarian institutions exist with the object of ameliorating the condition of the particular section of the community that they represent. So far their influence has not extended very widely nor have their activities been other than very circumscribed. The *Kayastha Sabha, Anjuman Gurba* and *Bhumihar Babhan Sabha* are the most important of these societies.

The Marwari community keeps up the *Gaurakshini Sabha* which shelters and feeds infirm cattle. The anti-cow-killing riots in 1893-94 are thought to have been the outcome of the activities of the emissaries of kindred *sabhas*.

The Bhāgalpur Institute possesses a library. Its subscribers indulge in billiard-playing, newspaper-reading and seditious agitation. In 1908 its finances were in a distinctly unsatisfactory state. The *Banga Sanmilani Sabha* aims at having the so-called "partition" of Bengal modified. The Marwari Young Men's Association is said to be a collection of Extremists, and disciples of Tilak.

The Bihari Literary Society and the *Sahitya Parishad* are non-political associations that aim at literary and social improvement.

CHAPTER IV.

PUBLIC HEALTH.*

CLIMATE AND VITALITY.

At the end of Chapter I above meteorological observations are alluded to. On the whole this district is healthy. Its mean annual death-rate is 35·79 per mille, that for the whole province being 35·41 per mille for the quinquennial period ending with 1908.

The healthiest months are February, March and July—the average death-rate in these months not exceeding 2 per mille.

In April, May, June, August and September the average death-rate is about 2·25 per mille. In October, December and January it is about 2·5 and in November—the least healthy month—it is as high as 3·23 per mille.

The highest death-rate recorded is 41·3 per mille in 1894. That for 1908 was only 33·22 per mille.

The increased mortality noticed towards the close of the year is correctly attributed to malarial fevers. Of course the term "fever" in the mortality returns covers very many diseases other than malarial fevers, characterized by febrile symptoms. The village chaukīdār is not an expert in diagnosis and beyond small-pox, cholera and plague his opinion as to the cause of the deaths reported by him at the police stations does not deserve much consideration.

The least healthy part of the district is the area in the northern half that is exposed to the action of the Kosi floods. Kishanganj thāna suffers more than any other tract. Thana Bihpur comes next in point of unhealthiness.

In the south of the district, an acute type of fever prevails in the area bordering on the Rajmāhal hills in the autumn. In 1872 an outbreak of "dengue" fever occurred. It has not since reappeared. In Hunter's "Statistical Account" a full description of it is given.

Exhaustive statistical researches have failed to establish any clear connection between the birth-rate, mortality-rate and climatic conditions of different years.

---

* I am indebted to Captain Barnardo, I.M.S., Civil Surgeon of Bhāgalpur, for the revision of this Chapter.

The death-rate is practically dependent on the fever-rate, though cholera in bad years may cause an increase of from 2 to 5 in the number of deaths per mille. Generally speaking the unhealthiest years appear to be those in which the rainfall is deficient, though in 1894—a conspicuously unhealthy year—it was practically normal. In 1890 and 1891 the death-rate was identical. In the former year the rainfall was 12 inches in excess; in the latter 5 inches in defect. The fever-rate was actually less in the more rainy year and the larger number of deaths from cholera in that year brought it up to 1891 in point of mortality. In 1908 the rainfall was extremely low and the death-rate was well below the mean for the whole province, 33·22 as against 35·41 per mille.

The average is kept up by cholera when rainfall is deficient and by fever (malarial) when rainfall is in excess.

The highest birth-rate occurs in 1897—a famine year—which followed on a very unhealthy year. The birth-rate in general maintains a fair average for the district though it varies from 19·20 in Bhāgalpur town to 50·55 in Bihpur thāna. The birth-rate in 1908 was 36·38, the quinquennial average up to that year being 38·29.

An examination of the number of deaths at each age appears to yield fairly definite results. It can be stated with absolute certainty that the greatest mortality in every year occurs in children under one year, next (though in a much less degree) in children from 1 to 5 years. In children from 5 to 10 years and youths from 10 to 20 years the mortality is about the same.

The mortality from 20 to 30 years increases; it falls slightly from 30 to 40 years and still more from 40 to 50 and 50 to 60 years, after which it increases a little. Briefly the first year of life is the most dangerous and this danger continues, though it gradually lessens, up to the age of ten years.

The next decade is the least dangerous. Then there is an increase in danger up to the age of forty years after which there is a progressive fall, decade by decade. At every age, more males die than females, the present annual means being 39·41 males and 32·61 females per mille.

Principal diseases.

"Fever" accounts for about 80 per cent. of the reported deaths, but it is a very comprehensive term in the mouths of the agency on which reliance has to be placed for the collection of vital statistics. Cholera occurs in localised epidemics, the virulence of which varies greatly, almost every year from April to June and from August to October. The mortality from cholera was very high in 1882 (7,719 deaths): in 1890 (10,190 deaths): in 1894 (7,594 deaths): in 1900 15,583 deaths from cholera were reported, and in 1903, 8,558 deaths. Other bowel-complaints such as dysentery and diarrhœa are very common and severe and the mortality figures for epidemics of cholera are enormously increased by the inclusion of many cases of dysentery and diarrhœa.

Cholera in Bhāgalpur town is usually prevalent from April to June, when the water-supply, never very satisfactory, begins to fail. The wells in the poorer *mahallas* are then called into use and their unsatisfactory condition leads to trouble.

Cholera prevails in the district from July to the end of the year chiefly commencing with the ingestion of the products of the *makai* crop, indifferently cooked, among the very poor whose systems have been more or less debilitated by systematic under-feeding.

Small-pox in 1908 accounted for only ·15 deaths per mille. No attempts at segregation of infected persons can be made.

Small-pox has ceased to be endemic. Inoculation has given place to vaccination, and the degree of protection (255 per mille), which is already fairly high, increases year by year with the dying out of the old people who are unprotected. In the period 1901—1908 the average death-rate from small-pox was less than 1 per 10,000 of population. Most cases occur in the hot weather.

Prevalent fevers. The following account of the prevalent types of fevers has been adapted from a note contributed by Captain Woolley, I.M.S., Superintendent of the Central Jail at Bhāgalpur:—

Malarial fever. "This is the most prevalent kind of fever met with in this district, and in one or other of its forms is extremely common among both natives and Europeans. The former, owing to their primitive habits of living, and disregard of ordinary sanitary precautions, are more prone to the disease, living as they invariably do in villages, in which their houses are closely crowded together, with tanks and stagnant pools in close proximity. Malaria is much more common in some parts of the district than in others; people living in the eastern portions in the direction of Rajmáhal suffering considerably during the autumnal months when malaria is at its height. The inhabitants of the jungly areas also, north of the Ganges extending to the Nepal Terai, suffer greatly from fever during August, September and November. The inundation of the Kosi river near Pertapgunj with the consequent raising of the sub-soil water level in thanās Madhupur and Kissengunj leads to very virulent and persistent malarial epidemics which at times practically prostrate the whole neighbourhood. The town of Bhāgalpur itself is not very malarious, standing for the most part as it does on elevated ground. The western end of the town is rather lowlying, and during the rains large areas are flooded. When the river begins to fall, these localities are malarious, as is the case in other similar places.

Malaria as seen here may be classified into—

(*i*) Simple tertian;
(*ii*) Double tertian;
(*iii*) Malignant tertian.

The two former are what is known as ordinary fever. In themselves they are not very serious, but repeated attacks, extending over lengthy periods, in persons living always in malarious localities, in badly constructed houses, etc., cause debility, lessen the vitality, predispose to attacks of the malignant form (iii) and may thus indirectly end fatally. The typical temperature chart of (i) Simple tertian is seldom seen: what is generally shown is a short fever with an irregular curve lasting two or three days and which after this may resemble a simple or double tertian. The reason the typical charts of these two simple forms of fever are not seen is that the universal practice of taking *quinine* interferes with the cycle of changes in the parasite in the blood,—the result being an irregular temperature for a few days; the temperature may become normal for some days, and rise again, and this may continue for a long time in cases of feeble health, or in persons whose system is full of the disease. Both these simple forms of the disease are controlled by quinine, and provided this drug be given according to Koch's directions, *i.e.*, two large doses of 30 grains for two days with half this amount for the following three days, most of these cases can be cured comparatively easily.

The parasites of malaria are found in the peripheral blood of these cases in the red corpuscles, but if quinine has been given, they tend to disappear and are found more rarely.

Malignant tertian. This is a much more severe form. The temperature rises and remains sometimes at a high level 104 degrees, never coming down to normal, and remains thus for varying periods,—a week, a fortnight or three weeks, or in some bad cases even longer. The spleen becomes enlarged, and some persons who have had many attacks of this disease have enormous spleens and are much debilitated. Another serious symptom seen in these cases is intestinal derangement. The parasite is not usually seen in the peripheral blood in the red corpuscles, but there is usually much enlargement of certain white corpuscles, which become distended with pigmented bodies, and being very friable are often seen broken up when blood preparations are made for diagnosis.

Another important distinction from simple forms of fever is that quinine, which is so useful for the former, is useless in malignant tertian fever. This form of fever must be regarded as serious; it not unfrequently terminates fatally, especially in persons who have had previous attacks and continue living in marshy places. It is not very common in this district, but typical cases are by no means rare. A considerable number of cases of Deishman Donovan infection (Kala-azar) are noted in Bhāgalpur itself. These nearly all end fatally and resist the most modern method of treatment. Enlargement of the spleen with little or no enlargement of the liver is their characteristic feature and the disease has been recognized as "Bhāgalpur spleen" for many years.

Enteric or typhoid fever. Among the native inhabitants this is an extremely common disease and one which takes an extremely heavy death toll yearly. Doubtless most of the deaths between the ages of 1 and 5 years attributed to "fever are due to enteric but are not recognised. In the town itself where the eyes of medical practitioners are more keenly open to the recognition of the disease, it is very common. During the months of April, May and June 1909 when the water-supply failed the town, the poor classes were visited with cholera while the better classes suffered from a true infection by the enteric bacillus; at one time no fewer than 200 cases were reported by the doctors of the town.

Cerebro-spinal fever. This is a form of meningitis which has frequently occurred in the Central Jail since 1897. It is a very fatal disease, about 70 per cent. of cases terminating fatally. The causation is doubtful. It is a disease of prisons and crowded communities such as barracks, but at least one case has been detected among the free population and possibly it may occur in crowded villages in the district, without being given its correct name. The specific organism is the diplo-coccus meningitides, which has been found in recent cases in the Central Jail.

A tendency towards this disease has been noticed especially among those convicts whose labour necessitates their working in a dusty atmosphere.

Isolated cases at intervals of a few years have occurred at the Police Training School at Nathnagar.

Plague. The history of plague in this district has many features in common with its history in other districts of Behar. It first appeared in the early part of 1900, and the mortality from it in that year was four only. It followed what is now known to be its usual course—gradually subsiding as the hot weather approaches, dying out altogether during the rains and re-appearing, oftentimes with renewed virulence, in the ensuing cold season. At first, evacuation of houses, segregation and disinfection were tried. There was the same opposition experienced here as elsewhere to all remedial measures, resistance, sometimes active and sometimes passive, being offered by those whose fatalism rendered them indifferent to the risks of infection and the possible results of an attack of the disease.

The mortality, year by year, from this disease has been as follows:—

Year.				Deaths.
1900	...	...	...	4
1901	...	...	...	50
1902	...	...	...	4
1903	...	...	...	265
1904	...	...	...	1,518
1905	...	...	...	2,369
1906	...	...	...	243
1907	...	...	...	37
1908	...	...	...	816
1909	...	...	...	131
		Total	...	5,437

Inoculation never made any headway in this district, until the early part of 1907. While the outbreak lasted in that year, 1,558 persons were inoculated with very satisfactory results. In 1908, 2,200 persons were inoculated with equally good results. It is noteworthy that not a single domiciled Bengali consented to be inoculated. On the contrary, the Bengalis opposed inoculation, not because they doubted its efficacy, but because it was "official" and therefore anathema to them. In the municipal area of Bhāgalpur town, the disease has been most virulent especially in the Marwari quarters where sanitation and cleanliness are non-existent. Voluntary evacuation of houses has become the rule now on the appearance of the disease. Early in 1907 about three-fourths of the houses were deserted.

It is interesting to note that plague has never visited (in epidemic form) any town or villages north of the river in this district with the exception of Narayanpur which had a visitation from pneumonic plague, an infection from an isolated case from Begusarai in 1907. This accounted for 40 deaths in two weeks.

Disinfection by means of crude oil emulsion—which is far more deadly to rat-fleas than the corrosive sublimate and other disinfectants previously employed—was carried out wherever the occupants of houses consented to its being done. A crusade for the extermination of rats was carried on by poison and by offering rewards for all rats and mice brought in alive. In the season ending 31st March 1907, rewards were paid for 134,301 rats destroyed.

It is obvious from what has preceded that plague is responsible for only a nominal number of deaths in comparison with fever and cholera. It is noteworthy that the number of inoculations performed against plague has been far higher in this district than in any other district of Bengal. The comparative immunity of Bhāgalpur from plague is a matter of great interest and at present the Plague Commission are at work on the question. The immunity of the district may depend on an immunity of the local rats to plague themselves, and 300 rats have recently been forwarded to Bombay for the purpose of testing their blood in this respect.

It is noteworthy too that Bhāgalpur lies at the apex of a triangular area. The further westward one goes the greater is the plague infection which attains a maximum in the most westward and most densely inhabited district of this province, namely, Saran In this connection it may, too, be noted that mud walls and tiled roofs begin to be in common use just below the apex of the triangle in which Bhāgalpur lies, *i.e.*, at about Sahebgunj.

Other diseases.

The records of admissions to the various hospitals and dispensaries when analysed show that the following diseases occur fairly often in the district:—(1) Primary and secondary syphilis and gonorrhœa. These account for about a thousand admissions per annum. (2) Worms, for which admissions average 2,000 per annum. Badly cooked food and dirty water are the main causes. Tape worm occurs among all classes. (3) Rheumatic affections account for about the same number of admissions per annum. They are rarely acute, generally mild and chronic. (4) Pneumonia and asthma are by no means prevalent. The out-of-door life of the inhabitants protects them, and the strong rays of the sun undoubtedly act as a sterilizing agent on the dust which seems at first sight an excellent medium for conveying this infection. (5) Pulmonary tuberculosis is remarkable on the increase and steps will shortly have to be taken to combat its ravages, otherwise it will assume alarming proportions. It is extremely common in Bhāgalpur town and especially so among the Muhammadan community. (6) Goitre is very common especially in the sub-montane tracts in the north of the district; operative treatment for its reduction is never submitted to. (6) Skin diseases and ulcers are very common; they are due to a low standard of personal cleanliness and septic surroundings. (7) Leprosy is not very prevalent. It occurs both in tubercular and anæsthetic forms. The 1901 census figures show about a thousand lepers in the district. They are most numerous in the Bānkā subdivision. No support to the "fish-eating" theory as a cause of leprosy is forthcoming in this district from the local distribution of those afflicted with this disease. (8) Diseases of the eye are very widely prevalent. Many sufferers from cataractous lens present themselves for operation as the disablement is so complete and the relief so immediate and certain. But at present the modern method of extraction has not earned such popularity as to be able to drive the "coucher" or "rawal" off the field of practice. Thousands of eyes are ruined annually by this unscientific and obsolete method of treatment especially in the northern part of the district. (9) Diseases of the ear are also widespread.

Surgical operations. The surgical operation most frequently performed is the extraction of the lens for cataract; next is the removal of stone in the bladder by lithotomy or by crushing the stone when possible.

Infirmities. According to the census of 1901 blindness is the most prevalent infirmity, the number of persons afflicted being 112 males and 96 females per hundred thousand of the population. Its prevalence among the labouring and agricultural classes suggest that the glare and dust to which the generally sandy nature of the soil exposes them, renders them more subject to this affliction.

Deaf-mutism afflicted 127 males and 73 females per hundred thousand of the population in 1901.

Sanitation. Outside of the municipal areas, sanitation is non-existent. In Bhagalpur, there is a municipal water-supply and the usual system of surface drains. Nightsoil is disposed of in trenching grounds. There is a good natural fall towards the Jamunia and Ganges in some parts of the town. This no doubt helps to explain the fact that the introduction of the water-supply in Bhagalpur has not been attended by the usual rise in mortality—usual, that is, where a complete drainage scheme has not been completed prior to the introduction of the water-supply. Thus, in the five years prior to the introduction of the water-supply, the death-rate of the town was 40·4 per mille. The annual mean death-rate since its introduction (March 1887) has fallen to 31·7. In Chapter XII some further details on this subject will be given. The water scheme has been extremely expensive for the municipality.

The latest amendments to the Local Self-Government Act (1908) provide legal authority for enforcing sanitary measures in rural areas. Time alone will tell how far the objects of these amendments will be fulfilled.

Medical institutions.

In this district there are at present seventeen dispensaries, out of which ten have no accommodation for in-door patients. Over 61 per cent. of the income is derived from private sources, a point in which Bhagalpur sets a very good example to most other districts.

Some of those institutions deserve more detailed notice. In Bhagalpur town the Municipal Charitable Dispensary has existed since 1842. It is thus one of the oldest in Bihar. Its popularity has been steadily increasing—the total number of patients treated in 1909 being 913 indoor and 14,476 outdoor. In 1872 the attendance was 267 indoor and 5,039 out door; in 1901 it was 380 indoor and 13,323 outdoor.

In 1868 a new dispensary building was added by the munificence of Babu Sardhari Lal, in 1888 a new surgical ward was erected as a joint memorial to the late Mr. G. N. Barlow, I.C.S., (for twelve years Commissioner of this Division) and to the late Major Beatson, I.M.S., for many years Civil Surgeon of the district.

The lack of funds to keep the building and operation room up to date is regrettable as a recent note of the Inspector-General of Civil Hospitals, Bengal, shows it to be one of the least up-to-date in the province at the time when a large amount of surgical work is done and the popularity of the dispensary is growing by leaps and bounds. A contributing factor to this lack of funds is the famine condition prevailing during the years 1906–1909 and also the fact that many of the chief landholders of the town support in the outlying parts dispensaries of their own.

The local branch of the Lady Dufferin Hospital is known as the "Rani Shibtarini" Hospital. It was founded in 1893 by Rājā Shib Chandra Banerji, and is called after his wife. The attendance is always good. It has been remarked that very few cases fit for operation are brought in. The bulk of the income of this institution is derived from subscriptions from the principal zamīndārs of the district.

The "Victoria Memorial Hospital" has recently been erected for purdahnashin female patients alone at a cost of Rs. 25,000. This is doing good work and is well patronised.

The Mohadinagar dispensary was established in the south of the district by Babu Tilakdhari Lal, the son of the late Babu Sardhari Lal, in memory of his father. It is entirely supported by him, and has an endowment derived from some landed property duly devoted to this purpose.

Babu Surendra Mohan Sinha in memory of his father Babu Ramoni Mohan Sinha has established a very fine hospital at Nathnagar, one of the best equipped in the district. Its out-practice almost equals that of the Sadar Dispensary at Bhagalpur itself. A large indoor hospital is shortly to be opened adjoining this.

At Barari on the extreme east of the town there is a charitable dispensary for out-patients only, which is entirely supported by two brothers, Babu Pran Mohan Thakur and Babu Ugra Mohan Thakur. The Baneli Rāj established a dispensary in 1901 at Sultanganj, the headquarters of Banka subdivision. There is a charitable dispensary which was established in 1867. At Bausi, Rani Makum Kumari of Lachmipur supports a dispensary from her own income.

North of the river there are dispensaries at the headquarters of the two subdivisions—Madhipurā and Supaul. Also there is one at Pertabganj established in 1872 by Rai Dhanpat Singh Bahadur in memory of his father Partab Sing, and maintained at his sole expense till 1888, when it was taken over by the District Board. Since 1901 it has been managed by a Committee; and a new building was erected for it by Babu Ganpat Sing, brother of Rai Dhanpat Sing Bahadur, in 1902.

A dispensary was started at Kishanganj—the least healthy tract in the district—in 1893 and it was rebuilt in 1901 by the District Board.

In 1908 a new dispensary was opened at Sonbursa which is completely maintained by the Sonbursa Rāj.

In 1909 a new dispensary was commenced at Bhimnagar on the borders of Nepal 14 miles north-east of Pertabganj which will fill a long-felt want.

Thus the whole district is extremely well supplied with medical aid and the out-practice of each shows what valuable aid is rendered and how much they are appreciated by the inhabitants of outlying districts.

The District Board also established a dispensary in 1901 at Bangaon. It was very badly needed there.

The Darbhanga Rāj maintains a dispensary at Bhaptiahi in the north of the district at its sole expense. This is not supervised by the Civil Surgeon of the district.

Leper Asylum. A leper asylum at Bhagalpur is maintained by the Church Missionary Society. It provides accommodation for 400 lepers.

Medical Aid. Exclusive of medical officers directly employed by Government or by local authorities, there are many native medical practitioners who follow European methods. In most villages are to be found practitioners who follow indigenous systems—baids, hakims and kabirajes. Barbers are very important socially as well as professionally. Satyas or couchers are generally itinerant practitioners. Their methods are of the crudest.

The Ayurvedic system of medicine is held in the greatest esteem, not so much from religious principles as from the idea that the more drastic operation of European medicines is not so suited to the more delicate Indian constitution.

Among the lowest classes, exorcism by charms and spells is firmly believed in, as all diseases are attributed to the malevolent influence of evil spirits. Cholera in particular is attributed to Kali Mai, and no one ventures abroad at night during a cholera epidemic for fear of meeting with this angry goddess and being infected with the disease by her baneful influence.

However, the constantly increasing numbers that resort to the charitable dispensaries afford ample proof that their benefits are gaining an ampler recognition. Thus from 1890 to 1894 the daily average attendance at all dispensaries was 223 only. In the period 1900 to 1904 it had risen to 584 per diem: though the number of institutions increased somewhat in the interval, the number of patients treated increased in a far higher ratio.

In 1909 the figures have risen to 123,987 yearly for the whole district averaging 1,014 per diem. Surgical treatment is at present in disfavour, but the abandonment of drugs and a willingness to submit to the knife is gradually being noted and the time is not far distant when the enlightenment of the general public in this respect will be in no way inferior to that of the same classes in Europe generally.

CHAPTER V.

AGRICULTURE.

The portions of this district lying north and south of the Ganges differ considerably, regarded from the standpoint of the agriculturist. The northern portion is purely alluvial. The southern portion comprises, in addition to alluvium, various geological formations, as already described in Chapter I. The outstanding feature that distinguishes the agriculture of the southern portion from that of the northern is that in the latter irrigation is only needed when the rainfall is in large defect or very badly distributed; in the former, the southern portion, irrigation in one form or another, is very widespread and is indispensable. Bunds are thrown up across the streams that flow northwards from the hilly southernmost portion of the district, and a network of distributaries, taken from this, lead the waters from field to field. Custom regulates the question of the supply. During the cadastral survey operations that have recently been brought to a close, an attempt was made to record the customary rights of various tenants and villages with regard to the use of the stock of water. It is, however, stated that the villagers generally speaking did not evince much interest in this part of the proceedings. At the end of this chapter are to be found details as to the various methods of irrigation in vogue. Natural divisions.

The total area of the district may be classified as follows from the point of view of agriculture. The actual figures are those furnished by the Settlement Department. Total area.

Total area ... 2,654,620 acres.*

		Acres.
Uncultivable area	... ...	261,016
Cultivable waste other than fallow	...	396,327
Current fallow	... ...	63,561
Net cropped area	... ...	1,684,107

* This includes 249,609 acres which were only surveyed topographically, for which no detailed records were prepared and no statistics compiled. About half this area would be entirely uncultivable and the other half "cultivable waste".

The municipal areas, 6,400 acres, are also included in this total. No agricultural statistics were compiled except for the purely rural areas of the municipalities.

Areas cultivated for each harvest.

Following the usual division into *rabi* (spring), *bhadoi* (autumn), and *aghuni* (winter) harvests, the following areas are cultivated for each of these harvests:—

		Acres.
Rabi crops	... ...	731,560
Bhadoi ,,	... ...	458,477
Aghani ,,	... ...	1,070,265
Total area under crops	...	2,260,302

As usual, a large proportion of the lands can bear two harvests. In the year for which figures are quoted, not less than 576,195 acres bore two crops. Deducting this from the total just shown we arrive at the net cropped area of 1,684,107 acres.

Main crops.

The following table gives all the principal crops grown in the district, with the assumed normal area under each crop, and the actual area sown with each crop during the settlement operations.

Class.	Name.	Assumed normal acreage.*	Actual acreage.
Cereals and pulses.	1. Rice ...	1,615,200	997,760
	2. Wheat ...	203,200	110,518
	3. Barley ...	68,900	62,739
	4. Millet (*cholum* or *joar*).	22,000	10,373
	5. Marua ...	123,100	142,683
	6. Maize ...	242,600	114,375
	7. Gram ...	73,700	99,203
	8. Pulses, etc. ...	203,100	435,145
Oil-seeds ...	9. Linseed ...	14,100	94,622
	10. Til ...	2,900	4,256
	11. Mustard ...	38,200	85,524
	12. Others ...	17,200	17,372
Condiments and spices.	13. Various ...	1,000	2,672
Sugarcane ...	14. Sugar ...	63,700	10,768
Fibres ...	15. Cotton ...	14,000	503
	16. Jute ...	22,400	816
Dyes ...	17. Indigo ...	13,000	5,408
Narcotics ...	18. Opium ...	600	463
	19. Tobacco ...	8,000	2,302
Orchards and gardens.	20. Various ...	22,700	39,795
Miscellaneous ...	21. Food-crops ...	69,600	21,515
	22. Non-food crops	87,600	1,590

* Normal areas are taken from the "Agricultural Statistics." Probably they will be readjusted now on the basis of the more accurate settlement figures.

In spite of some marked variations from the normal it is obvious that the rice crop is far and away the most important crop in the district. Under the heading "Oilseeds" there is a marked tendency to an increase and probably the accepted figures for normal acreage will need to be revised soon in respect of these crops just as a permanent diminution is indicated under the headings Indigo (17) and Sugarcane (14).

The principal types of soil in this district are clay, loam and sandy soils. The different kinds of clay soils are as follows, according to a note on the soils of Bengal, published by the Department of Agriculture:— **Soils.**

(a) *Kharar* or *Kaiari*.—This soil is blackish in colour: it is sticky when wet and rather difficult to plough when dry. It is best suited for the growth of winter rice. When the rice crop is reaped, peas of various sorts, *khesari dal*, gram and linseed are sown broadcast in the mud before it dries up and luxuriant crops are frequently raised in this way at practically no cost beyond that of the seed. **Clays.**

(b) *Khewal*.—This soil is also of a blackish colour, but is more friable when dry than *kharar*. It is suitable for almost all crops except maize, *kurthi*, etc. If it lies very low and goes under water when the Ganges is in flood, the land is called *char*. Such soils grow only *rabi* crops.

(c) *Gorimati*.—This soil is of a reddish yellow hue, and produces all kinds of crops if irrigated.

(d) *Harin chikai* and *pas oti* are whitish in colour and are suitable for winter paddy.

(2) Loamy soils are known as *doras*. If low-lying, winter rice is grown on them generally; if high, various *bhadoi* and *rabi* crops do well on them. This class of soil is found around old village-sites where it receives cow-dung and all sorts of household refuse. It is then generally called *dih* or *goora*, and it is sown with potatoes, vegetables, tobacco, chillies, etc. In low situations, loamy soils are called *tari*, and all crops except maize, *kurthi*, etc., will do well on them. **Loams.**

(3) *Balmut* is a sandy loam that will grow anything. *Dhus* is the name given to sandy loam in the Gangetic diara. As it is submerged when the river is in flood, it is used for *rabi* crops only. These crops thrive in it exceedingly. **Sandy soils.**

Soil that is almost pure sand is called simply *balu*. When a thin layer of silt (three to six inches thick) is deposited on the top of sand, it is called *patpar*. In this state it grows mustard well, but as the layer of silt gets deeper it becomes also fit for barley, oats, etc. Diara lands covered with sand are called *balu burd*.

Water-melons do very well in such lands as the melon, when formed, can lie on the sand without rotting, while the roots are far down in the clay beneath.

Diaras.

The gradual growth of *diaras* is an extremely interesting process of soil formation. Where an eddy in the current is the result of a curve or backwater in the stream, the velocity of the water is checked sufficiently to allow the suspended matter to be deposited. The building-up process continues until the sand bank appears at ordinary water-level. The water lying stagnant deposits clay and silt on the sand, and each succeeding flood deepens the layer of clay until at last the *diara* rises above flood-level. If from any cause the deposit of clay and silt is arrested, the *diara* remains mere barren sand. Excellent crops can be raised from such lands, but there is no stability nor certainty about *diara* cultivation. When unable to bear a crop, no one troubles about them. When fertile, they are not infrequently the source of sanguinary riots and the cause of perpetual litigation.

Inferior soils.

(4) Soils over which there is a saline efflorescence due to the presence of alkaline salt, *reh* or sodium salts, etc., which are called *usar*, *kharwa*, etc., are unfertile. Washermen use *kharwa*, so it may be inferred that sodium carbonate or 'black alkali' is found in that earth. · In *usar*, it is probably the 'white alkali' or sodium sulphate that is found. The want of subsoil drainage, owing to impermeable strata beneath, causes the accumulation of these alkaline salts.

In the extreme south of the district is found a reddish gravelly soil of lateritic origin. It produces *arhar*, castor, etc.

Climatic influences.

The prosperity or otherwise of the agriculturists—and by far the greater portion of the population is dependent for its livelihood on agriculture—is determined by the rainfall. It must be adequate and seasonable. As rice is the most important crop grown in the district, the rains that benefit this crop exceed all others in importance. For the winter rice crop, rain is needed early in June to facilitate the preparation of the ground and the growth of the seedlings. In July and August rain is needed to prepare for the transplantation. Finally copious rain is essential about the time of the *Hathiya* asterism, at the end of September or early in October, as without this the rice never comes properly to maturity and the produce is inferior in quality and indifferent in quantity.

Rain at these same intervals is also extremely beneficial for the *bhadoi* and *rabi* crops. For the latter especially, the September-October rains if copious give the supply of moisture essential for a good spring crop.

There are numbers of proverbial sayings and agricultural maxims prevalent among the people telling of the favourable and unfavourable climatic influences which bring prosperity or the reverse. A few of the most interesting are reproduced here: AGRICULTURAL PROVERBS.

(*a*) Ek pani jon barse swati
Kurmi pahire sona pati.

i.e., if one shower even falls in *Swati* (a lunar asterism of Kartik, *i.e.*, October-November), even Kurmi women can wear gold earrings.

(*b*) Sati pake sat din
Barkha hoye rat din.

i.e., *sati* paddy ripens in sixty days if it rains continuously day and night.

(*c*) Bed bidit na hokhe an
Bina tula nahin phutai dhan.

i.e., the words of the Vedas are infallible, and paddy cannot ripen before the Balance (*i.e.*, Libra or Kartik=October-November).

In praise of the agriculturists' life the following is interesting:—

(*d*) Uttam kheti, madham ban,
Nirghin seba, bhik nidan.

i.e., agriculture is the highest profession; next is fighting; next is service, and last of all is begging.

The three great harvests of the year are known here, as elsewhere in Bihar, as the *rabi* or spring crop, *bhadoi* or rains crop, and *aghani* or winter crop. The main *aghani* crop is *aghani* rice. This is sown about May and reaped in the following December or January. At first the plants are raised in seedling beds, and they are transplanted later on into the low-lying, wet fields in which the crop eventually comes to maturity. This crop is very largely grown all over the northern portion of the district and covers, according to the latest statistics, an area of about 850,000 acres. The average outturn per acre in a normal year is about fifteen maunds worth, say, twenty rupees. The tenant looks to the result of the *aghani* rice crop as his resource for paying his rent and his mahajan. If the winter rice crop fails, distress in a more or less acute form is bound to supervene. HARVESTS. *Aghani.*

The question of rents is dealt with in Chapter VII below.

The *bhadoi* rice crop is also known as the *sati* crop, as it matures in about sixty days. It is not transplanted but is sown broadcast, generally on fairly high land, not suitable for the slower growing winter rice. The *bhadoi* crop furnishes the food-supply for the year for those cultivators who can afford to eat *Bhadoi.*

rice. It yields considerably less per acre than the transplanted *aghani* rice, but its cultivation is much less laborious and it reaches maturity in a very much shorter time than the winter rice. Also, the rent payable for such lands is appreciably less than that paid for the land that can bear a winter rice crop. *Bhadoi* rice is grown on about 152,900 acres.

Maize or *makai* is of much importance as a *bhadoi* crop also. It is grown on 114,375 acres It is sown in April and May and ripens in August, but it is often exposed to destruction in that month by floods.

Various millets are grown of which *marua* (*eleusine corucana*) normally sown on 123,100 acres, is the most important. It is largely used as a food-stuff, as it is very prolific and not expensive to cultivate.

Rabi crops. The most important spring crop is wheat. It covers an area of 110,500 acres in normal years. Barley, covering an area of 62,739 acres, comes next. *Dals*, both *khesari* and *masuri*, are largely grown. The former is sown broadcast on silt left behind by receding floods or on wet lands from which winter rice has been reaped. It is believed to cause paralysis owing to the presence of some parasite, but this parasite is killed if the *dal* is cooked by thoroughly boiling it.

Indigo. Among the many other crops that are grown indigo, tobacco and sugarcane deserve mention. Indigo was introduced into the district about the end of the eighteenth century. The first indigo factory was founded by Mr. Glass, then Civil Surgeon of Bhagalpur, in 1793. For many years its cultivation extended and a large number of factories came into existence all over the north of the district, with some along the banks of the Ganges in the southern part. At an early date, however, the reverses that have overtaken indigo planters everywhere since, were noticeable in this district, and the ruined and abandoned factories to be met with in the northern part of it tell the tale of a once prosperous industry that has passed away. In 1901 there were eleven important factories at work in the district, the largest being at Colgong employing over 700 hands. In years gone by, an area of about 13,000 acres was considered normal for indigo. Of late years this has diminished sadly and little more then 5,000 acres are now devoted to this useful crop. Its influence on the soil in which it is grown is extremely beneficial for subsequent crops, as it tends to increase the nitrogenous matter available for the cereals by which it should be followed in rotation.

Tobacco. Tobacco is mostly grown near homesteads and covers about 2,800 acres only. It is a valuable crop.

The area under cane fluctuates greatly. It is an expensive crop to raise, witness the Bihari proverb :— Sugarcane.

Sau chas ganda | Tekar adha mori ;
Pachas chas manda ; | Tekar adha tori.

i.e.,—For cane, a hundred ploughings ;
For wheat, fifty ploughings ;
Half of that (25) for rice ;
Half of that ($12\frac{1}{2}$) for mustard.

It occupies the ground for a very long time, usually fourteen months. It must be fenced ; it cannot stand water-logging (at least not the varieties most common in Bihar), and its market price fluctuates considerably. Still, dealers in *gur* are always ready to give advances against the crop and this renders it popular, in dry seasons especially. Its normal area was taken at 63.700 acres, but only about 10,000 acres are now found under the crop.

Oil-seeds rank high in value among the *rabi* crops. The acreage under them shows signs of a steady increase. This indicates (what Saran district proves conclusively) that valuable non-food crops tend to replace food-crops. It is found economically advantageous to grow the oil-seeds for export and to buy food-grains. It must not be forgotten, however, that, in recent years, the rainfall has for some time been in marked defect. This would tend to an increase in the area under *rabi* crops, which would thrive in places incapable of yielding a satisfactory rice crop. Oilseeds.

From the figures already quoted it would appear that out of a total area of 2,405,011 acres, 261,016 acres are considered to be entirely unfit for cultivation, while about 396,327 acres, though cultivable, are as yet uncultivated.* The average number of persons to the square mile is 494. This is very far below the average in several Bihar districts and it indicates that there is still room for expansion. The density of the population is least in Bānkā subdivision, but the soil there is undoubtedly less fertile than that of any other part of the district, speaking generally. Extension of cultivation.

It is of course impossible to give exact figures from Hamilton's statistics for the present district area. Still, for the area dealt with by him, he estimated that over 50 per cent. was waste and entirely unfit for the plough : that about 2 per cent. was fit for the plough but fallow, and that about 48 per cent. was cultivated. A very considerable amount of jungle must have been reclaimed and brought under the plough since that estimate was framed. Buchanan-Hamilton's estimate.

After the Revenue survey (1846–50), a detailed geographical and statistical report was drawn up in 1852 by Captain Sherwill The Revenue Surveyors' report.

* These figures are to be taken subject to the footnote on page 69 above.

for the portion of the district that lies south of the Ganges and by Mr. Pemberton for the area lying north of that river. Unfortunately the columns designed to show the proportions of cultivated to unculturable and uncultivated areas are blank for the southern area.

Mr. Pemberton remarks that the general assessment is extremely low. "In 1798 [1793(?)] when the last settlement took place, nearly two-thirds of Bhagalpur north of the river was grass or tree jungle: the assessment of these areas was for the most part nominal, and even the cultivated parts were settled very favourably for the owners of the soil and on mere estimated areas . . . Many vain regrets obtrude themselves here respecting the perpetual settlement of Bengal, knowing as I do the wonderfully improved state (as to cultivation) of these parganas: but it is useless to indulge in them or to comment on the thousand per cent. loss Government is sustaining in consequence of this settlement."

Mr. Pemberton's figures for the four parganas lying north of the river then show nearly 85 per cent. of the area as cultivated, 14 per cent. as culturable waste and 1 per cent. as unculturable and barren waste. But only the parganas Malhani Gopal, Naredigar, Nisankpur Kurha and Chhai were under consideration.

Increase of cultivation. It is amply established that there has been an enormous increase in the cultivated area of this district since 1793. The present figures for land revenue demand and for annual rental value, for cess valuation, illustrate this.

The land revenue demand is Rs. 6,05,746.

The cess valuation (annual rental) is Rs. 56,81,997.

Comment is needless.

Scientific Agriculture. Bhagalpur district now possesses, at Sabour, the Provincial Agricultural College, which will, it is hoped, prove a centre from which improved agricultural methods will gradually be diffused over the whole Province. Its foundation stone was laid on August 17th, 1908, by Sir Andrew Fraser.* Its main object is in the first place to provide a suitably trained agency for carrying out the propaganda of the lately constituted Department of Agriculture, and next, to provide a research station for solving problems presented by the agricultural conditions of this Province. In addition to purely agricultural instruction, provision has been made for departments under an Agricultural Chemist, an Economic Botanist, a Mycologist and an Entomologist. Also, a workshop for the manufacture and repair of agricultural implements will be maintained.

---

* *Vide* the Quarterly Journal of the Department of Agriculture, Vol. II, No. 2, October 1908.

District Agricultural Association.

To carry out more effectively the objects aimed at by the Department of Agriculture, associations have been formed in most districts of this province. That in Bhagalpur was inaugurated in May 1908. Each member of the District Association is expected to co-operate in furthering the improvement of agriculture in his own neighbourhood by disseminating a knowledge of the results obtainable by improved methods. The following courses have been suggested as suitable means to this end:—

(a) Wealthy proprietors could start a demonstration farm on their own estates, to give object lessons to their own tenants and other cultivators.

(b) They could encourage cultivators to adopt improved methods that have been already demonstrated satisfactorily on their own account and assist them (by loans or otherwise) to meet the initial expenditure.

(c) The purchase of new or improved varieties of seed and its introduction and distribution.

(d) The purchase of suitable manures and their distribution.

(e) To encourage cultivators to visit demonstration farms.

(f) To distribute widely vernacular pamphlets on agricultural subjects.

(g) To promote cattle shows and agricultural exhibitions generally.

(h) To enable promising young men to get practical instruction at the Sabour College by giving scholarships, etc., etc.

It is too soon yet to expect much practical result from the activities of this Association. The scheme is excellent and the motives are most commendable. The future will show how far its objects are attained.

Veterinary Assistance.

The Bhagalpur District Board maintains an itinerant veterinary assistant, the value of whose services is gradually receiving due recognition by the cultivating classes. In Banka subdivision there was an outbreak of rinderpest in 1907 and the inoculation treatment was successfully practised.

Veterinary Hospital.

A public-spirited zamīndār, Babu Surendra Mohan Sinha, lately built and completely equipped a veterinary hospital and made it over to the District Board. It cost nearly Rs. 12,000 and is known as the "Ramani Mohan Sinha Veterinary Hospital," being so called after its founder's elder brother. This institution fills a long-felt want and has a sphere of action of unquestioned utility and of boundless extent before it.

NOTE ON IRRIGATION.*

How artificial irrigation is generally effected. *Daurhs* and *Singhas*.

Artificial irrigation which is indispensable over a large area of South Bhagalpur is generally effected by leading off from a natural stream or from a head of water collected in a *bandh* or tank. The channels are called *Danrhs* and their smaller branches are called *Singhas*. They are maintained and repaired by the *maliks*, the raiyats supplying labour in case of small and ordinary repairs. *Danrhs* and *Singhas* are used mainly for the irrigation of paddy fields from *Asarh* to *Kartik* (July to November).

Wells occasionally used for special crops.

Wells are also used, but only for the irrigation of special crops, *e.g.* sugarcane or *Kachu*. They are cheap and are dug by the raiyats at their own expense. In some villages *pukka* wells are dug at the expense of the *malik* for the irrigation of sugarcane fields.

Irrigation for *Rabi* crops.

The *Rabi* crops are often irrigated from *Danrhs* if water is available in them at the time. But the *maliks* do not take any interest in this and only the raiyats occasionally dig holes (called *Bhaw*) here and there in the sandy bed of a *Danrh* and draw out water with buckets, etc., for irrigating *Rabi* fields in the dry season. Little importance is attached to this kind of irrigation. It is only during the irrigation of rice fields from July to November that disputes arise, and it is to this irrigation only that all rules and limitations of rights of different parties, whether established by custom or by contract, refer.

Irrigation records prepared for irrigation-canals with all connected *bandhs* and tanks

Irrigation records have been prepared only for *Danrhs* or water-channels with all connected *bandhs*. The total length of these water-channels is 892·65 miles, and 646 villages with an area of 406·20 square miles are dependent on them for irrigation. The thanawar distribution is as follows:—

	Villages.	Area.	
Thana Bhagalpur	61	30·40	square miles.
" Amarpur	300	179·70	"
" Sultangunge	64	33·53	"
" Banka	183	139·68	"
" Colgong	38	22·88	"
Total	646	406·19	"

This covers the area about 10 miles on either side of the river *Chandān* north of the subdivisional headquarters of Banka and some area to the west of the river Chir which flows along the

* Furnished by the Settlement Officer, Bihar.

boundary of the Southal Parganas. For the purpose of comparison the following figures from the Darbhanga and Muzaffarpur Settlement Reports are quoted:—

	IRRIGATED AREA—				
	Wells.	Tanks.	Canals.	Other sources.	Total.
Darbhanga	10·4 sq. miles.	73 sq. miles.	5 sq. miles.	82·3 sq. miles.	170·7 sq. miles.
Muzaffarpur	29 ,,	37 ,,	1·6 ,,	[illegible]·8 ,,	97·4 ,,

The irrigation record is separate from the ordinary village record. An independent irrigation scheme has been treated as unit and the record divided into two parts. Part I gives a description in detail of the water-courses, *bandhs*, etc., the plot numbers in the 16-inch map being quoted. It is illustrated by a 4-inch to the mile *mufassil* map showing the boundaries of all the villages concerned, the position of the waterways, *bandhs*, roads, sites of *basti*, etc. Special methods of irrigation, if any, are also described in this part. Part II consists of general rules of irrigation from the scheme, the rights of different villages to use the water, and liabilities as to maintenance and repairs. **Irrigation records prepared with scheme as unit are separate from the ordinary village record.**

The unit thus adopted for the irrigation record usually consisted of a number of irrigation works forming one system with a natural source for its supply of water, not dependent on any other artificial scheme. All schemes have local distinctive names and there was not much difficulty in ascertaining how much was to be included in one record and how much should form a separate record. In cases where two or more independent schemes happened to be connected with each other, inquiries were made as to their origin and history, their owners and such other facts as might throw light on the matter. **Definition of "Scheme" taken as unit for record.**

Exceptions were made in two or three cases where a very large number of small water-courses all commencing from the river ended within the same village. In these cases one record was prepared showing all canals together as more convenient and intelligible to the people concerned. In fact, the village or *mauzawar* system is more convenient in all cases of small schemes terminating in the same village or in a group of villages owned by the same *malik*. The system with scheme as unit has been found convenient only in those cases where numerous villages with conflicting rights as to irrigation were concerned. But in other cases it involved useless and tiresome multiplicity of work; at the same time many minor improvement works had to be left unrecorded. **When *Mauzawar* system is preferable.**

Altogether 301 records were prepared. Two of them could not be draft published as several villages lay in thana Katauria, which had not been dealt with then. The remaining **Three hundred and one schemes dealt with.**

299 schemes give the total length of water-courses 892·65 miles. The average figures per scheme are :—

Average length of water-course .. ... 3 miles.
„ number of villages irrigated ... 4
„ area irrigated .. .. 2 sq. miles.

The subjoined table gives the details that are necessary for a proper understanding of the nature and extent of some of the most important irrigation schemes in the south of the district.

District No. of scheme.	Name of scheme.	Length of water-courses in miles and decimals.			Number of villages concerned.			REMARKS.
		Main canal.	Branches.	Total.	Irrigated.	Not Irrigated.	Total.	
10	Raj *Danrh* urf Mahashayji.	28·46	53·21	8·67	75	21	96	Owned by Mahashay Tarak Nath Ghose and dug in 1809 A.D.
79	Naya *Danrh* ...	21·38	36·64	58·02	28	16	44	Owned by Mahashay Tarak Nath Ghose and dug in 1844 A.D.
3	Raj *Danrh* urf Bilasi.	19·30	38·40	57·70	49	1	50	Owned by Raj Baneli (old).
	Raj *Danrh* (Panjwara).	9·48	18·76	28·24	20	2	22	Old.
98	Kajhia *Danrh* ...	...	...	25·68	15	...	15	Owned by Lachmipur Estate (old).
87	Jhikta *Danrh* ...	7·84	18·21	25·55	58	2	58	Owned by Raj Baneli (old).
85	*Danrh* Dogbai ...	5·46	15·97	21·43	18	1	20	Owned by Nand Lal Choudhry (old).
69	Chaksafia *Danrh*	8·08	12·35	20·43	13	3	16	Owned by several *maliks*, dug in 1846.

Mahashay Tarak Nath Ghose is a brilliant example to other zamīndārs and he has acquired proverbial fame for the special interest he takes in the proper irrigation of the lands lying in his estate. *Danrhs* owned by him are always kept in excellent repair.

Classification of *schemes* according to source of water-supply.

For convenience of description all *Danrhs* may be classified as follows :—

Class A.—Those commencing from a river (shallow broad stream like the Chanan).

Class B.—Those commencing from a *kharra* or *jore* (deep channel with high bank).

Class C.—Those commencing from a head of water protected by a *bandh* or from a tank.

The methods of lifting water into the three kinds of *Danrhs* are different although the way in which it is ultimately utilized for actual irrigation is the same. The following figures show how the 299 schemes for which records have been prepared fall in these three classes:—

Class.	No. of schemes.	Length of water-courses (miles).	No. of villages concerned.		
			Irrigated.	Not irrigated.	Total.
A.—Wide river ...	179	650·08	620	169	789
B.—Narrow deep stream.	47	148·89	202	26	228
C.—Reservoir ...	73	93·68	143	17	160

All important irrigation canals fall in class A.

Schemes—Class "A."—All commence from the rivers Chandan (flowing right through the middle of the district) and Chir (flowing along the boundary of the Southal Parganas) and their tributaries and branches. The Chandan has three tributaries in the district—(1) The Orni in thana Banka, (2) the Bilasi in thana Amarpur and Sultangunge, (3) the Dakai in thana Banka. On the southern boundary of thana Bhagalpur, the Chandan branches out into four streams—(1) the Andhari, (2) the Māhmudā, (3) the Hāhā (Paijormāri) and (4) the Chandan. The nature of these streams and how they afford special facilities to the opening of irrigation canals are very well described in a report of the Superintending Engineer, dated May, 1864:— Description of the rivers in the area.

"At its greatest width the Chandan is about 1,500 feet from bank to bank. From the long-continued practice of embanking, its bed is actually higher than the lands on either side and more specially than that on the eastern bank. Being a hill stream, it is liable to sudden and violent inundations, but except when in flood, the channel is a dry bed of gritty sand, bounded on either side by an artificial embankment pierced through with innumerable cuts for irrigation purposes". These remarks apply equally now. The embankments still exist on either side of the river throughout its length in thana Amarpur and the innumerable cuts are the mouths of innumerable irrigation canals. The lands on either side are nowhere much higher than the bed of the river and at places actually lower, so that it is not necessary to make irrigation canals very deep. The mouths of the *Danrhs* in the embankments are protected by pipes (made of palm trees) and in several cases by masonry work. In 1864 there were only 6 such *pukka* bridges; now there are over 20. The bridges are provided with sluice gates either of wood or iron, which are let down when the rush of water threatens to damage the crops. In the case of pipes, bundles of straw are sufficient to keep off the water. In some cases where the bed of the river is comparatively low the mouths of the *Danrhs* are open, *i.e.*, not protected by pipes or *pukka* bridges. This is however a source of danger in years of unusual flood. The Superintending Engineer attributed to this the origin of some of the branches of the Chandan, which he says are probably diversions of its course along some ancient *Danrh* in some years of heavy flood. The Chandan flood has done great damage even in recent years (1897) when it burst through the embankment on its eastern bank, and it is a matter of public importance that the mouths of all irrigation canals opening from it are well protected either by pipes or by masonry work.

Mouths of canals protected either by pipes or masonry work.

Necessity of such protection.

Sudden floods lasting usually for four or five days at a time occur occasionally in these hill streams from the month of June to October. During such floods, water would naturally flow into the *Danhrs* without any artificial training devices. But when there is no flood, or when there is not sufficient water in the river, the following devices are adopted:—(*a*) A small canal is dug along the bed of the river flanked by *ails* of sand thus diverting a portion of the current into the mouth of the *Danrh* These are called *Janghās*. (*b*) Pits (called *Bhaw*) are dug in the apparently dry bed of the river and the water thus obtained is lifted by means of buckets, swing baskets, or spoons worked on lever, etc. This kind of water is commonly called *Jharna* or *Jhilākā Pāni*. When there are two *Janghās* close by, water in the higher one would naturally ooze through the *ail* into the lower one. This is insignificant, but yet has a local name *Pasaba* or *Kasaba ke pāni*. The term is also used to the water which oozes through the *ails* of one field into a neighbouring field which is lower.

Devices for lifting water into Danrhs.—(a) Janghā (b) Bhaw.

Description of the Janghā

The *Janghā* is most important. As floods do not last for many days at a time, or may not come when water is most necessary, people have constantly to work at the *Janghā*. The *ails* of the *Janghā* are made only of such loose earth as is available on spot (only occasionally protected by boulders of stone) in the bed of the river, and they are invariably washed away during floods. The raiyats of the villages concerned usually dig and maintain the *Janghā* at their own expense. In the zamindary of Mahashay Tarak Nath Ghosh the practice is to pay and feed them when *Janghās* are raised for the first time in the year. Subsequent to this they are supplied only with fuel, wood and leaves. When, however, the raiyat works for more than a day, he is given food by the *maliks* and this is the general rule in the estates of the Baneli Rāj, Mr. Dip Narain Singh, the Barari Thakurs and others. The local agents of the zamīndār fix the terms by which raiyats of different villages should take charge of the *Janghā* and the general rule followed has been worded thus for use in Part II of the record:— Responsibilities of raiyats and *maliks* as regards construction of *Janghās*.

"The raiyats of all the villages having right of irrigation from the *Danrh* at first raise the *Janghā* and then the raiyats of particular villages keep it in order during the time their respective villages are irrigated. (Rule 16, Part II, Irrigation Record, Appendix A.)"

Special labour is thus necessary to carry water into the *Danrh* only when a *Janghā* or *Bhaw* has to be dug, and it is to the water thus obtained that all disputes, limitation of rights to use water such as *Paris*, etc., are mainly confined.

Disputes arise when any party attempts to open a new *Danrh* or a new *Janghā*, or to alter the number or position of pipes placed at the mouth of the *Danrh*, or to substitute a *pukka* bridge in place of pipes. It is commonly believed that the law does not allow such innovations but it is doubtful if the law can interfere and prevent by injunction the completion of any such salutary innovation unless it causes specific damage or injury to a third person.* Disputes regarding *Janghās* and *Danrhs*.

Rivers with high banks of the kind usually called *Kharrās* or *Jores* are numerous especially to the east of the Bhagalpur-Bausi Road. There are also some to the west of the river Bilasi in the western parts of thanas Amarpur and Sultangunge. In these cases the river is completely blocked by strong *bandhs*, sometimes of considerable length and thus the water is raised to the level of the fields on either side and to the level of the *Danrhs* which lead off from the sides of these *Bandhs*. When the rush of water Schemes, class B, require strong *bandhs* across the streams.

* The High Court decision reported at page 825 of volume XIV of Calcutta Weekly Notes (1910) is of much value in this connection. *Inderjit Pertap Bahadur Sahi* v. *Krishna Doyal Gir*.

is too great it is let out by means of openings in the *bandhs* which are called *Kānuās*. Sometimes the *Kānuās* are protected by masonry work with sluice gates or simply with *pukka* walls rising up to certain heights, leaving a free passage for the water above (the latter is called *Chhikta*, *i.e.*, weir).

Disputes about schemes, class B.

Disputes arise when an attempt is made to raise a new *bandh* in any village, or when a village lying lower down the stream cuts open a *kanua* in an old *bandh* before the owner of the *bandh* has chosen to do so. Disputes in such cases are known as far back as 1836, and in all these suits intricate questions of riparian rights and limitation were involved. In many cases the parties came to terms agreeing that openings of certain widths or weirs of certain heights should be kept for free passage of water to the lower villages. In one case the proprietors of Dhurya were permanently restrained from raising a new *bandh* in the river Gahira on the ground that such *bandh* would affect the prescriptive rights of villages lower down the river.

Some important schemes of class B.

The most important of these *bandhs* are :—

(i) The *Bari Bandh* on the river Bilasi in village Bhaluhar about ¾ths of a mile in length, owned by the Thakurs of Barari. It has four *pukka* bridges and *chhiktas* at four places.

(ii) The *Gopalpur Bandh* belonging to Mr. Dip Narain Singh about ¼th mile in length. This has got a *pukka kanua* with 11 openings.

(iii) The *Jhikta Bandh* in village Jhikta (about ¾ths of a mile in length) belonging to the Baneli Rāj. There is no masonry work in it.

Schemes, class C, correspond to *Ahars* with *pynes* in other districts.

Schemes—Class "C."—These are not of much importance as no great supply of water can be had from them. They correspond to what are called *Ahars* with *pynes* in Monghyr and Patna. *Bandhs* there are large and small in every village all over the country, but most of these only form reservoirs to store water obtained from a *danrh* or *singha*. Such *bandhs* have been treated as parts of the record of the *danrh* from which they are supplied with water. But there are still a good many *bandhs* in which only the water which drains down the surface of the country during the rainy season, is stored. This water is then led off through cuts (in many cases provided with pipes) in the *bandhs*, and then by means of *Danrhs* or *Singhas*, or simply from field to field. So also in the case of *danrhs* commencing from tanks. When there is not sufficient water swing baskets (called *Sine* or *Sine-karin*), or *Donas* worked on levers are used. These *Donas* are usually made of palm trees, but iron *Donas* have also come into common use.

Disputes which arise about these reservoirs usually relate to the damage which they cause to a higher village, when there is too much water in them. The higher village cannot derive any benefit from the reservoir, while the lower village may not require all the water accumulating in it. These result in criminal cases when the higher village forcibly cuts the *bandhs* to let down the water. In such cases the recent records attempt to define the area which properly forms the reservoir by reference to the plot-numbers on the map and thus fix the limit up to which the owner of the *bandh* has by long use got right to store the water even if the result is damage to the lands submerged, whether they belong to him or to some other *malik*. Disputes about Schemes, class C.

It has now been shown how water is conveyed into the three classes of *danrhs*. The methods employed for carrying this water from field to field, or to distant villages and fields are the same. The canals usually run along the highest convenient ridges in the country so that water may easily be taken to the lands on either side. Branches and sub-branches are then opened to take the water of the main channel to fields and villages which are away from its course. Where a branch or sub-branch opens, the place is usually protected either by masonry work or by pipes. The width of the opening or the number and position of the pipes define the quantity of water which the particular branch or sub-branch has right to take. All these are fully described in Part I of the record. Branches called *singhas* carry water to distant fields and villages.

There are two methods by which water is taken to the fields for actual irrigation, (*a*) the *Banokhar* system, and (*b*) the *Mulari* system.

The *Banokhar* system consists in constructing dams across the *Danrh* or *Singha*. The level of the water in it is thus raised to that of the fields on either side. The *ails* of these fields are then cut and water is let into the plot of land close by. When this plot has been irrigated the next lower field cuts its *ail* and takes down the water and so from field to field till all the fields which can be irrigated from the dam have been irrigated. This method of damming is also applied in taking water into a branch (*Singha*) from the *Danrh* or from a branch into a sub-branch. The dam is commonly called a *Dhatti* or *Banokhar*. (*Cf.* Muzaffarpur Settlement Report, 1892–1899, page 259.) The dam or *Dhatti* absolutely stops the flow of water further down the *Danrh* or *Singha*, so that there must always be some restriction of the time during which a particular dam may be Two systems of irrigating fields. *Banokar* system—*Paris.*

kept. This restriction is imposed either (*i*) by *Paris* (turns), or (*ii*) by limitation of irrigable area in a village or Patti. A village or a Patti or a group of several villages or Pattis held by the same *malik* is usually taken as unit in fixing *Paris*. The reason is that all these arrangements are at the entire control of the *maliks* and the raiyats have very little hand in them. These *Paris* are described in full, village by village, in Part I of the irrigation record. In paragraph 3 of Part II, an abstract is also given for convenience of reference. When the *Pari* of one *patti* or village, or group of *pattis* or villages expires the *patti* or village having the next *Pari* cuts the dam and takes down the water to its own dam already raised by this time. The *Paris* however are not adhered to when owing to flood, etc., the *Danrhs* and branches are quite full with water. If the first village of a *Pari* is situated at some distance from the mouth of a *Danrh* so that some time is necessary before the water of the river can reach the outskirts of the village, a period of grace is allowed to this village. It is called *Khurvijan*, and it is after the expiry of this period (usually a day) that *Paris* actually commence. A day means day and night and it is taken as equivalent to 8 *Pahars* and not 10. *Paris* commence when the first *Jangha* has been completed at the mouth of the *Danrh*.

The *Mulari* system. Where a village is irrigated by the *Mulari* system it has no right to raise any dam across the water-course and has thus to wait till the water in it is sufficiently high to come over to the fields. It is, however, the *Banokhar* system with *Paris* which is most prevalent.

Questions arising with reference to right of irrigation in a village. In dealing therefore with a scheme with ramifications extending over several *pattis* or villages owned by different *maliks* the principal questions that arose were (*i*) which of these villages had right of irrigation; (*ii*) whether such right was only confined to take *Mulari* water or whether a village or patti had right to raise *Dhatti* or *Banokhar*; (*iii*) in the latter case—what were the *Paris*; (*iv*) if no *paris*—what were the ways by which the time for which the *Dhatti* could be kept was defined, *i.e.*, whether it was well known that only a certain area could be irrigated and that after this was done the dam was to be removed, etc.

Contrivances where two water-courses cross each other. When two water-courses cross each other, one is made to pass over the other by means of *Donas* or *pukka* bridges with walls, or pipes are placed underneath one for the water of the other to pass through. The number and position of these pipes and *Donas*, and the widths of the openings in the bridges have in many cases been the subject of hot dispute. There seems however to be no restriction in carrying the water from a field on one side of the canal to a field on the other side by means of *Donas* or pipes and there cannot be any reason for such restriction so long as no obstruction is caused to the free flow of water in the irrigation canal.

Khetbaran.

The method by which water is carried for irrigation from field to field without any definite water-course is called *khetbaran*. Where irrigation is done in this way, it has been so described in Part I of the record.

Relative position of the raiyats and *maliks* with regard to irrigation.

The whole arrangement is entirely under the control of the *maliks* and their local agents. The following rules embodied in Part II of the Irrigation Record explain the relative position of the raiyats and *malik* in this respect:—

"*Rule 11.* When there is not sufficient water for the irrigation of all the lands in a village the *malik's* local agents fix *Paris* amongst the raiyats in such a way that all the fields may be equally irrigated. Or, if there is any surplus water in any field the *malik's* local agents arrange to get that water for the irrigation of any other field which could not otherwise be irrigated, in such a way that the former field may not be in any way injured.

"*Rule 12.* Internal disputes amongst the raiyats of a village about irrigation are decided by the *malik's* local agents."

Neglect by zamīndārs to repair irrigation work.

It may be apprehended that such arrangement may develop into an effective source of oppression by the *maliks*. But the management and regulation of irrigation schemes must in any case, of necessity, rest with the *maliks*. The rules above describe the existing facts. It is only when the *malik* neglects to look after the irrigation work or keep them in repairs that any hitch arises between him and the raiyats. Such instances were met with in several cases in thana Amarpur. A zamīndār after purchasing an estate tried to enhance the rents of the raiyats but was unsuccessful. He then began to neglect the several *Bandhs* and *Danrhs* in the villages, so that in a short time they had become almost entirely useless.

Customary rights to use of water.

It may be laid down as a general rule that every raiyat in the village has right of irrigation from a scheme belonging to the *maliks* of the village. It is therefore no vague statement when it is noted in the record that a particular village has or that a particular village has not right of irrigation. When the right is confined to any limited area it has been so described in the record, but such cases are very few.

Responsibilities of raiyats and *maliks*.

Rules 13, 14, 15 and 16 in Part II of the record (see Appendix A below) describe the responsibilities of the raiyats and *maliks* as regards maintenance and repairs. These rules were framed after very careful enquiry and they describe the relation of the parties with sufficient accuracy. Rule 13 is to be read with reference to the *Banokhar* and *Mulari* systems described before :—

"The *maliks* of those villages which have right of irrigations from the scheme, are responsible for its repairs and maintenance. They meet the expense in proportion to their respective *Paris* of irrigation, and where the *Mulari* system prevails according to the areas irrigated. If a *malik* does not pay his share of the expenses, he may be sued in court, but the irrigation of the lands in his village cannot be stopped on that account."

This is a general enunciation of the principle which underlies the prevailing custom. There are, however, cases in which the *maliks* have made special arrangements amongst themselves, *e.g.*, one may have been allotted a fixed sum of money every year, or another may have entirely been exempted. Total exemption from responsibility for contributing to the cost of maintenance may in most cases be traced to the origin of the scheme when this concession was allowed as compensation for damages to land when the scheme was opened at the expense of another *malik*. For instance the *Naya Danrh* belonging to Mahashayji passes through 9 villages of the Lachmipur Estate at its source. These villages have been given one day's *Pari* in the week and the Lachmipur Estate has not to bear any portion of the cost of repairs or maintenance.

Importance of the Bhagalpur-Bausi road with reference to irrigation.

An important part is played by the embankment of the Bhagalpur-Bausi road which runs almost parallel to the river Chandan about six miles to the east of its eastern bank. This embankment serves not only as a protection to the country to the east against the violent floods of the Chandan, but it is also a high level irrigator, regulating the water necessary for the irrigation of the large area extending up to the borders of the Sonthal Parganas. Numerous important canals (for example, (*i*) the Raj Danrh Mahashayji, (*ii*) the Naya Danrh, (*iii*) the Shampur Danrh, (*iv*) the Dogbai Danrh, and (*v*) the Katiawa Danrh) are crossed by this road at several places and at each place there is a *pukka* culvert or bridge for free passage of water. In two places these culverts are provided with sluice gates which are maintained by private zamīndārs. Besides these principal gates every culvert in the road affords an opening for the irrigation of the lands to its east. The great importance of keeping free openings in the embankment of the Bhagalpur-Bausi Railway, now under construction, thus becomes apparent. This embankment runs close by and parallel to the Bhagalpur-Bausi Road and it does not seem to be impossible to provide openings in the Railway embankment corresponding to those in the road. If this is not done, the agricultural prospects of the large area to the east of the line will be adversely affected. It is further necessary that in keeping these openings the Railway Company should not deposit boulders of stone in the beds of canals and raise up their level.

The following procedure was adopted in drawing up the irrigation records. The work was taken up when attestation camps were all practically closed. It consisted in calling up the men of the several villages concerned with any scheme at the same time and ascertaining from their statements and close examination of the maps the position of the scheme, its branches and their accompanying *bandhs*, tanks, etc., the draft record was then read out to the people and, if admitted, attested at once. If disputed, the dispute was entered in the dispute list, inquired into and decided immediately or after local enquiry. Part II of the record was also amended to suit the particular case and attested as above. A map on the scale of 4″ to a mile of the irrigated area was then prepared by pentagraph reduction from the 16″ maps already prepared. **Procedure adopted in drawing up to record.**

APPENDIX A.

PART II. GENERAL RULES OF IRRIGATION FROM *Danrh.*

1. The water of the river comes naturally into the *Danrh*,
   (1) when there is flood in the river; and
   (2) when without flood there is sufficient water in the river.

Besides these, there are three other means by which water can be obtained into the *Danrh* even when there is not sufficient water in the river (1) by making a *Jangha, i.e.,* a small channel in the bed flanked by a low *bandh* to divert a portion of the current into the *Danrh*; (2) by digging into the bed of the river and then drawing up the spring water thus obtained; and (3) by taking advantage of what is called *Pasaba* or *Kasaba* water (literally water which oozes through), *i.e.* water which naturally oozes through the sandy *ail* of a higher *Jangha* into a lower *Jangha* or *Danrh.*

2. There is no definite usage regulating the construction of new *Danrh* fed by new *Janghas* from a river which passes through the properties of several *maliks*. The only rule is that if a new *Jangha* is made close to an old one, it must be made in such a way as to leave free passage of water to the latter.

3. The several villages interested in the *Danrh* are irrigated according to the following *Paris.*

4. The *Paris* above mentioned are adhered to only when there is a limited supply of water and not when irrigation is being carried on with flood-water or heavy rain-water. When the *Pari* of one village has come to an end, the village whose turn is next has the right to remove the *bandh* (*Dhatti*) made by the first village.

5. When two or more villages are being irrigated from the *Danrh* at the same time, the upper village (*i.e.*, the village through which the water flows first) cannot take water from the *Danrh* except by means of *Singhas* and the use of contrivances such as widening the *Danrh*, digging a hole near it and drawing water therefrom by means of buckets, etc., is forbidden.

6. No village can increase the number of its *Singhas* or *Dhattis* or alter their position without the consent of the other villages concerned.

7. No adjoining village unconnected with the irrigation scheme can insist on the *Nigarhs* or passages for outlet of surplus water from any village being opened. The number and position of these *Nigarhs* cannot be altered except by the mutual consent of both the villages.

8. Water is taken to every plot or *chakla* of land in the village by cutting open the *ails*.

9. A raiyat of a lower field can open a passage in the *ail* of a neighbouring field which is higher, only when that field has been irrigated or when the flow of water is such that the opening of such passage is not likely to cause any diminution of the quantity of water necessary for that field.

10. If there is any surplus water in the field of any raiyat it is let off by its *Nigarh* or passage for exit of water.

11. When there is not sufficient water for the irrigation of all the lands in the village the *malik's* local agents fix such *Paris* amongst the raiyats that all the fields may be equally irrigated. Or, if there is any surplus water in any field the *malik's* local agents arrange to get that water for the irrigation of any other field which could not otherwise be irrigated, in such a way that the former field may not in any way be injured.

12. Internal disputes amongst the raiyats of a village about irrigation are settled by the *malik's* local agents.

13. The *maliks* of the villages having the right of irrigation from the *Danrh* are responsible for its maintenance and repairs. They meet the expenses in proportion to the periods of their respective *Paris*, and where the *mulari* system prevails in proportion to the areas irrigated. Any defaulting *malik* may be sued in court by the rest, but water for the irrigation

of the village or Patti of that *malik* cannot be stopped on that account.

14. Ordinary repairs of the *Danrh* are made by the raiyats who do not receive any wages for this. But when extensive repairs are made the *maliks* meet the expenses.

15. According to established usage all the *maliks* either jointly or separately repair or cleanse the *Danrhs*. The earth required for repairs is taken from the lands on either side of the *Danrh*, and the earth removed from the *Danrh* is also deposited on such lands, within such limits as are determined by usage. The proprietors or tenants of these lands cannot object to it whether they have any right of irrigation from the *Danrh* or not.

16. The raiyats of all the villages having right of irrigation from the *Danrh* at first raise the *Jangha* and then the raiyats of particular villages keep it in order during the time their respective villages are irrigated.

APPENDIX B.

Vocabulary of Irrigation terms commonly used in south Bhagalpur.

Ahar.—A reservoir of water protected by a *bandh*.

Ail.—A small ridge between plots of land in the field.

Banokhar.—A dam of earth made across a canal.

Bhaw.—Hole dug in the bed of a river or water-course to obtain spring-water.

Barish.—Heavy rain.

Boha.—Flood.

Bandh.—Embankment.

Chhikta.—Passage of water left in a *bandh* at a certain height so that water can pass out only when it exceeds that height.

Dona.—Sloop or spoon made of palm tree or of iron.

Danda Khamba.—The contrivance of drawing water with double or treble buckets at a time from a well or with *Donas* worked on lever.

Dhatti.—Same as *Banokhar*.

Danrh.—Irrigation canal.

Faras.—Level of the bed of a water-course.

Indara.—A *pucca* well.

Jore.—A narrow stream with high and steep banks.

Johari.—Water which naturally flows down the gradient of the country during the rainy season.

Jangha.—Temporay channel dug in the bed of a river flanked by small *ails* to divert a portion of the current into the irrigation canal.

Jharna. } —Spring.
Jhila. }

Kua.—Well.

Karin.—Or *Sine-karin* means swing-basket.

Kharra.—Same as *Jore.*

Kasaba.—Or *Pasaba,* applied to water which oozes through the *ail* of one *Jangha* into another, or through the ridge of one field to another.

Kanwa.—Opening in a *bandh.*

Khurvijan.—Period of grace given to the first village of a *pari* to allow the water of the river to reach the boundary of that village.

Mulari.—Applied to the system of taking water from a canal without damming it.

Narbaha.—The ordinary village establishment of the *malik* to look after irrigation works. He is a labourer paid at Rs. 3 to Rs. 5 per month, and is also supplied with a *kodali.*

Nal or Nar.—Pipe.

Pokhar.—Tank.

Pyne.—A water-course.

Pul.—A bridge.

Paghra.—Applied to water coming down a hill.

Pasaba.—See *Kasaba.*

Pari.—Turn.

Sine.—Swing-basket.

Singha.—Smaller branch water-courses (artificial).

Sulus.—A sluice gate.

Talab.—A tank.

CHAPTER VI.

NATURAL CALAMITIES.

THE earliest famine in this district, regarding which any authentic information is still extant, was the great calamity of 1770; but, as at that time Bhagalpur had not been made a separate revenue centre, being subordinate to the Supervisor of Rājmahāl, no records exist in the Bhagalpur Collectorate referring to that disastrous year. The proceedings of the Provincial Council of Murshidābād however show that, in April of that year, the condition of the district was very bad. Mr. Harwood, the Supervisor, referring specially to Bhagalpur, reported that "the zamīndārs are ruined, the lands not having yielded half produce for the last twelve months." He had already, on the 28th March 1770, in alluding to some lenient revenue arrangements, written:—"Had the misery of the inhabitants been reported to you sooner, and had the ryots received this ease at the proper time, your beneficent intentions would have been fully answered, and many thousands who are now reduced to poverty might have enjoyed ease, if not affluence. But from motives of false policy and self-interest, the (native) collectors in the different parts, during this calamitous season, have pressed so hard upon the ryots to oblige them to make good their engagements to Government, that their total ruin has invariably followed." It is a matter of history how the famine progressed, till the beginning of the new year brought relief in the form of an abundant harvest. In November, Mr. Harwood, in forwarding the abstract revenue settlement for the current year, attributes the deficit to the "impoverished, ruined, and miserable state" of the district.

During the fifteen years following, there are frequent references to drought and scarcity. In September 1775, the Collector reported to the Governor-General and Council that, "as the drought still continues, the approaching harvest affords a very bad prospect throughout my districts, but particularly in those *parganās* where the chief cultivation is the early grain. The late crops were good; but grain has for some time past sold at an advanced price, from the unfavourable appearance of the next harvest. The settlement has been made good, but I very much apprehend great deficiencies in the revenue in the ensuing year. The growth in the most plentiful year not being sufficient for the consumption of the inhabitants, the price grain bears in the markets of my district depends in a great degree on the adjacent provinces from which supplies are drawn." The statement that the grain outturn of the most plentiful year fell short of the consumption, will startle those who are acquainted with the present large export from this district, but it must be remembered that the tracts in the north that are now highly productive were then attached to Darbhanga and Purniah, that the low country south of the headquarters station was a swamp cultivable neither in summer nor winter, and that the jurisdiction of the Collector then included the rocky waste of Rājmahāl.

In May 1779 a severe drought is reported. "As there is no appearance of a change in the weather," writes the Collector, "it is with much concern I am under the necessity of representing to the Honourable Board, that the severe drought which we have experienced in this part of the country for some time past, has alarmed the landholders in general to so great a degree, that they absolutely refuse to make themselves responsible for the current year's revenue, without a considerable remission; or upon such terms as must in the end prove very disadvantageous to Government. The country is certainly in a most alarming situation. The lands which ought to have been cultivated six weeks or two months ago, are still lying waste for want of rain, as a result of which little or nothing is to be expected from the *bhadoī* harvest; and the *aghanī* or principal rice harvest, which should be sown by this time, will suffer materially if we have not a change of weather very shortly. To add to the distress which the inhabitants must necessarily experience from the extreme heat, the tanks and wells in the interior parts of the country are entirely dried up; scarce a village in the district has escaped being burnt to the ground; the cattle are dying for want of grass; and grain in general, notwithstanding every method is taken to supply the markets as usual, is every day apparently more difficult to be procured, and of course rising in price. The country being in this situation, I have in vain used my endeavours with the zamīndārs to prevail on them to renew their leases for the present year's revenue, agreeably to your orders. They absolutely refuse, except on terms which will reduce the revenue about one-eighth, or from Rs. 1,71,771 to Rs. 1,50,300."

Again, in 1783, the same officer, in noticing a partial failure of the crops, gives the following interesting information concerning the food supply of the district:—"The produce of this district consists chiefly of wheat, barley, *kalāi*, *būt* or *gram*, and mustard seed, the greatest part of which is generally exported in the months of May, June and July to Murshidābād and Calcutta; and so trifling is the proportion of rice that none is ever exported, and above three-fourths of what is consumed in the district is imported from Purniah. This resource, however, has of late fallen off very much, and rice is certainly become scarce; but the *bhadoi* harvest which was cut in August and September, and consists of Indian corn, *maruā*, and other small grain, will effectually secure us from any real distress." At the same time, he declared himself unable, without taking special measures, to supply from local sources any troops or travellers passing through his district. He accordingly obtained sanction for the purchase of 20,000 maunds of rice in Purniah, for which he paid Rs. 21,800. In 1795, a similar difficulty presented itself; and 50,000 maunds of rice were stored at different points along the main road through Rājmahāl to Monghyr.

The famine of 1866.

No special reference to any drought is to be met with in the subsequent records, and distress is not again mentioned till 1865, the year of the great Orissa famine, when it was much less severe in Bhagalpur than in more southern and westerly districts. The following paragraphs are condensed from the report of Mr. R. F. Cockerell, c.s., who was specially deputed in the following year to inquire into the famine in Bihar. The extreme pressure of want in this district was confined to the northern *parganās* of Nāredigar, Malhanīgopāl, Nāthpur, Nissankpur-Kūrhā, Uttarkhand, and Kabkhand, bordering on the Nepāl territory, and mainly due to the complete failure of the rice crop, which there constitutes the chief cultivation. In other parts of Bhagalpur, there was only that general distress which is caused by high prices of food unaccompanied by an increased demand for labour, and consequently no rise in its value. In the northern *parganās* these difficulties were enhanced by the failure of the *maruā* crop, which, in its season, forms the mainstay of the poorer classes, and which was almost entirely destroyed in 1865 by the exceptionally heavy rainfall in the month of July. Severe distress was felt in October 1865, at which time the commonest kind of rice had risen to the rate of 11 seers for the rupee. The usual temporary relief was obtained during the rice harvest season and lasted up to the gathering of the spring crops in April, after which prices again increased, and the greatest want prevailed. In June, the Commissioner of the Division directed the attention of all the local officers to the threatening state of things; and a public meeting was held at Bhagalpur, at which a general subscription was set on foot, and relief committees were formed.

On the north side of the Ganges, relief depôts were supplied with grain imported from other districts. The highest average number of persons relieved gratuitously throughout the district during the months of August and September, when the distress was greatest, did not exceed 1,108 persons; and the largest average number employed on labour, supplied as a means of relief during any month, was about 700. The latter were paid at rates varying from 1½ to 1 anna (2¼d. to 1½d.) per diem for each person. No epidemic disease prevailed in any part of the district during the period of distress. There was, however, a good deal of sickness in the town of Bhagalpur amongst the paupers who had been attracted there by the relief measures from all parts of the district. It was generally stated that the mortality was not great in this district, as compared with most of the other districts of Bihar; and it seems probable that the relief measures adopted, though somewhat delayed in their inception, were carried out on a not inadequate scale.

On the south of the Ganges, high prices were chiefly due to large exportation to the Patnā Division. The Deputy Collector of Bānkā wrote:—"I think the high price of rice, and of pulses too, is owing mainly to the *mahājans* buying up the grain for export to the western provinces. I believe the general outcry at present is not of bad crops, but of the scarcity of grain caused by export. If grain continues at its present price up to the harvest time, the lower classes in this subdivision will not suffer extreme want. I cannot say what the consequences of a bad harvest and exportation combined will be next year, but I think famine in such a contingency is not improbable." In the months of September and October 1865, 46,185 cwt. of grain were exported from the Bhagalpur station of the East Indian Railway, against 13,783 cwt. during the same period of the previous year.

The average prices of food grain in 1865, as returned by Mr. Cockerell, were—rice, 13 seers for the rupee, Indian corn, 18 seers for the rupee, and pulses, 11 seers for the rupee. In the previous year, 1864, they had been—rice, 25 seers for the rupee, Indian corn, 31 seers for the rupee, and pulses, 24 seers for the rupee. The rates in 1863 and 1862 were nearly the same as in 1864, but slightly cheaper. These are average prices. The highest price for rice was 8¼ seers per rupee in July and August 1866. Pulses sold then at the same rate. Maize sold then at 16 seers the rupee. There were 1,019 persons on gratuitous relief in September 1866. This is the greatest number recorded. The numbers on relief works were never higher than 441 in August 1866. All forms of relief ceased with the close of the year. The mortality due to starvation as reported by the police was 97 deaths, of which 12 occurred in August, 24 in September, 27 in October, and 14 in November. At the same time, 309 deaths were attributed to disease engendered by want, of which 50 occurred in August, 58 in September, 75 in October, and 51 in November. With regard to these deaths, which were mostly in the north of the district, it must be remarked that Mr. Duff, an experienced planter, gave his opinion with regard to the two *parganās* of Nāredigar and Malhanīgopāl, that "if any cases of death did occur, the persons who died were strangers from the western districts, such as Tirhut and Champāran." On the other hand, Mr. Christian, the lessee of the Government estates in *parganās* Kabkhand and Uttarkhand, stated that from two to three per cent. of the population had perished of starvation. During the whole period of distress, a sum of Rs. 17,416 was available for purposes of relief, of which Rs. 13,561 were realised by local subscription, and Rs. 3,854 were assigned from local funds. Nothing was obtained from Government or the Calcutta Relief Fund. Of the above total, Rs. 12,871 were expended in gratuitous distribution of food and relief works, Rs. 8,287 on the former, and Rs. 4,583 on the latter, leaving Rs. 4,545, unexpended on the 1st January 1867, when the scarcity had ceased to be felt.

The famine of 1874.

The following description of the famine of 1874 is derived, for the most part, from the reports, monthly and fortnightly, of the Collector of the district and his subdivisional officers. They have been condensed as much as possible, only the more important passages being reproduced as quotations. As in the case of all previous scarcities in this district, drought was the originating cause. The rain ceased early in September, and the last heavy shower of the year fell on the 13th of July. The monthly rainfall for the entire year was:—January, ·40; February, *nil*; March, ·60; April, ·55; May ·15; June, ·5·37; July, 11·07; August, 6·68; September, 4·47; October, *nil*; November, ·06; December, ·32; total rainfall, 29·23. In the last year of drought (1865) it had been 64·35, and in 1864, 49·80. In 1872 it was 37·53. The scarcity which followed the comparatively large fall of 1865 was caused, not by any deficiency in the total quantity, but by its irregularity as well as by the partial destruction of the autumn crops by heavy rain in July and August. The fall was small in September and there was none in October; and in the words of the Collector, "no amount of early rain prevents a bad rice harvest. Without rain in

October the crop cannot be a large one." In 1873, the rain was yet more unseasonable than in 1864, and was extremely deficient, the total being only 29·23 as against 51·52 in normal years. The two tracts into which this district is divided by the Ganges are distinct not only in physical aspects, but in their products and in the manner of living of the people. The northern,—comprising the subdivisions of Madhipurā and Suapul, and Thana Bihpur police division in the headquarters subdivision,—has an area of 2,394 square miles, and produces to main food staples, rice and *maruā*, in the proportion of ten to six. The latter grain is grown most in the *parganās* of Harāwat, Kabkhand, and Uttarkhand, rice being very largely cultivated in the *parganās* bordering on Purniah. Some wheat is also produced, chiefly in *parganā* Chhāī. The *maruā* crop is almost entirely reserved for home consumption, and is distinctively the food of the poor. There are two rice crops, the *bhadoī*, reaped in August and September ; and the *aghanī*, harvested in November and the early days of December. The area in the northern portion of the district under *aghanī* is three times as large as that under *bhadoī*. The latter is exported perhaps to the extent of one half ; whilst the former, if not already hypothecated to the grain-dealer and money-lender, is immediately sold to meet the landlord's demand for rent, and finds its way both up and down country by boat and by rail, the largest purchasers being the merchants of Bhāgalpur and Monghyr, who carry on a large trade with most of the chief towns of the North-West Provinces and Oudh. The wheat is in large part sent to Calcutta for export. Little of the rice is fine enough to suit the European market.

It has been observed that in 1865 the *maruā* was nearly a total failure, being drowned by excessive rain in July and August, but that the *bhadoī* rice was a fair average crop, " the same as in other years." According to the before-mentioned estimates of these two crops, on which the people depend for food, the one that failed bore the proportion to that which was saved of 12 to 5 ; in other words, more than two-thirds of the food supply was cut off. A comparatively good *aghanī* harvest followed ; at least, one which had only failed to the extent of one-third. However, just as this relief came in, the great distress in Orissa and other rice-consuming districts of South Bengal began to be felt ; rice was largely exported and its price in Bhāgalpur quickly rose to a point beyond the means of the poorer classes, and particularly of the numerous day labourers. These classes were further unfortunate in not sharing in the benefits of the high prices, as they do not sow much *aghanī* anywhere, and in the *parganās* above mentioned, not more than sufficient to pay the rent. They were left to depend on the one-half that remained of the *bhadoī*, and one-eighth of the *maruā* crop. In 1873 the Collector reported on the 15th November, "the *maruā* is, on the whole, good"; and estimated the outturn at nearly three-fourths of a full crop, or what is over a number of years, a fair average crop. Three-fourths of the *bhadoī* rice, on the other hand, had failed, but fortunately as regards the poorer classes, the food supply destroyed was to that which they had to depend on as 5 is to 12, or the converse of the proportion in 1865. The *aghanī* in 1873 was the shortest crop. In the words of the Collector, "the rice of the whole north and west cannot yield more than a one-eighth crop, though in the east and south a half crop may be hoped for." This failure of the *aghanī* crop forced many people accustomed to consume that rice, to subsist on the coarser kinds, and so diminished the food supply to which the poorer classes had to look for support.

The most authoritative account of the state of affairs during the early months of the scarcity is the Minute by Sir Richard Temple, dated 19th February 1874, which is reproduced here:— "The Collector, Mr. V. Taylor, assures me that in those parts of the district which lie south of the Ganges and those which are situate on the basin of the river Kūsī, there is no reason to fear any serious distress; and on the north bank of the Ganges the crops are excellent. Here and there, owing to the high range of prices all over the country, there may be scattered outbreaks of distress. Otherwise, the prospect of widespread and protracted suffering is restricted to the tract which lies on the eastern or left bank of the Tiljūgā, which tract extends eastward till it approaches the 'spill' or basin of the Kūsī, and on the west adjoins the Madhubanī and Darbhangah subdivisions of Tirhut. This tract includes the *thānās* of Supaul, Bangāon, Prātāpganj, in the Supaul subdivision; and the *thānās* of Madhipurā, in the Madhipurā subdivision. The population of these *thānās* is:—Supaul 279,102; Bangāon, 145,088; Pratāpganj, 141,577; Madhipurā, 251,683; total, 817,430. The cause of distress here is much the same as in North-eastern Tirhut—namely, the loss of the principal rice-crop, which failed from insufficiency of rain on a hard soil, peculiarly needing abundant moisture. The case is, however, slightly better than Eastern Tirhut because of the *maruā* crop of August being somewhat larger, the spring crop of wheat being somewhat better, and the supplementary crop, *chīnā*, sown since the recent rain, being susceptible of irrigation. Still, allowing for all these circumstances, the nature of the case in most parts of the above-mentioned *thānās* does not materially differ for the better from North-eastern Tirhut. There is reason to fear that for several months the distress will be severe. The Commissioner of the Division, Mr. Barlow, has given me a careful and elaborate calculation, which he made after consulting the Collector and the subdivisional officers. He reckons on a possibility of 171,651 persons needing assistance for a period of five months; from which he deduces a requirement of 500,000 maunds at ¾ *seer* or 1½lb. per head per diem, to which he adds 100,000 maunds as a margin of security. My own opinion, after the best consideration which I am able to give to the subject, is that some of the percentages assumed in Mr. Barlow's calculation may be exceeded in many parts of this tract, when the worst season of distress arrives. All things considered, I estimate that in *thānās* Supaul and Bangāon 50 per cent. of the population may need assistance in the most distressed half, and 30 per cent. in the other half; that in *thānā* Pratāpganj, not quite so distressed, there would be 30 per cent.; that in Madahpurā, in one-half badly distressed, there would be 50 per cent., while the other half may escape from distress altogether. This estimate gives a total number of 274,650 persons who might need assistance for three and a half months, from 1st June to 15th September; while half this number might need assistance for April and May, and one quarter of this number for March. This calculation at ¾ *seer* per head per diem, gives a total requirement of 733,732 maunds. Looking then to the comparatively isolated situation of this tract, far from the Ganges, close to the hill frontier, having few roads passable in the rains, and few facilities for private trade, adjoining other tracts even more distressed, I consider it essential to the safety of the population concerned—817,430 souls—that 730,000 maunds should be brought within its limits by the 15th June."

The necessary action was taken under this decision and all danger of famine was removed. The railway continued to pour rice into the district; and on the 18th June the Collector reported that of 769,956 maunds, the total allotment finally decided on, 748,994 maunds had been stored, of which 166,728 had been distributed. Seventy-eight miles of road-work had been, up to the same date, completed or taken in hand, on which a daily average of 20,000 persons were employed. In the north of the district, in the four distressed police divisions, 28,217 persons were receiving gratuitous relief; and 16,905, principally women, were employed in light labour, for which they received full wages in rice or money. Before this date the cold-weather crops had been reaped, and their outturn is thus described by the Collector at the beginning of April:—"The spring harvest is now almost over; and in *parganā* Chhāī and the head-quarters subdivision, the crop may be safely put down as a very good one indeed, and above an average crop of ordinary years. In Bānkā subdivision it has also yielded above an average crop. For Madhipurā, taking the whole subdivision together, I am not wrong in putting it down as a three-fourths one. The Supaul officer admits a three-fourths or an average crop. The *chīnā* cultivation which is far beyond anything ever seen in this district, is not, taken into account; it is still in all stages of growth." On the 21st of the same month he adds:—"The irrigated *chīnā* has been cut, and has proved a very good crop, so much so that ryots themselves admit that those who were fortunate enough or wise enough to sow it this year, are in comfort." He then goes on to describe the position of the people at that period, and incorporates with his own opinion those of the subdivisional officers. The Supaul officer reported:—"No cases of misery and starvation have come to light; a large proportion (on one occasion when an account was taken at the relief centre here, it was found to be nearly 50 per cent.) of our paupers come from Tirhut, and most of them are most worthy objects of charity. As yet very few others than the very lowest classes, and those who, in the best of years, would have been, to some extent, dependent on charity, have been attracted to our relief centres." "There have been a few deaths at some of the relief centres in the Supaul subdivision, which cannot in any way be put down to starvation, and are not to be wondered at when one sees the class of persons who come to them." "Five out of seven deaths were those of residents of Tirhut district; and in most of them I can certify that disease, in many cases of long standing, was the cause, though possibly the end has been accelerated by privation."

As early as the 30th of July the district officers were able to report signs of a speedy cessation of distress. The subdivisional officer of Supaul wrote on that date:—"The weather during the past fortnight has been everything that could be desired. It is on all hands admitted that a fuller and more promising *bhadoī* crop, both *maruā* and *rice*, has not been seen for many years past; it is, moreover, unusually forward, and will be generally ready for the sickle in about twenty or thirty days." To this the Collector added:—"From the Pratāpganj side matters are still better. New *maruā* is already in the market, and selling at 24 seers for the rupee; and when the crop comes well in we shall see it selling at not less than a maund for the rupee; and it must be remembered that this grain is the food of the poorer classes. Early *bhadoī* rice is also here in the market. It is selling unhusked at 35 seers; and the Deputy Collector reports that, before long, it is expected that it will be as cheap as 2 maunds for the rupee. Should this be a fact, the time must be close at hand when all idea of any distress in this portion of the district must be given up." The report of the Madhipurā officer on the same date is interesting:—"The crops are looking exceedingly well everywhere, only the lowest lands having been so far flooded as to injure the crop on them. A zamīndār who visited me the other day said he was astonished to find almost every field sown in this subdivision, and said he believed it was owing to fewer relief works having been started here than elsewhere. I have purposely lessened the works lately in this subdivision, in order to allow employers to get their usual labourers. I am glad the desired effect has resulted." Up to this period 422,577 maunds of Government rice had been expended in relief.

On the 7th of October the last fortnightly narrative was submitted. It gives, in appendix, the following details of expenditure on relief.—Disbursed by District Engineer for relief works, Rs. 1,88,000; by officers in charge of transport arrangements, Rs. 5,28,393; for construction of storehouses, Rs. 6,750; advances made to trustworthy residents for purchase of grain, Rs. 70,400; advances made to traders for purchase of grain, Rs. 1,600; advances to the Bhāgalpur municipality, Rs. 5,000; advances made to zamīndārs and others for land improvement, Rs. 7,625; advances to zamīndārs and others for helping their tenants, Rs. 1,03,900; total expenditure, Rs. 9,12,668. It must be remembered in calculating the entire cost of relief in the Bhāgalpur district, that the above total is exclusive of the cost of the Government imported grain; and also of its carriage by railway to the various railway stations of the district. On the other hand, a large proportion of the expenditure in money and grain consisted of recoverable advances which were afterwards largely realized.

The monthly average number of persons employed on relief operations varied from 1,351 in November 1873 to 32,637 in May 1874. The numbers gradually diminished after that month, but no big drop occurred till September in which month 12,002 was the average, the average for August having been 29,424. In all the equivalent of 1,77,847 persons for thirty days were relieved.

Scarcity in 1889.

In 1889 Supaul subdivision suffered somewhat from the loss of a large part of the winter rice crop consequent on a deficiency in the rainfall of 1888. In May and June there was considerable distress, but favourable rains set in and relieved the tension of the situation. Advances up to Rs. 17,458 were made under the

Agricultural Loans Act and this enabled the cultivators to sow for the ensuing harvest.

In 1892 a large part of Supaul and Madhipura subdivisions suffered from the scanty rainfall of 1891 and the consequent short crops. Relief works were opened in January. In March the average number on them was 3,494 per day. The numbers rose rapidly to a maximum of 12,370 in June and fell again just as rapidly. All relief works were closed at the end of June. Over Rs. 37,000 were advanced in loans. Private sources contributed Rs. 47,000 to the relief of this distress. **Scarcity in 1892.**

The scarcity in 1896-97 was due mainly to the general rise in prices consequent on the widespread failure of crops in Upper India which caused prices to advance rapidly. The free supply of food grains was exported, and in consequence the local supplies fell short. Between October 1896 and September 1897 the total exports of food grains from the district exceeded the imports by nearly 83,000 tons. The same is true of the scarcity in 1892 but to a less degree. The experience of those two years makes it difficult for local officers to calmly acquiesce in a policy of unrestricted export, in consequence of which hundreds of thousands suffer privations that a few bunnias may grow wealthy. It is the poorest of the poor that suffer the pinch of scarcity first and that recover from it last. At times the greed of the local grain dealers brings its own punishment. Thus in 1903 around Banka, in consequence of the failure of the rains, the local bunnias put up the prices. The result was an indiscriminate and unrestricted outbreak of grain looting that lasted for three days about. **Famine in 1896-97.**

In 1896-97 the area most affected was that bordering on Darbhanga on the west, with Supaul as a centre. The Supaul subdivision has always suffered most from famine and scarcity. The winter rice crop in 1895 was very short owing to early cessation of the rains. In 1896 there was a prolonged break in the rains from July till August 20th, and no rain at all fell after September 20th. Rice rose to 7¾ seers in June 1897, and maize to 9½ seers. These prices were phenomenally high. Relief works were opened in January and attracted labour till July. Early in May, the daily average on relief works reached 24,465. It declined thereafter.

It is very noteworthy that in this year the death-rate was only 27·03 per mille for the whole district. The figure for the previous year was 37·08 and for the previous quinquennium 34·09.

Relief from private sources was liberally given. Upwards of Rs. 26,000 were distributed in grain or money doles under the provisions of the Indian Famine Fund. The total expenditure was about Rs. 1,64,500 out of which Government met Rs. 56,400, and the District Board the balance.

Scarcity in 1902. Scarcity was apprehended in 1902 owing to the scarcity and ill-distributed rainfall of 1901. Supaul again was the centre of the area most affected. Mr. Shirres, the Collector, pointed out that labourers around Supaul are naturally indolent. Till comparatively lately they were mostly herdsmen in charge of grazing grounds, and they have not as yet become inured to really hard work. The mean rainfall for 1901 was only 35·5 inches against an average of 51 inches.

Floods in 1906. The tract of country around Supaul and Madhipura was devastated by exceptionally high floods in August-September 1906. As usual the distress was severe until the waters subsided. Agricultural loans were freely distributed. The receding waters left a fertile deposit of silt behind, which yielded an excellent *rabi* crop in the spring of 1907.

Scarcity in 1908-09. The mean rainfall of 1908 was only 24·4 inches—the lowest ever recorded and less than half the average. At Bhāgalpur itself only 18·04 inches were registered in the whole year. At Supaul 23·96; at Madhipura 22·00, and at Banka 33·6. The result was inevitable. The *bhadoī* crops failed entirely and the *aghanī* crop was a complete failure in many places. Fortunately, the Kosi floods gave bumper crops of *bhadoī* and *aghanī* in the eastern portions of the two northern subdivisions. This saved the district from what threatened to be the worst famine yet known.

The first warning of impending danger was submitted as early as August 1908 when it was obvious that there was a wide-spread failure of rains. After August, the only big fall of rain was registered at Banka, 10·97 inches having fallen in September and ·89 in October. But this was by no means a general fall as the northern portion of this subdivision suffered as much from short rainfall as the Sadar subdivision. South of the Ganges there were literally hundreds of square miles left absolutely fallow, without a crop of any sort being planted out. But the crops of previous years had been good and the cultivators were well prepared to stand a strain. The landless labourers cleared out in thousands to look for employment elsewhere. The luxuriant crops in the east of Supaul and Madhipura subdivisions, north of the river, attracted many : large numbers went into the lands on the Purnea side of the Kosi and many others went eastwards to get employment in the rice lands of Bengal proper. It was computed that in August and September about 70,000 people crossed the Ganges from south to north in search of work.

Agricultural loans were freely distributed to enable the cultivators to sow *rabi* crops, but unfortunately the failure of the hoped-for rains in December and January nullified to a large extent the beneficial results that were expected.

The local officers were able to induce zamīndārs and other wealthy persons to avail themselves of the abundant supply of labour for the excavation or re-excavation of tanks and wells: and for the construction of bunds and irrigation channels. The Banaili Rāj completed an embankment along the Tiljūga river at a cost of over a lakh and a half of rupees. This should protect a large area in future from the destructive floods that have worked such havoc in the past.

In the south of the district the irrigation channel known as the Mahashay Taraknath Ghosh's Raj Dourh from the Chandan river saved a large part of the Rajaun outpost area. Steps were taken to lead some of the Chandan waters into the beds of the Kadwa and Gahira rivers and irrigation channels were also cut from the Chir river.

In April 1909 about 485 tanks were in hand in the north of the district and the construction of the Pertabganj-Bhimnagar branch line railway embankment gave constant employment to over 2,000 labourers.

The Tiljūga and Dimra rivers were bunded up and every drop of water that could be got from them was lifted up by the usual *karins* (palm-tree trunks hollowed out) to the higher levels and used for irrigation. Water was led from the reservoir formed by damming up the Tiljūga as far as nine miles north and south, and four miles east and west.

The benefits of irrigation in those parts of the district, especially in the north of it, were so manifest that strong representations were made to Government to have the possibility of utilizing the Kosi waters for a general irrigation system with the existing channels as distributaries considered from a professional point of view. The suggestion was that head works should be constructed above Birpur where the channel of the Kosi does not fluctuate and oscillate over as large an extent of country as it covers lower down. At about 15 miles north of Birpur it emerges from a sharply defined gorge in the hills, and this exit is certainly fixed and invariable, but it is some distance outside the borders of British India.

This is the fatal defect in the scheme and on this account it was dropped after some preliminary investigation. To secure a sufficient head of water, the reservoir and training works should be constructed just where the river emerges from the hills—and as this point is in Nepal and as it was believed that the consent of the Nepalese authorities was not likely to be given, the matter went no further. This is regrettable, as a scheme that would irrigate nearly two thousand square miles would be at all times a boon.

A further objection was that a similar proposal to use the existing river beds as distributaries had been already tried in Saran and had failed utterly. Water could not be got along them when most needed. Finally the shifting and unreliable nature of the Kosi had to be considered. "The Kosi is an impudent hussy that leaves her bed at night and seeks strange beds so that every engineer will have nothing to do with her for fear of his reputation". This criticism by an experienced Irrigation officer caused the scheme to be dropped.

In the south of the district irrigation has been systematically practised for a long time as already described in chapter V. The river Chandan was restrained by a bund for this purpose but breaches of the bund by sudden floods are not uncommon.

Chandan Floods. About 1860, the great main road from Bhāgalpur through Deogarh to Sūrī was constructed across these lowlands. The work had scarcely been completed, when a great flood came down the Chandan, swept through the petty embankments of the zamīndārs, breached the new road in several places, and broke down some bridges. Attention was strongly called to the condition of the river, which was made the subject of a report, in May 1864, by the Superintending Engineer, Northern Circle.

From this report the following particulars are derived :—The Chandan is a river which has its source in the hills about Deogarh in the Sonthal Parganas, and, for the first half of its course, is fed by numerous tributaries, also rising in the hills. At about thirty miles from its embouchure into the Ganges, it begins to throw off branches to the eastward, and, twenty miles nearer its termination, also to the westward. It thus gradually loses nearly the whole body of water it brings down, the main channel at its junction with the Ganges being reduced to insignificant dimensions. At its greatest width, the Chandan is about 1,500 feet from bank to bank. From the long continued practice of embanking, its bed is actually higher than the land on either side. Being a hill stream, it is liable to sudden and violent inundations ; but, except when in flood, the channel is a dry bed of gritty sand, bounded on either side by artificial embankments pierced throughout with innumerable cuts for irrigation purposes. The principal of these, six in number, were then (1864) spanned by temporary bridges. The protecting embankments being entirely in the hands of the riparian proprietors, and under no systematic control, they were liable, from the ignorance and neglect of those in charge of the irrigation openings, to be extensively and frequently breached at the most inconvenient times and places, thus causing occasionally the divergence of the entire volume of the Chandan flood from its proper bed through one or other of those gaps. The Bhāgalpur to Bausi road runs parallel to the river for the entire distance, acting throughout as a high level irrigator to the neighbouring land; and the great number of bridges and culverts provided in the road embankment, shows how much water is required for the use of the country beyond. The six following *nālās*, or drains are each nearly as wide as the Chandan itself, at the points from which they respectively branch, viz., the Gūrdhāi, Phulbārī, Pinjamnārī, Purāinī, Kokārā, and Razalahār; and the aggregate cost of bridging these permanently, with due provision for the contingencies of flood, was estimated to be three or four times as much as that of bridging the Chandan about Purāinī. These cuts were all undoubtedly artificial in their origin, and have been gradually enlarged to their present dimensions by successive floods. To illustrate the position, the case of the Purāinī cut may be cited. Previous to the rains of 1863, it was only from thirty to forty feet in width. But, in consequence of a large and permanent breach formed in the embankment of the Chandan, it grew to three times that size; and nearly the whole river flood was diverted into it at a bend in its course, where it seems scarcely possible to effect any permanent repair. At the same time, three channels to the south of it became comparatively dry. The landowners gave no sign of any intention to repair the breach; and it was proposed that the management and control of the Chandan embankments should be vested in the Executive Engineer in charge of the road, the cost of repair, &c., being borne, as now, by the riparian proprietors. The water-supply required through the different branch channels having been once definitely fixed, with the concurrence of all interested, the openings into them from the river could be permanently arranged for, and subsequently the channels themselves bridged at a considerable saving to Government. The first cost of building up and securing the mouths of these escapes might be borne by Government, as the outlay would result in a saving in the bridging of the road; but all subsequent expenditure for keeping up the embankments should fall on the proprietors, being for the benefit of their lands. The Commissioner of the Bhāgalpur Division was favourable to the adoption of these proposals, provided the consent of the neighbouring landholders could be obtained. Nothing, however, was effected, except what the influence of the Commissioner and the Magistrate induced the landowners to do. The latter were most willing to bear any reasonable expenditure for the protection of their lands and the regulation of irrigation. The Magistrate thus describes the manner in which they had previously arranged for the repair and maintenance of these embankments. "When any expense of magnitude is incurred, the amount of benefit which each landholder will derive from the work when completed, is calculated; and the cost is then rateably divided on that basis among the proprietors. The money is collected, and all benefited send ryots to assist in the accomplishment of the work; these ryots are fed daily, but do not otherwise receive any remuneration, while the regular *beldārs* who may be employed are paid at the ordinary rates. Petty maintenance repairs are effected by the ryots themselves on each estate; and it is only when extensive works are required, that the above system is resorted to."

The lands are still exposed to ruinous floods; but the road having settled down and being better bridged, the attention of the executive authorities is less drawn to the permanent injury to the country caused by the floods. Down to the present time, only a cold-weather crop is grown on a tract of country covering some 150 square miles, chiefly because the danger of floods from the Chandan is so great, that no crop is grown during the rains. In many years the injury extends over a much larger area, and devastates a regularly cultivated country.

During the scarcity of 1874, embankments were one of the forms of earthwork labour on which the able-bodied recipients of relief were employed. Many were made by the resident landholders, with money borrowed from Government. The principal of these are—one in the Government estate of Rājanpur in *parganā* Kabkhand, erected by the Public Works Department, along the banks of the river Parwān; and one erected by Mr. Christian, indigo planter of Bangāon, on the banks of the river Dimrā, in the Uttarkhand *parganā*. The other embankments are of less size, and are scattered over the subdivisions of Madhipura and Supaul.

Cyclonic cloud-burst.

In 1899 (September) the eastern part of south Bhāgalpur including the country about Colgong suffered very severely from a heavy flood. Owing to the bursting of a cyclonic storm the river Chandan breached its embankments and flooded all the country in the neighbourhood of Gogha, washing away the railway bridge near that place. At least 1,800 lives were lost and 25,000 houses were destroyed. Numbers of cattle perished, and loans were freely given to enable the ryots to purchase new cattle.

CHAPTER VII.

RENTS, WAGES AND PRICES.

UNTIL the completion of the recent survey and preparation of a record-of-rights under Chapter X of the Bengal Tenancy Act, really accurate figures showing the incidence of rent on various classes of tenancies in the different parts of this district were nowhere to be found. Reference must be made to the Final Report on those operations for a detailed analysis of the rent question in this district. The following figures present a summary of the results arrived at. Cash rents.

The incidence of rent per acre in the case of raiyats at fixed rates was found to be Re. 1-4-0: for settled and occupancy raiyats it was Re. 2-10-6: for non-occupancy raiyats it was Re. 2-13-3: and for under-raiyats it was Re. 2-1-7: the average for these classes of tenants (excluding under-raiyats) worked out at Rs. 2-10-5 per acre.

The great bulk of the tenants (namely 96·38 per cent.) consists of raiyats with a right of occupancy (including raiyats at fixed rates and settled raiyats). The average rents per acre payable in each thana by those tenants varies considerably. Starting with the two subdivisions north of the river we find the average, thana by thana, to be as follows:—

Subdivision.	Thana.	Incidence per acre. Rs.	A.	P.
Supaul	Supaul	2	10	1
	Partabganj	1	9	7
Madhipura	Madhipura	2	5	1
	Kishanganj	1	14	0
	Bangaon	1	15	9

South of the river the details are as follows:—

Subdivision	Thana	Rs.	A.	P.
Sadar	Bhagalpur	5	8	8
	Colgong	3	4	8
	Sultanganj	5	2	10
	Bihpur	2	2	11
Banka	Banka	2	2	5
	Amarpur	4	10	8
	Katauria	1	7	11

Produce rents.

Produce rents are of more importance in the area lying south of the river Ganges than in the northern portion. Irrigation is more generally practised in the south, because it is always useful and even essential there. To the north it is of use only in seasons when the rainfall is abnormally short. The details show that an area of 157,073 acres is held on produce rent—the division of the crop into two equal shares being the commonest form of this rent. But instances in which the crop is divided into unequal shares are by no means unknown.

The Bengal Tenancy Act provides (section 40) a method by which tenants who hold lands on produce rent can have this commuted for a cash payment. Tenants freely avail themselves of the opportunity afforded by the presence in their villages of Revenue Officers to apply for commutation. Widely divergent views are held as to the advisability of this. Lately, owing to the high prices that prevailed, tenants were extremely anxious to get their rents fixed on a cash basis; but it is doubtful if they will be pleased with the results when prices have fallen to a normal figure. Another disadvantage resulting from wholesale commutations of produce rents for a cash payment is that the landlord becomes a mere rent-collector and is—or at least will tend to develop into — an impersonal head, utterly careless whether the raiyats get a good or a bad crop. When paid in kind, the landlord stands to lose very largely if the crops be indifferent over a large area and hence enlightened self-interest made landlords look after the maintenance of embankments, reservoirs and irrigation channels. It is to be feared that this stimulus will be wanting in future and that the ultimate results may prove disastrous.

Finally, there is an ineradicable conviction in the heart of the average unlettered tenant that he has no permanent rights in any lands held only on payment of produce rents. This belief encourages applications for commutation.

In the lately-concluded operations, applications for commutation were presented, in respect of an area of about 12,000 acres. The average rent per acre resulting from the commutation was Rs. 6-2-3. On the other hand, it must be borne in mind that the Bengal Tenancy Act lays down strict limits (often not observed, it must be admitted) as to the amount and frequency of the legal enhancements of cash rents that may be made. No such limit exists in the case of produce rents and wholesale extortion results when the produce rent is fixed not by a share of the produce but by a bulk amount of grain or its market value at the time of the harvest (*mankhap*), determined at random and variable at the whim of the local tahsildar. This system of produce rents embodies all the vices of the cash rent system without any of its advantages.

The figures given in the report of the Revenue Surveyor (1862) for incidence of rent in the various parganas show amounts varying from about 5 annas to about Rs. 2-10 per acre. The figures actually given are for bighas of which the area is not mentioned but as the bighas varied from 3,600 to 5,057 square yards (an acre being 4,840 square yards) it is impossible to select the particular bigha for which the rate is quoted. Former rents.

Buchanan Hamilton gives a very interesting account of the state of things at the time he made his survey (circa 1812.) He mentions the practice of not fixing the rent till the crop was grown as fortunately fallen into disuse. The *mustajiri* system was prevalent in the south of the district. He was convinced that the landlords made enormous profits but, owing to their apprehensions that the Permanent Settlement was not unalterable, they were at great pains to conceal the extent of their profits. They submitted statements showing that the retention of their *zamindaris* caused them a heavy loss, but he regarded such statements as totally unworthy of credit. In some places they avoided extensions of cultivation fearing to exhibit evidence of making much profit from their lands.

The money rent in several parganas was about one rupee for a bigha of 2,525 square yards—or a little over half an acre: this is approximately two rupees per acre. The lands were usually leased out on short terms but tenants rarely cultivated the same lands for more than two years. Apparently it was the custom to accept a nominal rent for the first year when soil was newly broken (called *khil*) and taken under cultivation for the first time. In the second year a slightly higher rent (called *kam*) was taken. This was meant of course to attract new settlers but it certainly tended in practice to letting lands run into fallow after two years' cultivation. It is obvious that such a custom could prevail only where almost unlimited facilities for taking up new lands of fair quality were afforded to the cultivators. These reserves of unbroken lands no longer exist, with the obvious result that the tenants are more than ever at the mercy of their landlords. The demand for tenants that prevailed in years gone by has now given way to a demand for land and this naturally produces rack rents. The vast extension of cultivation that has come about in the last century may be inferred from this alteration of agricultural conditions.

Buchanan Hamilton also remarked that labour was scarce at the time of his investigations. It was then considered extremly disgraceful to work for hire, so much so that few tenants of land would admit that they ever worked elsewhere than on their own lands. No doubt the existence of bondsmen or slaves, as he calls them plainly, helped to make daily labour appear an indignity. Some men cultivated the landlords' land for a share of the crop. Some were hired for the season or for a month or for a day. Subletting by actual cultivators was very rare: in the extreme south it was known and these under-raiyats as they would now be called were then known as *koliaits*. This term is known at present in parts of Purnea district.

Towards the east, only one crop a year was grown. Very little preliminary cultivation was given to the ground, and the cultivators were content to get enough only to live upon from their efforts.

In the south of the district subinfeudation was rather common. Very often the middleman made no profit whatever out of the rents he collected from under-tenants, but had to pay it all over to his landlord, as well as pay him a rent for the lands he personally occupied. This system is a survival of an old method of settlement whereby one man was held responsible for the rent of the whole village. Formerly he may have been a man of some position and influence, but now there is little if any prestige attaching to such a post.

Slavery. Slaves were called *nufur* (male) and *laundi* (female). They were found mostly in the part of the district near the Monghyr border. They were mostly employed as agricultural servants and if there was no work to do on their owner's farm they might take up casual employment elsewhere. Slaves were always of Dhanuk or Rawani caste. They could be sold at the whim of their master, but they were not often brought to sale. As a rule slaves were intermarried if possible. If a slave youth married a free girl or a girl slave of another master, the youth's master had no claim on the children. If a slave girl married either a free man or the slave of another man, her master claimed all the children. The free man who married a slave girl was himself sometimes, but not generally, degraded to slavery: in other cases he became a *chutiya-gulam* (cunno servus) and worked for his wife's master for the usual daily allowance of six pounds of grain. He could not however be sold by the owner of his wife.

Peculiar tenancies. A peculiar form of tenancy is that known as *halhasila*, is found in Bhagalpur. The tenant pays rent for the lands cultivated by him according to the nature of the crops grown on them and for fallow land, at the rate paid for that land in the previous year or at a special rate for fallow land. Sometimes the rent is levied on the area actually cultivated, irrespective of whether it bears a crop or not: and sometimes on the cropped area only.

Agricultural labourers are still paid in kind almost universally at about two seers of paddy per day. Hence they are untouched by the variations in prices of food crops as long as there are any agricultural operations in progress yielding a crop worth harvesting. The following table shows the average daily rate of wages for men of the artizan class at intervals during the last 15 years:— Wages.

	1895. Annas.	1900. Annas.	1905. Annas.
Carpenter—			
Superior ...	8	8	8
Common ...	5	5	5
Blacksmith—			
Superior ...	8	8	8
Common ...	6	6	6
Gharami, (*i.e.*, thatcher, etc.) ...	6	6	6
Cooly—			
Man ...	3	3	3
Woman ...	1=6	1=6	1=6
Boy ...	1=6	1=6	1=6

These rates appear to have been fairly constant. The number of labourers does not appear to be in excess of local demands.

Taking four staple articles of every-day consumption we find the following prices in seers per rupee prevailed in the years given, at the end of March each year, in Bhagalpur:— PRICES.

	Wheat.	Rice.	Gram.	Salt.
1895 ...	14·8	17·10	18·15	10·1
1900 ...	13·4	13·14	17·4	10·0
1907 ...	7·8	8·3	8·12	20·
1908 ...	9·8	8·14	12·10	20·

The very marked rise towards the last years quoted is due directly to the extreme local scarcity that prevailed in those years and less directly to the general rise in prices that has been noticed all over India. Various explanations based on diverse economic theories have been put forward to account for this very wide-spread increase in the cost of the barest necessaries of life

Perhaps the soundest, if not the most plausible as well, is that based mainly on considerations of currency.

Mr. Shirres gave the following explanations for the rise in prices in 1902:—(1) An unprecedented succession of bad harvests affecting an abnormally large proportion of the cultivated area of India as a whole. (2) The extension of jute cultivation which now covers more than 3,500 square miles of land capable of bearing rice. This explains the exceptional rise in the price of that grain. (3) The diversion of labour from agriculture to industry; (4) The continuous import of money which has apparently influenced prices for the last century.

It may be observed that the second explanation is untenable if it is understood to mean that the growing of a crop of jute necessarily excludes the possibility of raising a rice crop from the same field in the same year. This can be done. It requires very hard work, it is true, but it *is* done when the price of jute is low.

A further explanation is that during the last five years the price of jute has been so high that a great amount of money has been poured into the jute-growing districts. With his pockets full after a successful jute season, the cultivator will not grow more rice than is required for the support of his family. Consequently there is only a very small surplus on the market for sale, and those who must purchase their rice in the open market have to pay accordingly.

Material condition of the people.

It is generally admitted that there has been an all-round advance in the general condition of the people in this district as well as in Bengal generally. The standard of living is gradually rising and the petty luxuries of yesterday are becoming the necessities of to-day. The progress is slow but it is none the less sure. The improvement of inland communications facilitates the gradual spread of imported commodities and competition for markets on the part of manufacturers in the western world keeps the prices at a reasonable figure. It is extraordinary what a variety of imported articles can be found even in the remotest country bazaars, and as a rule, a very large proportion of them are of other than English manufacture. Cotton piece-goods, kerosine oil, sugar, salt, umbrellas, shoes, cigarettes, soap, scents, enamelled ware vessels for domestic use and various imported miscellaneous articles are everywhere exposed for sale.

The agricultural classes enjoy a modicum of comfort if not of prosperity. The labouring classes can find a constant demand for their services in other districts. It was remarked in the Census Report of 1901 that Bhagalpur shows a larger amount of inter-migration with contiguous districts than any other district of Bihar. In every 10,000 of the enumerated population, 514 were immigrants, mostly from contiguous districts. But a considerably larger number (595 per 10,000) of persons born in this district were enumerated elsewhere—most of them again in contiguous districts. The actual net excess of emigrants over immigrants was over 20,000 individuals.

No doubt the decay of the indigo industry has lessened the demand for labour in certain localities among day labourers and carters, but facilities for temporary emigration are now far greater than formerly and they are availed of freely when occasion compels. It has already been noted that during the scarcity in 1908, very large numbers (possibly as many as 70,000) of unemployed went from the south of the district across the Ganges into that part of Madhipura thana in which a good rice crop created a demand for labour.

The mahajan class prospers here as everywhere else at the expense of the old landed proprietors whose improvidence, extravagance and consequent gradual impoverishment make them an easy prey to the usurer's wiles. The usual stages in the downward course are as follows. First stage, a loan on mortgage, without possession: then a mortgage with possession of part of the property. Then possession of more, and eventually sale of it. Owing to the heavy incumbrances, no one finds it worth their while to bid except the money-lender. The phenomenon is not infrequent of a *kaya*, as these money-lenders are generally called, beginning with a small cloth shop and rising in a few years to a position of very marked affluence.

Among the professional classes, the lawyers and doctors do fairly well. The increased cost of living has however told very hardly on the struggling members of these professions and on all classes of Government servants whose income is stationary or practically so, as their expenses have gone up in a very marked manner. Fortunately, at present (1909-10), thanks to the plenteous harvests of the last year, the prices of food stuffs have fallen to a reasonable level.

Relations of landlords and tenants.

The following extracts from the reports of the District Magistrate (Mr. F. F. Lyall) for the years 1907-08 and 1908-09 need no comment. They show that in many instances landlords who ought to know better are absolutely devoid of conscience in dealing with their tenants. It has been said elsewhere that the law interferes and punishes the man who steals even an anna's worth of his neighbour's property, but it protects the man who robs half a countryside, with or without the appearance of a technical legal sanction for his acts of oppression. No where has the legal maxim "*summum jus summa injuria*" been more sadly exemplified.

1907-08. "Further acquaintance with the north of the district shows me that though the settlement may have settled up old standing disputes, it has, in many cases, only been done by the zamindars having forced the tenants to accept the very rent which the Settlement Department had refused to allow and sometimes much more. Babu Rash Bihari Mandal not only forced all his tenants to accept the former cash rent which was 20 to 33 per cent. in excess of what the survey fixed, but actually secured in addition in many villages a half share in 2 cottahs in every bigha, the produce of the bigha for purposes of levying his rent being fixed at 12 maunds. The Maharaja of Sonbarsa similarly threw all the demands the settlement had cut down into 'miscellaneous,' and forced the tenants to accept them. Babu Rajendra Narayan Singh has been attempting the same game: and enquiries are being made how far he has gone. I mention these names only, but I fear that many landlords not mentioned are in a similar category. The system worked was first to get back practically all rent receipts the tenants had, then to levy rent without giving receipts, then to demand the illegal high rate of rent, and if a man refuse, to sue him for four years' rental and use the decree as a threat to force him to accept. I have secured papers of Babu Rash Bihary Mandal indubitably proving this. The Maharaja's registers now in the Court of Wards also prove this. This wholesale oppression could in my opinion only have existed owing to rent suits being decided by Munsifs—officers who are bound by a technical code of procedure and never have opportunities of going into the mufassal and seeing the evil their orders bring about. I have constantly heard it said that if a man cannot produce a rent receipt, the zamindar must get a decree, and no plea of payment without obtaining a rent-receipt is ever listened to or accepted. I have myself read the appellate judgment of a Subordinate Judge in such a case in which he has come to the clearest and strongest finding that Babu Rash Bihari Mandal had filed forged zamindari papers to support a claim to the illegal rate of rent he claimed: yet the plea of payment is dismissed with the remark that the defendant can file no receipt to prove it. This may be law, but surely it is not justice, which would clearly seem to point to the fact that a man who can stoop to forging papers to support his claim for an illegal rate of rent would not be above stooping to fraudulently suing a man for rent he had received to force him to accept this illegal rate of rent. The plaintiff's whole *bonâ fides* is tainted by this act of forgery—the defendant is not shown in any way to be a man of doubtful credit, yet a decree is given as if it were a matter of course. I am personally of opinion that one of the greatest reforms that could be introduced into these Bihar districts is to place all rent-suits in the hands of Deputy Collectors. I do not see why this would entail any extra cost, for the number of Munsifs would be decreased, it would bring the parties into direct touch with the Collector, and once it was known that local hearing of these cases was possible and probable, I have no doubt that 30 per cent. of the litigation now going on would be stopped because the masses of false cases now brought would never come to Court.

"My plea is for justice, and for giving the go-by to all this procedure. No one who has not heard at first hand such tales as I have, can imagine the utter and cruel injustice now habitually worked in the name of justice through our Civil Courts, simply because all this tangled web of procedure has put the poorer man, the less educated, at the mercy of any unscrupulous man who chooses to ruin him by litigation. The fact that our Courts are here to administer justice seems to be lost sight of by almost every officer presiding in them, and their eyes are rivetted only on questions of whether some rule of procedure has been transgressed or not.

"In the condition of things that has now arrived it is small wonder if we hear less and less of open fights between the landlord and the tenant; but surely that was preferable to the present system when the zamindar utilises the Courts as a cat's-paw to ruin his tenantry for him, and then if the tenant does turn, he is run in for resisting Government authority, and not the zamindar. Small wonder if the tenants begin now to vaguely voice their belief, as I heard one man say, that the Courts are blind—'*tab na aisa ho sakta*' (for only then could such things be); but unless some steps are taken to see that justice, as against procedure, is dispensed, to re-introduce the personal touch between the Courts and the people, in place of the Courts seeing nothing but what pleaders and mukhtears allow their clients to bring to the Court's notice, I think the vague misgivings and hopelessness will be replaced by an active desire among the tenantry to remedy such a state of things. A large section of the bar is engaged in spreading disloyal sedition on the one side; on the other, it is engaged in fostering and thinking out all the cruelly false and criminally fraudulent litigation that is going on and by the injustice, they conspire to bring about, and actually *bring about*, they are leading the people to look with contempt and hatred on our Courts as things which are powerless to bring criminals to justice, and are in fact but means of affording criminals a safe means of revenge on any who dare to cross their paths.

"There would be no stronger advocate of the separation of Judicial and Executive functions than myself, were any concurrent measures taken to enable the judiciary to hear and know what goes on in the villages, and judge what comes before them more with a view to what justice demands, and less with an ear to the quibble that any astute lawyer can put forward to defeat justice; and without the strongest control of the judicial side from an administrative point of view, any change made will only lead to further injustice being perpetrated. If this cannot be done, then I can look for nothing but a more marked decline in the relations between the people, the landlords and the Government."

* * * * * *

1908-09. "Another year's experience only corroborates the very strong remarks I made last year—which, I would respectfully urge, may be again read—as to the evils our system of dispensing law by rule of thumb is bringing about between landlords and tenants. I quoted some specific instances last year; I could quote many more. A typical one I may note is where a Muhammadan-landlord was anxious to oust some Sonthal tenants of his district. A creature was got up to sue them on a forged bond in Purnea, and the defendant was sold up.

"On being told of the case, I arranged for the plaintiff in the case to be made to identify the defendant in the presence of the Munsif, and it was found he could not. The whole proceedings had been fraudulent! Now, how is the Sonthal to get justice? He cannot get it by just asking the Munsif to sanction the prosecution of the plaintiff: the Munsif's decree, palpably gained by fraud, bars the way. The Crown cannot move for the same reason, and can in fact do nothing unless the plaintiff agrees to be used as a pawn in the game, and be pushed forward to ask for a review in one Court, to oppose an appeal in another, and if he secures the review, to give evidence. Then, if he gains the review, or if he has to bring a title suit to declare the bond forged and wins that suit, still nothing can be done by the Crown unless the complainant will put in a final petition before the Munsif, asking for sanction to prosecute, and then move the Magistrate. Is it any wonder that the most impudent forgery is committed every day, and that a zamindar considers himself absolutely immune from any loss but that of his court-fees, if he attacks an enemy in the Civil Courts?

"When I first came to the district I never heard of such cases. The action taken on Rash Behari's and Girdhari Marwari's case now often brings me two or three men a day asking me to redress wrongs thus done them. The matter is one calling for the very serious attention of Government, for what loyalty can there ultimately be to a Government which allows itself to be used as an instrument whereby the strong can oppress the weak? The difficulty is, I am aware, very great. I would suggest, as a temporary palliative, that where the plea set up in a written statement of the defendant is one of forgery, the Magistrate should be informed with a view to an enquiry and to his intervening with any evidence the enquiry secured before the decree was passed. This, of course, does not reach the many *ex-parte* cases there are.

"For the rest, things have now greatly improved between landlord and tenant. Rash Behari Mandal was forced, through the knowledge he could not escape conviction for forgery, to apply to be declared a disqualified proprietor*. His prayer was accepted, and now the Court of Wards is managing. Babu Rajendra Narain Singh of Koriapatti, through fear of future similar criminal cases against him, voluntarily appointed a reliable European manager and cut himself off from all management."

The Final Report on the settlement operations gives detailed descriptions of similar instances of misconduct, proving the supremest disregard for law and justice on the part of many landlords of this district in their dealings with their tenants. Fortunately there are a few brilliant exceptions.

Unfortunately the deplorable state of things here described is by no means new or of recent origin. As long ago as the days of Buchanan Hamilton's survey (*circa* 1812) the state of things then prevalent was described as follows:—

"What I have said in Dinajpur and Rangpur concerning the illegal exactions alleged to be taken by the zamindars or their agents are entirely applicable to this district. . . . . I am persuaded that in general the people are worse used than in that district, and to this chiefly must be attributed the miserable condition to which many parts of it are reduced."

However, it is to be hoped that the educative influence of the settlement operations under Chapter X of the Bengal Tenancy Act, carried through in spite of opposition, both active and passive, on the part of the landlords of the district will bear its full fruit in time. Mr. Lyall's remarks show that in this district as elsewhere the landlords began at once to ignore the entries in the

* Fuller details of the proceedings against him are to be gathered from Indian Law Reports, 1908, 35 Cal., p. 1076.

record-of-rights. The amendments made in the Tenancy Act by Act I of 1907 [in particular, by sections 147A, 147B, and 148B(1) and B(2)] are designed to counteract some of the devices resorted to by dishonest and unscrupulous landlords. It remains to be seen how far Civil Courts will give effect to these provisions, and how far they will fulfil the purposes for which they were framed.

It is difficult to estimate the actual indebtedness of the people of this district. The statistics compiled during the settlement operations indicate that sales outright are more frequent than mortgages with possession.

Co-operative Credit Societies.

The Co-operative Credit Society movement, with its unlimited scope in an almost purely agricultural community such as that in Bhagalpur district, has not as yet spread very widely, but the prospects for the future are distinctly promising. This is a matter in which example is far more useful than precept and a few prosperous societies will exercise an influence which could not be expected from a number of weak associations of doubtful solvency.

The Registrar of these societies has kindly furnished the following note on the present state of this propaganda in Bhagalpur :—

"The Co-operative Credit Movement has so far made very little progress in the district of Bhagalpur. The chief reason for this is want of local helpers. There are at present only 5 societies all located in one area, viz., near the headquarters of Madhipura subdivision, where the work commenced in the year 1907. The combined capital is Rs. 2,100, the bulk of which has been lent by the Banaili Raj and the rest by some of the local residents. Within limits the societies are doing useful work but their capital is very small and ought to be increased.

"A scheme has been drawn up for developing this area round Madhipura and gradually extending it from that centre. The Subdivisional Officer, Babu Saroda Prasad Sircar, has been the means of starting these societies.

"Another area is being opened up in Banka by Moulvi Abdus Salek, Subdivisional Officer, who has written a pamphlet on Co-operative Societies and has taken a great interest in the movement. One society was registered there late in 1909 and a few more are in process of formation in this subdivision.

"At the instance of the Commissioner of the Division the clerks of the Government offices in Bhagalpur town have recently formed themselves into an Urban Co-operative Credit Society.

"Generally speaking, Bhagalpur district offers a good field to the movement; but owing to the fact that no permanent local resident has come forward to help the Co-operative Credit Society movement we have been unable to take full advantage of its possibilities"

CHAPTER VIII.

OCCUPATIONS, MANUFACTURES AND TRADES.

GENERAL. BEFORE proceeding to quote figures for the numbers of persons that follow a particular occupation, it is advisable to utter a note of warning. The figures quoted are all taken from the Tables of the Bengal Census of 1901 and the introductory paragraphs of Chapter XII of that Census Report show that no great reliance can be placed on the figures ascertained under the heading "Occupation." Still, as the census figures are the most accurate at present available, they are given for what they are worth. Their unreliability is due in part to the unscientific method of classification adopted. For example 'rent-receivers' and 'rent-payers' are shown as separate classes: but it is obvious that these terms are purely relative terms and that tenure-holders and raiyats and even under-raiyats are often simultaneously both rent-receivers and rent-payers. Again the labourer and especially the landless labourer follows a varied number of occupations, even simultaneously, and his classification under one or other of these several heads depended ultimately on the idiosyncracy of the enumerator in whose schedule the individual in question was returned.

AGRICULTURE. By far the greatest part of the population is dependent, directly or indirectly, on agriculture, no fewer then 1,432,000 people being supported by it, amounting to 68 per cent. of the total population. Forty-two per cent. of agriculturists are actual workers and 58 per cent. dependents. Industries (including the 'preparation and sale of material substances') support 10 per cent. of the population. Commerce supports only 1·2 per cent. and the literary and learned professions support not quite one per cent.

As just stated, out of the number dependent on agriculture 42 per cent. are actual workers and in their number are included 12,545 rent-receivers, 1,210,200 rent-payers and 221,453 farm servants and labourers. Of the industrial population, 41 per cent. are actual workers. Included in this number are, in round

Industrial.

numbers, 24,000 cattle breeders and stock raisers; 16,000 cow and buffalo keepers and milk and *ghi* sellers; 8,000 vegetable and fruit sellers; 15,000 grocers and condiment dealers; 21,000 cotton workers; 11,000 potters; 8,500 carpenters; 7,000 basket and mat makers; 10,000 shoemakers and leather workers; 25,000 fishermen and fish dealers; and 3,600 oil pressers.

Professional. Among the professional classes, 46 per cent. are actual workers including 8,000 priests, 2,000 teachers and 2,000 musicians. Finally, general labour accounts for 255,000 of the population. These figures include of course male and female workers and dependents of both sexes.

Occupations and caste. It has often been observed that there is a marked tendency of late for the traditional caste occupation to fail to command the unswerving allegiance of all born within that caste. This applies most markedly of course to the functional castes—evolved in past ages to satisfy the essential needs of a self-contained village community. Thus, the Ahirs or Goalas are theoretically and traditionally dairymen; but in Bihar as a whole, about 80 per cent. of them have become agriculturists pure and simple. This no doubt is the result of cultivation encroaching on pasturage. Again, Chamars are essentially leather workers; but now about 66 per cent. of them are agriculturists; 20 per cent. are general labourers and only about 7 per cent. still believe that there is "nothing like leather." Of the Potters' caste, only about half make pots and other earthenware articles: the rest are agriculturists. Among the Telis or oil pressers about one-third of the whole community follow their traditional pursuit; over half of them have taken to agriculture. Among the Weavers, only 11 per cent. of the Tantis (Hindu weavers) and 25 per cent. of the Jolahas (Muhammadan weavers) still adhere to their ancestral craft, but it is highly probable that a very large proportion even of these attenuated numbers look on agriculture as at least a subsidiary means of livelihood.

The reasons for this departure from the traditions of their ancestors are in all probability mainly economic. As well, the agricultural profession is undoubtedly regarded as occupying a higher position in the social scale than the calling of artizans and craftsmen and this too must be a contributary cause.

Industrial classes. The following are the chief classes engaged in industrial pursuits: the Jolahas and Tantis are weavers; the Dhunias card cotton (using an instrument not unlike a single stringed banjo for this purpose): the Rangrez are dyers. Bangles are made by Laheris and Churihars. Fancy silk strings and fringes are made by Patwars. Goalas (Hindu) and Ghosis (Musalman) deal in milk and curds. The Chiks and Kasais are butchers. The Telis are oil pressers; the Kandus parch grain (*chura*); and the Halwais are confectioners. Liquor vendors are usually Pasis and Suris. Chamars and Muchis are leather workers and cobblers. Barhis are carpenters. Domes and some others work bamboos into mats, baskets, etc. The Sonar is a goldsmith and often a 'fence' or receiver of stolen property. The Lohar is a blacksmith. The Kasera is a brass founder or tinsmith and the Kumhar is a potter.

Commercial classes. The Marwaris, Agarwallas and Banias are all born traders agents, bankers and money-lenders. They occasionally acquire large estates which come into their hands at first on mortgages and finally as their sole property by purchase at sales in execution of their own decrees against the improvident or unwary zamindar whom they have enmeshed.

Brahmans are professional priests, though nowadays numbers of this caste are mere agriculturists, who make no pretence to a liberal education and never attempt to exercise their priestly functions.

Professional classes. Kayesths are born for clerical work and nothing that a clerk can do comes amiss to them. In village parlance the *kayeth* is the village accountant or patwari as inevitably as the "Dusadh" is the village watchman or chaukidar. Neither Brahmins nor Kayesths are greatly loved by others of the Hindu confraternity. Many bitter incisive proverbs are current at their expense.

Manufactures. As Bhagalpur district depends still to such an extent on purely agricultural pursuits, the nature of its manufactures will neither be varied nor numerous. The Central Jail has 33 power looms and 34 hand looms at work in it, run by convict labour. Blankets are supplied from it to the Supply and Transport and Ordnance Departments of the Army. Winter clothing and blankets are supplied to all the prisons in this Province and in Eastern Bengal and Assam both for the use of the prisoners and of the warders' establishments. To a lesser extent, carpet making, carpentry, ironwork and bamboo and cane work are carried on in this jail.

***Tasar* silk industry.** The particular indigenous industry that is most closely associated with this district is the *tasar* silk industry. The following account of it is adapted from Hunter's "Statistical Account," altered where necessary to bring it into accordance with the facts of the present day.

"About 1810 Dr. Buchanan Hamilton estimated that there were about 3,275 looms at work in the district. Though this number has fallen off the industry is still considered an important one; though the processes of manufacture have not improved, and the looms are as rude as they were at the beginning of the century, being little more than bamboo frames. The kinds of cloth now, as then, most usually made are *dariyās* in which the warp consists of three parts of cotton, and two parts of *tasar* of the different colours. The woof is all cotton of one colour, so that the cloth is striped lengthways, being dyed entirely by the weavers in the thread. The pieces are from twenty to twenty-two cubits long, by one-and-a-half broad. A man can weave eight pieces monthly. *Namūnas* are pieces from twenty to twenty-two cubits long, and one-and-three quarters broad. The warp contains about 35 parts of cotton thread and 21 of *tasar*, disposed in stripes of a different pattern from those of the *dariyā*. The woof is all cotton. One loom can produce seven pieces a month. *Chārkhānās* are about 18 cubits long, and eight-sevenths of a cubit wide. Each loom weaves six pieces in the month. The warp requires ten parts of cotton, and fifteen parts of *tasar*, the woof ten parts of cotton and eighteen parts of *tasar*, so that the pieces are checkered. *Baftas* are pieces of a uniform colour, dyed after being woven, and of the same size with the *namūnas*. The whole warp is *tasar*, the woof is cotton. The foregoing kinds are mostly made for exportation. *Kharsārīs*, which are produced chiefly for home use, are like *dariyās*, but of inferior size and firmness, and afford occupation to a larger number of weavers than any other kind. They are made up in pieces about eight feet long and three wide, and are dyed by the weavers, who can make eight pieces a month. The pure *tasar* silk is called *tūl*. *Dhūpchāyā* is a *bafta* of a bright blue. *Maurkāntī* is a white silk figured in blue. *Lahan gowāl* is a figured silk worn only by Brāhmans, Kāyasths, and Rājputs. The *koa* or cocoons of *tasar* come from Sūrī, Bānkurā, Gaya and the Sonthal Parganas.* Patwās, Momims, Tāntīs and Tatamās are the weaver castes most employed in this trade. The winding of the silk from the cocoons is effected by a very simple instrument called a *tāriya*. Eight pounds weight of the cocoons are boiled with twice that amount of water, till all the water is evaporated. They are then left to cool, and next day are again boiled. The silk is then easily wound off, strands from five cocoons being generally used to form each thread. For cheaper work, three strand threads are used and for better work, seven

* *See* Chapter I, pages 11, 13 *ante.*

strand threads. They are twisted with the left hand on the left thigh, and wound on the *tāriya.*"

One cocoon from an *asan* tree yields about 10·2 grains (Troy) of silk: from a *bari* tree, about 7·6 grains. *Asan* cocoons sell at about 200 to the rupee and *bari* cocoons at about 300. At present about 1,000 looms are working and about 450 families (of which over 300 are Musalmen) are engaged in this industry. During the last few years the *swadeshi* movement has created a larger demand then there was before for these cloths and this has caused a slight revival in this industry.

In his "Review of the Industrial Position and Prospects in Bengal in 1908," Mr. J. G. Cumming, I.C.S., remarked as follows on this industry:—

"Like practically all the cotton weavers, the *tussar* silk weavers are in the hands of their *mahajans*; but they are probably a little better off, midway between cotton weavers and silk weavers..........................

"What the *tussar* weaving industry requires is a fly-shuttle mechanism for working *tussar.* I have tried several dodges myself but have not been successful. Infructuous efforts to introduce a fly-shuttle loom were made at Bhagalpur. One weaver of the Mourbhanj State, Bamdeb Uriya, is asserted to have succeeded; but I could not get this verified. The weavers of Kalipur Kodiya in Birbhum district succeeded only with a cotton warp and a *tussar* weft. The complaint is that the reeds of the sley fray the threads of the warp. The remedy may be in a device in the loom or in improved spinning. This is a problem for the new Government weaving institute to solve.

Mixed cotton and silk.

"Under the head of *tussar* can be considered *bafta* or mixed cloths. This is associated with Bhagalpur. A cotton *chadar* costs ten annas to Rs. 5 and lasts for two years; a *bafta chadar* costs Rs. 3-8 to Rs. 15, and lasts five or six years. In Champanagar I found that the *mahajans* were sweating the local craftsman; about eight annas was the labour return for four days' work. In Bhagalpur itself the Bihar Trading Company under Kabir Ahmad Khan of Mujahidpur is doing good work in advertising and circulating samples, issuing new designs to the weavers, and in financing them without extortion. This is a method which the middle class capitalist might follow with advantage where there is any colony of weavers who are at present following individualistic methods of purchase of yarn and sale of material."

Iron work.

In Buchanan Hamilton's survey there is given an exhaustive account of iron smelting as practised in Bhagalpur. The area alluded to by him is now in the Sonthal Parganas and is thus outside the scope of this book. At present there is no indigenous iron smelting carried on in the district. A small amount of iron-work is done in the Central Jail and in 1904, an enterprise called the Bihar Trunk Works was started in the town of Bhagalpur, to manufacture steel trunks locally from imported sheets.

The village *lohar* or blacksmith continues to practise the methods of his ancestors in making and repairing the plough-shares and other necessary articles for the agriculturist. But the iron employed is ultimately all imported.

Glass articles, more especially bracelets, were manufactured in Bhagalpur at least a century ago. Buchanan Hamilton gives a detailed description of the methods then practised. Impure carbonate of soda and river sand when melted and cooled several times yielded ultimately about half its own weight of black opaque glass called *kanch*. By a slightly more elaborate process and the addition of some colouring matter, shades of green semi-transparent glass, of deep blue and of a purplish brown were made. **Glassware.**

This industry has never been developed. In 1890 it was still in existence but in the twenty years that have since elapsed, it seems to have practically died out.

Just as the synthetic product has practically killed the indigo industry, so too the competition of cheap imported aniline dyes has almost driven the indigenous dyer and his methods out of the market. In 1901 aniline dyes to a value of 1.69 lakhs of rupees were imported from Belgium to Calcutta. By 1906 the value of similar imports had risen to 6·7 lakhs. **Dyeing.**

The indigenous dyes used in this district are as follows, according to Hunter's "Account":—

"The following are the chief materials used: the flowers of the *kusam* or safflower (Carthamus tinctorius); the flowers of the *singahār* (Nyctanthes arbor tristis), and of the *tūn* (Cedrela toona); the leaves of Indigofera tinctoria or indigo; *tairī*, the pods of Cæsalpinia sappan; the wood of the same tree; *kath* (catechu or terra Japonica), obtained from Acacia catechu; the root of the *haldi* (Curcuma zerumbet); the seeds of Bixa orellana; the fruit of the *karanja* or Galedupa Indica; the bark of the *ām* or mango (Mangifera Indica); the flowers of the *palās* (Butea frondosa); the root of *manjīt* or Indian madder (munjista); *singrif* or vermilion; *zangār* or verdigris; *sajīmatī*, an impure carbonate of soda; and *kassis*, a white and powdery sulphate of iron.

"The following are the principal colours derived. The order given by Dr. Buchanan Hamilton is followed.—(1) *Kakreja*, a dark brown, inclining to purple, is obtained by infusing 9 oz. of *tairī* in 10 lbs. of water for two hours; the greater part of the water is strained off, and the cloth soaked in the remaining dye. Then, 1¼ oz. of *kassis* is dissolved in 10 lbs. of water, and the cloth put into the mixture for a few minutes, after which it is dried in the sun. Other mordants may be used. Next, 1¼ oz. of alum is dissolved in a little hot water, added to 10 lbs. of cold water; and in this the cloth is thoroughly soaked. Then boil 5½ oz. of *sappan* wood in 30 lbs. of water for six hours, cool the decoction and steep the cloth in it for half-an-hour; add to it 2½ oz of lime, stir quickly, and put in the cloth again. Then wring and dry in the shade. (2) *Agāri*, a brown, without any tinge of purple, is produced from 19 oz. of bruised *tairī*, infused in 10 lbs. of water for about an hour and-a-half; in this the cloth is soaked, *kassis* being the mordant used. Then, infuse 7 oz. of terra Japonica in 10 lbs. of cold water; add a little lime-water, and stir the infusion; dip into it the cloth, wring it and dry it in the sun. (3) *Udā*, a bright purplish brown, is derived from a weaker solution of *tairī* than is necessary for the last mentioned colour, and is similarly fixed by *kassis*. Afterwards, soak the cloth in the solution of alum, such as is first used in obtaining *kakrea*; and then place it for half an hour in a decoction of 10 oz. of *sappan* wood, boiled for seven and-a-half hours in 40 lbs. of water, to which a little lime is added. (4) *Baigani*, a shade lighter than the above, and approaching to claret colour, is produced in the same manner as the last, except that the decoction of *sappan* is less strong. (5) *Habasi*, a blood red, is produced by much the same treatment as the above, but alum is freely used, and the *sappan* infusion is prepared in the same manner as in the case of *udā*. (6) *Shotari*, a light brownish drab colour, is obtained from 5 oz. of terra Japonica infused for a whole day in 1 lb. of water; in this, when diluted, the cloth is steeped. The mordant is usually *kassis*. (7) For *taranji*, a bright gamboge yellow, 5 oz. of turmeric are infused in 10 lbs. of cold water. The colour is fixed by alum mixed with 20 oz. of sour curdled milk. (8) *Asmāni* is a light sky-blue, made from 1¼ oz. of native indigo infused in abundant water. (9) In preparing *fakhta*, a bluish ash colour, first put the cloth into an infusion of 20 oz. of *tāirī* in 10 lbs. of water, and next into a solution of 2½ oz. of *kassis* dissolved in a similar quantity of water. Then dry in the sun, and taking an infusion of 2½ oz. of powdered *haldi* root, steep the cloth in it. (10) In the case of *shishaha*, a pale blue, somewhat resembling the colour of lead, the process is the same as in producing *fakhta*, except that the cloth after being taken from the infusion of *kachur*, is put into an infusion of 5 oz. of native indigo in 10 lbs. of water. It may be also made by omitting the *kachur* infusion. In the whole of these processes the dyers use well water alone, most of which near Bhagalpur is hard.

Allusion has already been made to the blanket weaving and carpet making in the Central Jail No other industry prevails to any great extent. As the indigo industry is decaying, it is unnecessary to go into any account of its manufacture. In 1908-09 only 5,400 acres were under this crop as against 13,000 acres in 1900. Indigo.

Only a small area is now sown with opium, namely, 400 acres in 1908-9. In 1900 the corresponding area was 900 acres. This reduction is part of the general policy of contraction of the area settled for opium cultivation. Moreover, the quality of Bhagalpur grown opium was not very good and its cultivation was of late less popular than ever, owing to its fixity of price comparing unfavourably with the general advance in price of all other commodities grown by actual cultivators. Opium.

Bhagalpur from its situation is eminently calculated to be a place of considerable trade, and the elaborate statistics available for rail- and river- borne traffic in Bengal and of trans-frontier traffic with Nepal amply bear this out. Usually an enormous quantity of rice is exported from the district but, owing to the prevalent scarcity in 1908, the excess of exports over imports of rice is comparatively small. Trade.

The following table shows in a very compact form the figures for Import and Export of thirty staple products for the last two years and for 1896-97, for purposes of comparison. The contraction in the exports of rice and indigo is very marked.

A large part of the exports goes to Nepal. Stations for registering this traffic are maintained on the main trade routes through the north of the district.

Name of Article.	Imports (in maunds).			Exports (in maunds).		
	Total.			Total.		
	1896-97.	1907-08.	1908-09.	1896-97.	1907-08.	1908-09.
	Mds.	Mds.	Mds.	Mds.	Mds.	Mds.
1. Rice	28,545	52,287	335,613	1,215,486	1,171,372	578,820
2. Paddy	14,289	57,831	428,704	515,383	481,908	235,103
3. Wheat	1,702	33,009	24,406	113,177	43,734	104,843
4. Gram and pulses	22,471	223,413	108,529	459,469	168,841	303,116
5. Other food-grains	11,468	251,205	747,028	1,233,542	724,837	612,267
6. Jute, raw	333	794	616	16,293	128,548	198,657
7. Gunny-bags ...	69,516	46,387	46,420	7,901	7,970	21,752

Name of Article.	Imports (in maunds). Total.			Exports (in maunds). Total.		
	1896-97.	1907-08.	1908-09.	1896-97.	1907-08.	1908-09.
	Mds.	Mds.	Mds.	Mds.	Mds.	Mds.
8. Linseed	415	6,078	7.092	1,10,907	1,43,477	2,49,255
9. Mustard	2,263	13,435	29,696	1,48,109	1,74,628	2,86,589
10. Tea (Indian) ...	14	74	122	...	...	...
11. Cotton, raw ..	10,713	2,968	3,117	872	29	232
12. Silk, raw	623	882	1,890	125	79	97
13. Sugar (refined) ..	13,548	19,393	45,555	719	1,184	1,089
14. Sugar (unrefined)	20,372	34,679	24,857	20,956	1,696	5,218
15(a) Gur	...	67,867	0,73,000	...	23,186	33,356
16. Tobacco (manufactured).	183	1,799	1,495	186	279	374
17. Tobacco (unmanufactured).	16,999	27,339	32,257	4,759	5,496	12,353
18. Indigo	24	2	147	2,876	260	755
19. Cotton piece-goods (European) in bales.	64,366	70,814	64,423	1,112	2,160 (combined 2,225)	2,169 (combined 2,173)
20. Cotton piece-goods (European) in boxes.	36	...	2,323	...	65	4
31. Cotton piece-goods (Indian) in bales.	3,105	8,167	3,094	529	1,161 (combined 1,169)	1,842
22. Cotton piece-goods (Indian) in boxes.	53	...	6	1	8	
23. Cotton twist (European).	842	835	26	4	3	...
24. Cotton twist (Indian).	11,240	11,895	4,319	373	223	756
25. Salt	3,22,998	3,51,241	3,16,793	944	3,156	3,522
26. Kerosine-oil ...	2,996	89,083	71,449	70	961	3,706
27. Coal and coke ...	3,51,637	4,65,186	5,75,517	606	2,841	6,244
28. Ghee	...	...	531	...	...	2,640
29. Lac	...	...	1,534	...	...	1,488
30. Til	...	...	537	...	...	617
Total ...	9 70,771	18,36,563	29,75,396	38,54,399	30,88,360	26,67,484

CHAPTER IX.

MEANS OF COMMUNICATION.

The river Ganges was for a long time the main route for all travellers to and from Bhagalpur. It still is of much importance as a trade route for steamer traffic. Its boat traffic is probably not as great as it formerly was, owing to the competition of the river steamers and the railway lines that run along both banks of this river.

The first steamer that plied on the Ganges came up from Calcutta about 1828. The road along the south bank of the Ganges was of course a much used highway but its importance as a through trade route has gone.

The East Indian Railway was extended to Bhagalpur very early in the sixties. This line alongside the river—now known as the Loop line—was laid much earlier than the Chord line from Lakhisarai to Khana which just touches the extreme south-west corner of the district, near Baidyanath Junction. The line parallel to the river is about sixty miles long. The chief railway stations on it, beginning at the western boundary, are Sultanganj, Bhagalpur town, Sabaur, Gogha, Colgong and Pirpainti. A branch line from Bhagalpur to Bausi is under construction. It is probable that it will be continued to Deoghur on one side and to Naya Dumka and Suri on the other. With the completion of this line, the southern part of the district will be very well served by the railway.

A branch line on the metre gauge has recently been constructed by the Bengal and North-Western Railway Campany from Bhagalpur town *viâ* Bhagalpur Kachahri to Barari Ghat. A waggon ferry plies between this Ghat and Mahadevpur Ghat on the northern bank of the Ganges, and this connects Bhagalpur directly with the whole of the Bengal and North-Western Railway Company's system north of the Ganges.

North of the river parallel to the Nepal Frontier this same Company has a line from Nirmali *viâ* Raharia, Bhaptiahi, Raghupur, and Partabganj to Balua. Formerly this line went on to Khanwa Ghat and a ferry boat connection was maintained with Anchra Ghat station on the Eastern Bengal State Railway system on the Purnea side of the Kosi. Owing to the difficulties of crossing, the through traffic was always inconsiderable and of late years, the ghât lines have been abandoned on each side. The bridging of the Kosi between Katarea and Kursela stations opened up an unbroken connection between Somastipur and Katihar and so drew all traffic away from the frontier route.

A cross-link from north to south between Bhaptiahi and Mansi (in Monghyr district) *viâ* Supaul, with a branch line to Madhipura, has opened up this northern portion of the district, which was hitherto inaccessible at times. Since its opening. Bhagalpur as a district enjoys exceptional railway facilities. On the north bank there are now about 120 miles of line open. In the event of a widespread failure of crops, the value of these lines north of the river could not be over-estimated. They are all on the metre gauge. A glance at the map shows their position and the configuration of the country through which they pass quite clearly. There are no special engineering features to note except the Kosi bridge. This bridge between Katarea and Kursela, consisting of 15 spans with a waterway of about 1,100 yards, crosses the only outlet for the drainage of a huge extent of country. The Bagmati and Tiljuga drain the south-east of Darbhanga, and the north of Monghyr, eastwards from Khagaria. Their united waters under the name of the Ghagri, joined by the Tilawe, Parwan, Dhusan and Loran from north Bhagalpur, unite with the Kosi streams that drain a belt 30 miles wide in the western portion of the Purnea district a couple of miles above the bridge and the whole drainage of this tract, the area of which may be put roughly at 4,000 square miles, finds its outlet to the Ganges by this one comparatively narrow opening. The current flows very rapidly under the bridge. It is a most exciting experience to cross the river in a ferry boat even before it has risen in flood.

When the Ganges is in flood the drainage cannot get away rapidly enough and the whole country goes under water. It is sometimes possible to go almost straight across country by boat from Madhipura to the railway line near thana Bihpur ; only the village sites keep above the flood level, and that not always. An attempt was made in 1902-03 to open up a steamer route on the Ghagri from the Kosi bridge, but it did not succeed. There is a certain amount of boat traffic on the various streams that flow into these rivers. An elaborate report was prepared on the navigability of these streams during and after the famine of 1874, but the extension of railway communications has rendered the local authorities independent of waterways as a means of conveying grains-upplies into affected tracts. Moreover, as famine in north

Bhagalpur is always directly due to insufficient rainfall, and as many of the tributary streams dry up entirely in the late hot season, even in years of normal rainfall, it would probably be found that the river beds were dry just when the need for them was sorest. Moreover, the villagers are accustomed to throw small embankments across the streams when the rainfall is insufficient so as to enable them to irrigate at least a portion of their lands as long as the water lasts. These embankments would oppose an insuperable obstacle to navigation in seasons of scarcity.

The effect of the embankments of the Bengal and North-Western Railway line, which runs across the districts of Monghyr and Bhagalpur, on the agricultural prospects of the localities the line traversed, has been discussed at length of late years. These bunds serve to keep out the Ganges floods from the lands lying north of the embankment ; but the water lies deeper on the lands between the embankment and the river. Also, when a flood comes across the country from the north owing to excessive rain in the hills, the embankment undoubtedly prevents the flood waters from getting to the Ganges as quickly as they otherwise would. If the floods are not very high and if they come late in the season when the rice crop is well established, this may be of some benefit to the rice lands.

Sections 11(*1*)*b* and 11(*3*)*b* of the Indian Railways Act require Railway Administrations to provide sufficient waterways to enable the water to drain off lands near or affected by the railway as rapidly as before its construction. It is more than doubtful if this is ever done or if it is possible to do it.

In 1906, detailed enquiries were made into this whole question. The general opinion of those most affected was to the effect that the benefits resulting from keeping back the Ganges floods more than outweighed the disadvantages resulting from the obstructions caused by the embankment to the free passage of floods from the north. The area south of the embankment admittedly suffers more than it did before. But it has always been subject to floods, and *bhadoi* crops sown there were invariably "catch crops" the harvesting of which was highly problematical at the time the seed was sown. It was ultimately decided to take no action towards providing additional waterways to allow the freer escape of floods from the north of the railway embankment.

There are now about 64 miles of metalled roads, 1,685 of unmetalled roads and 40 miles of village roads maintained in this district. This mileage works out at 2·4 lineal miles per square mile. There is in addition a perfect network of village **Roads.**

tracks that are not maintained from local funds. In 1874 there were only 36 miles of metalled roads and 641 of unmetalled roads maintained.

Birbhum road.

The most important road on the south of the Ganges is the Birbhum road which runs almost due south from Bhagalpur town *viâ* Bausi to Suri. About 42 miles of it lie in this district. The remaining metalled roads are only short lengths, *e.g.*, that from the Central Jail *viâ* Nathnagar to Champanala, a distance of six miles; from Sultanganj to the Monghyr boundary, three miles, and from Dhaka to the Chandan river (three and a half miles) on the Dhaka-Simultala road.

Other main routes.

Other trunk routes on the south of the Ganges are Bhagalpur to Banka, Banka to Simultala, Banka to Jaypur, Ghogha to Bausi, Banka to Sagrampur; also the main routes west from Bhagalpur to Monghyr, and east to Sahebganj *viâ* Pirpainti.

North of the river, there are no metalled roads. The main route is Lakhipur to Madhipura *viâ* Jhurki and Phalaut, a distance of 43 miles. A continuation of this *viâ* Singheswarthan, 21 miles long, leads to Supaul. From Supaul a road runs north-east *viâ* Partabganj to Birpur on the frontier, a distance of 45 miles. Another runs from Supaul *viâ* Bhaptiahi to Kanauli which also is on the Nepal Frontier. There are routes across towards Purnea district, one *viâ* Singheswarthan and Dhalesori to Keotgaon; another *viâ* Murliganj from Singheswarthan. But these are impassable except in the end of the cold season and the early part of the hot weather. They are largely within the area subject to the devastations of the Kosi and it is practically impossible to keep them up satisfactorily. The map shows the situation and general direction of these and other roads.

Conveyances.

There are no special features about the conveyances in common use in Bhagalpur. Bullock carts of various more or less glorified types and pack-ponies do most of the business of the interior. The pony *ekka* is in common use and surprising distances can be covered by these weedy ponies drawing this very primitive and extremely uncomfortable vehicle.

Palanquins of various sorts are used but not as much as formerly, owing to the extension of roads.

Post and Telegraph offices.

At present in the district there are sixty-seven post offices. Every railway station is of course a telegraph office as well, but there is no direct telegraphic communication between the north and south of the district. Madhipura, Supaul, Partabganj, Sonbursa and Nirmali are connected by wire but telegrams from Bhagalpur to Madhipura travel *viâ* Bankipur and Muzaffarpur.

CHAPTER X.

LAND REVENUE ADMINISTRATION.

THIS chapter is intended to give only a bare outline of the Land Revenue Administration, as naturally those who wish for a detailed account would refer to the recently published Final Report on the Survey and Settlement proceedings in this district. Scope.

Owing to changes in the area of the district it is now impossible to ascertain exactly what was the assessment by way of land revenue on the actual present area of the district at the time of Todar Mull's settlement about 1582. Sarkar Monghyr in Subah Behar is shown in the Ain-i-Akbari as assessed at Rs. 7,41,000: probably part of the present district south of the Ganges fell in Sarkar Jannatabad (Gaur) or Sarkar Tanda (Pandua), but this is only a conjecture. Early Revenue History.

About 1722 Murshed Kuli Khan, whose name survives still in Murshidabad, revised the whole assessment of Bengal, but it is impossible to unravel the exact proportion of the enhancement that was levied in this district. However, from old records of the Murshidabad Diwani office it appears that the *asl jamá tumári* or original crown rent of the forty estates, included in the area which formed the jurisdiction of the first English Collector at Bhagalpur, was Rs. 8,98,950. In 1765, when the Company assumed the administration, this constituted the reorganized assessment, of which Rs. 90,950 had been alienated in grants of rent-free lands, *nánkár* estates, and other charges connected with the collection. The system of collection followed was then, as now, carried out through the *zamindárs*; but as they had not then been recognised as actual proprietors, their operations were supervised by Government officers called *kánúngos*, one of whom was attached to each large estate, or to two or three minor ones.

In 1787, the Collector of Bhagalpur furnished to the Board of Revenue a report on the constitution and duties of the *kánúngo*. It commences with the following vernacular list of books and papers, composing his records, (1) *Dastúr-ul-aml*, a collection of rules for the use of revenue officers, originally issued in the time of Akbar; (2) *aml-dastúr*, the book in which orders superseding the rules of the *dastúr-al-áml* were entered—the current circulars issued by the *ámil* for the time being in power; (3) *firisht-i-dihát*, or list of villages; (4) *awárija*, ordinarily a rough note-book, but in connection with land revenue an account book specifying first the unproductive lands of each village, and then those paying revenue field by field, arranged under the names of their occupants; (5) *sháhi ámdani*, the royal revenue derived from all sources; (6) *dául-i-tashkhis-i-bandobást*, particulars of the assessment and settlement; (7) *jamábandi khás*, account of the revenue assessment of lands in charge of Government officers; (8) *jamá sair-i-chabútrá-kotwáli-mái chaukiyát o guzarghát*, miscellaneous revenue derived from markets customs, and ferries in the head-quarters police division; (9) *jamá mahál mir bahri*, literally an account of harbour dues, but in inland places referring to mooring dues on rivers; (10) *jamá pánchautrá*, a transit duty of five per cent. on merchandise; (11) *jamá mahál badraki*, from *badrak*, an escort,—a charge of one per cent. on merchandise, levied as the expense of keeping the highways and rivers free from robbers; (12) *ism navisi zamindárán*, list of names of *zamindárs*; (13) *hakikát bázi zámin*, particulars of land exempted from the payment of revenue under various denominations; (14) *jamá mukarrari-o-istimrári*, fixed and permanent revenue; (15) *wasil báki*, an account of collections and balances; (16) *hakikát rozinadárán*, particulars of pensioners.

The Collector's Report proceeds as follows: "These accounts, when faithfully taken, gave the complete annual history of a *zamindári*—comprehending the ground in cultivation, particularising the portion of it which paid rent to Government, and that which was held free; the customs and usages established by former *ámils*, and those introduced by the *ámils* for the time being; the amount of rent in demand from every *raiyat*, with the balance remaining against any of them at the end of the year; the whole amount of the *zamindár's* or farmer's collections, specifying the particular sums under every head in which those collections were made, together with his expenses of collection. In short, the object of the *kánúngo's* office was to supply such information respecting the country, that no circumstance of advantage in the administration of it should be concealed, nor the *zamindár* enabled to appropriate any more of the produce of it to himself, than the share allotted to him by Government; that no lands might be separated from the *jamá* or rent-roll without authority; and that the real value of the land yielding revenue might be known at the end of one year, and either farmed or kept in the hands of Government for the next; either of which modes it was the right of Government to adopt. At what period the *kánúngo's* office was instituted, or how long the regulations above specified were strictly observed, it may not now be easy to determine. It is probable that under a Government subject to convulsions, they were occasionally violated for the advantage of the *ámils*, the *zamindárs* and the *kánúngos* themselves; and that the office, from neglect, has fallen gradually to decay. In Bengal little remains, besides the name and the salaries annexed. In Behar, where the ancient usages of the Province have undergone fewer alterations, the *kánúngos* have retained more of the exercise of their functions, although, as might be expected, these have often been made subservient to the purposes of the *zamindárs*. The *kánúngos* of Behar are, however, well informed of those functions, agree in their definition, and are ready to resume the strict exercise of them to any extent that it may be the pleasure of the Government to require."

It may be noted here that the present Banaili Raj family is descended directly from one Dular Sing (or Chowdry) who was a *kánúngo* in the north of Purnea, and Mahashoy Tarak Nath Ghose, at present one of the leading zamindars, is directly descended from Poreshnath Ghose who was *kánúngo* in 1793.

It may be assumed that the nominal revenue roll was Rs. 8,98,950 when the *dewani* was taken over by the East India Company in 1765. In 1772 the Company "stood forth as *dewan*" and it was then promptly discovered that the revenues of the parganas Bhagalpur, Colgong and Chari amounting to Rs. 5,28,580 annually had been embezzled for the previous seven years, under the false pretence that these parganas were a *jaigir* (or revenue-free grant) in favour of Nazim-ud-Daula, son of Mir Jafar, some time Nazim of Bengal. It was also alleged that in 1765 these parganas had been transferred from Subah Behar to Subah Bengal, but this was demonstrably untrue, and in 1773 the district was formally severed from Subah Behar and annexed to the *dewani* lands of Bengal.

In 1774 Mr. Barton was appointed supervisor. His methods of encouraging the administration of justice would not find favour in the present advanced era. On one occasion when the Muhammadan judicial officers failed to inflict justice on a body of murderers, he went so far as to have three of the judges flogged in public.

In 1790 the decennial settlement was ordered to be carried out generally but in this district great difficulties were experienced in inducing local zamindars to take settlement. The result was that the permanent settlement of 1793 did not affect the majority of the estates in Bhagalpur, most of which were permanently settled long after 1793. In 1793 only a revenue of Rs. 38,129 was permanently settled; by 1820, the revenue permanently settled was Rs. 3,64,078. The current demand in 1790 was far less than it had been in 1765, but in spite of that, it fell to Rs. 3,09,730 by 1799. The Revenue Survey of 1846 to 1850 and the subsequent legal proceedings for the resumption and assessment to revenue of lands which had so far escaped assessment or were not validly exempted from assessment resulted in an increase of revenue to Rs. 5,79,040 in 1860. In 1872 the revenue demand was Rs. 7,21,600. Some slight changes in the revenue demand followed the changes in jurisdiction. At present the total land revenue demand is Rs. 6,05,746. On an area of 4,426 square miles, this gives an incidence of revenue per acre of only 3·5 annas, which is abnormally low.

At the time of the permanent settlement, ten per cent. of the assets of each estate, after deducting the cost of collections, were left to the zamindars. At present, the annual rental value in this district is Rs. 56,81,345 according to the Road Cess Valuation returns, so that the zamindars enjoy now an unearned increment of over fifty lakhs of rupees per annum; in other words, the zamindars collect from their tenants and enjoy themselves assets averaging over two rupees per acre and their liability for Government revenue is only three and-a-half annas per acre. When such a profit is made by them out of their tenants, it is sad to see their mutual relations described as has been done in Chapter VII. There are, however, a few brilliant exceptions among the zamindars whose relations with their tenants leave nothing to be desired.

Number of estates. Temporarily settled estates and estates held direct by Government.

At the time of the permanent settlement, there were only forty estates in the district. Since that time the number has increased rapidly and at present there are 4,643 permanently settled estates in the district, In addition there are 18 temporarily settled estates and 63 estates held direct by Government.

The majority of the estates in this district pay less than 100 rupees revenue. According to an analysis made in 1901, there were 3,954 estates held by proprietors who paid less than Rs. 100 for each estate as land revenue. The average area of each estate was 84 acres and the average assessment of each estate was only Rs. 19. In all, these small estates covered an area of 332,312 acres.

At the same time there were 699 estates that paid each between Rs. 100 and Rs. 5,000 as land revenue. These covered 813,239 acres. Eleven estates covering 624,119 acres paid between Rs. 5,000 and Rs. 50,000 each and only one estate paid more than that amount. It covers 1,113,500 acres and is assessed at Rs. 72,498.

The number of revenue-free estates is 1,320 covering 49,990 acres, the average area of each estate being 38 acres. **Revenue-free estates.**

The modern tendency is obviously to increase the number of estates and to reduce correspondingly the average assessment of each. This is the result of the importation of Western notions of individual ownership, and the operation of the law for the partition of estates. Bhagalpur is still, fortunately for those entrusted with its revenue administration, far behind several other Bihar districts as regards the number of estates borne on its revenue-roll. **Result of partitions.**

The total demand for the 18 estates that are temporarily settled is at present about Rs. 1,950 per annum: and for the 63 estates held direct by Government it is about Rs. 38,700 per annum. The areas affected are mainly riparian and as they are not of very great importance no detailed account of them is given. **Amount of revenue from areas not permanently settled.**

Two very unusual sources of Government revenue are found in this district. They are described as follows in Hunter's "Statistical Account":— **Unusual *Mahals*.**

"Two remarkable tenures, in the nature of servitudes, exist in *parganá* Colgong, which formerly constituted part of the *samíndárí* rights of the landlord of that *parganá*. One is called *mahál boro-ajawán*, and the other is known as *mahál bhaisunda*. Both of them are held direct from Government as ordinary estates in perpetuity, the revenue assessed being payable in instalments corresponding with those of the land revenue. The former, *i.e.* the *boro-ajawan mahal*, (derived from *boro*, a species of paddy, and *ajawán* or coriander), is a right of sowing broadcast the rice called *boro dhán*, the coriander seed and a species of mustard, *rái* or *ráinchí*, on newly formed land on the banks of the Ganges, while the soil is still too soft to admit of ploughing. The right ceases the moment the land hardens and can bear the weight of the plough and cattle; whereupon the landholder, to whom the land belongs under the ordinary law, assumes his right of cultivation and lets it to tenants. The other right or *bháisundá*, so called from *bháis*, a buffalo, consists in the levying of a tax, the amount of which is regulated by custom on each head of cattle grazing on all lands included in *parganá* Colgong. It does not detract from the right, that the land grazed over is the property of the owner of the cattle, or whether they graze in jungles or in cultivated fields. Whatever may have been the former limits within which it was exercised, its present extent does not now coincide with the whole *parganá*, and it is said that it is yearly becoming more and more restricted."

The following explanation of the origin of these curious rights is given in the same place :—

"This *parganá* formerly belonged to a single family of Chaudharis who, besides owning the land, exercised many rights which were all capable of money valuation. After the Permanent Settlement they repeatedly fell into arrears, and their property was year after year sold in lots. In this way, three of their then prescriptive rights as *zamindárs* being acquired by persons different from the purchasers of the land, obtained a separate existence which they had not before. One is the fishery right of the Ganges where it bounds the *parganá* on the north, and the other two are the rights just described. Being separately sold, they were formed into distinct estates, bearing their own numbers on the *tauji* or rent-roll."

Tenants and tenancies. Since the passing of the Bengal Tenancy Act in 1885, the tenants of this Province fall naturally under the head of tenure-holders of various degrees intermediate between the proprietors and the actual cultivators *or* under the head of raiyats, with underraiyats to whom they may have sublet part of their holdings. The settlement report shows that no very serious difficulties were experienced in endeavouring to fit all classes of tenants into these two main heads. Generally speaking sub-infeudation is not very common beyond the first degree. The majority of raiyats hold directly under and pay rent directly to a proprietor ; when a tenure-holder intervenes, there is rarely more than one tenure-holder. Two main divisions of tenure-holders are found, namely, (*a*) permanent tenure-holders within the meaning of the definition in section 3 (*8*) of the Bengal Tenancy Act: and (*b*) those that are not permanent. The rents of "permanent tenure-holders" may or may not be fixed in perpetuity either under the terms of the document granting the tenure or by the operation of the legal presumption contained in section 50 of the Bengal Tenancy Act.

Tenures that are not permanent are frequently *mustajiri* or *ijara* leases for a short term of years. This system of sub-infeudation was greatly in vogue some time go. It was a favourite form of tenancy with managers of indigo factories. To secure local influence and prestige, the factory took a lease of several villages or even of a whole estate and then encouraged or persuaded tenants to cultivate indigo. The superior landlord often times lost all touch with the village but he got in his rents from the factory regularly and the tenants often found the factory a far easier landlord than the real proprietor had been.

Many hard things have been said about "middlemen" in every walk of life, and the holders of farming leases in this district have not escaped. In the Revenue Surveyor's Report (1853), Mr. Pemberton says :—

"The present system of *mustajiri* or middlemen, the bane of all agriculturists throughout the world, must be abolished before the power of the raiyat to improve his tenure can be fully developed. Time and more perfect civilization alone can accomplish this, and we must look calmly on until the Divine Disposer of all events sees fit to break the shackles of superstition and hereditary custom which at present bind the minds of our Indian fellow-subjects."

Buchanan-Hamilton also spoke of the *mustajiri* system as leading to abuse, especially in that part of the district in which produce rents were the rule. He says also:—

"Some of the estates under the immediate management of the landlords are badly enough conducted, but all, or at least most of those whose rents are farmed, are going backwards...... most farmers leaving the estate as bad and often a good deal worse than when they took it. Besides, many give large sums to the owner for the farm and of course make up this and a profit by vexing the tenants."

It is to be hoped that the exactions of middlemen will diminish as time goes on.

The bulk of the agriculturists of the district are occupancy raiyats, including settled raiyats. In the district, according to the figures of the Settlement Report there are 411,043 holdings in the possession of occupancy raiyats; that represents about 90·5 per cent. of the total number of occupied holdings; and 87·2 per cent. of the occupied area is held by these occupancy raiyats. **Raiyati holdings.**

The average size of an occupancy holding is just over 3 acres. The rents of almost all occupancy raiyats are liable to enhancement as only 951 holdings in all are held at a fixed rent, or rate of rents, and only 10,370 acres in all are so held.

Holdings of raiyats who have not yet acquired rights of occupancy amount in numbers to 15,480 and in area to 48,460 acres.

It will of course be understood that one raiyat may be the tenant of more than one holding and, accordingly, the actual number of occupancy raiyats and of the other classes of tenants under consideration is somewhat less than the gross number of holdings or tenancies.

Tenants holding under raiyats are very often farm servants or field labourers who are given a patch of ground on which to build a house by the tenant-farmer for whom they habitually work. In this district they number 47,484 holding 57,533 acres and the average size of each tenancy is one acre and a quarter.

Rent-free holders - as distinct from revenue-free proprietors above alluded to—hold their lands generally as religious offerings, due to the piety or remorse of preceding generations. There are various names for rent-free grants, indicative of the origin of the grant, *Birt*, *Sheopujai*, *mafi* and *barhmottar* are some of the commonest descriptions.

The whole area held rent-free is about 21,486 acres, the average area held by each rent-free tenant being only 2 acres.

Transferability of occupancy rights.

It may be noted here that in one estate (Sonbarsa) which has lately come under the Court of Wards, the late proprietor succeeded to an uncommon degree in restricting the acquisition of occupancy rights, or indeed of any status as tenants at all by persons whom he did not care to have resident within the limits of his estate.

The question as to whether a proprietor has the right to veto the transfer of occupancy rights within his estate is one that the legislature has left to be decided by local usage. From the enquiries made during the recent settlement operations it would appear that the right to transfer occupancy rights by purchase is becoming very generally recognized. It is no doubt inevitable that this should be so, seeing that the legislature has laid down in section 65 of the Bengal Tenancy Act, that an occupancy raiyat shall not be liable to ejectment merely for failure to pay his rent, but that his "holding" might be sold up: this recognition of a saleable interest in the occupancy holding would make the remedy inoperative unless the interest were transferable. Usually the value of occupancy rights in the open market far exceeds the three years' rent that may be overdue on account of the holding. Section 169 of the Tenancy Act lays down rules for the application of the proceeds of a sale in execution of a rent decree, and provides that when the landlord's lawful claims have been satisfied, the balance if any shall be paid to the tenant whose interest in his holding has been sold up.

Proprietors' private lands.

The area of "proprietors' private lands" in this district is only 6,584 acres in all. This amount can never increase and the difficulty of proving that any land is legally "proprietors' private land" within which occupancy rights cannot accrue under the ordinary law increases with each year that passes by.

CHAPTER XI.

GENERAL ADMINISTRATION.

For purposes of general administration the district is divided into four subdivisions, namely, Bhagalpur and Banka south of the Ganges; and Madhipura and Supaul north of the Ganges. At Bhagalpur are situated the main public offices, namely, the Collectorate and Magisterial offices in addition to the offices of the Commissioner of the Division. At each subdivision there is a Subdivisional Magistrate (generally a Deputy Collector of the Provincial Service) most of whose time is usually taken up with criminal work under ordinary conditions. Under stress of special circumstances such as floods or scarcity, the brunt of the work of putting into operation remedial measures falls on the Subdivisional Magistrate in his subdivision. Very little purely revenue work is done at the subdivisions. Administrative units.

At head-quarters, there are several Deputy and Sub-Deputy Collectors and usually one or two Assistant Magistrates. Each of these usually disposes of criminal cases in addition to holding charge of some of the many departments into which revenue work has now been divided, such as Road and Public Works Cess, Income Tax, Excise, Treasury, Land Registration, Certificates, Partitions, etc., etc.

For convenience of comparison, the area and population of each of the four subdivisions is here shown:—

Subdivision.	Area in square miles.	Population (1901).	Number of persons per square mile.
Sadar or head-quarters ...	934	585,244	627
Banka	1,182	433,499	367
Madhipura	1,176	559,310	476
Supaul...	934	510,900	547

Main heads of revenue.

The following table shows the amounts realized under the main heads of revenue at intervals of about 9 years: –

HEADING.	1892-93.	1901-02.	1908-09.
	Rs.	Rs.	Rs.
Land Revenue	6,02,302	6,08,868	6,09,806
Stamps	2,67,456	3,36,963	4,61,515
Income Tax	68,965	85,504	93,050
Excise	2,65,926	3,55,820	4,26,217
Opium	19,574	24,869	31,317
Miscellaneous	...	3,841	..
Road and Public Works Cess ...	3,00,836	3,29,825	3,34,025
Dak Cess	9,105	9,398	(Abolished.)*

It is obvious that there has been a healthy expansion unde practically every head. The Land Revenue demand being practically constant, no expansion is to be expected under tha head. The variations shown above are due simply to the different amounts collected each year. In one year, the whole of the current demand may be collected. From another, there may be left over a considerable balance of outstandings.

Stamp Revenue.

The growth in Stamp Revenue is very noticeable. This ultimately means more litigation, as the bulk of this head comes from judicial and court-fee stamps.

Excise.

Excise revenue is increasing more in proportion than the population increases. This suggests the inference that the use of exciseable articles is extending to classes of the population that held aloof from them hitherto. About half of the excise revenue comes from country spirit. Hemp drugs including *ganja* contribute about 36 per cent. of the remaining revenue, *tari* or palm tree liquor contributes about ten per cent.; opium about four per cent. The net excise revenue is now over three annas per head of the population. The average for the whole Province is 5·12 annas per head.

Cesses.

Road and Public Works cesses are levied at the maximum rate of one anna in the rupee, half of which is payable by landlords and half by tenants. In actual practice, however, many landlords have hitherto habitually extorted one anna in the rupee at least from their tenants on this account in addition to miscellaneous exactions under the general term "*abwab*."

It will be noticed that the cess demand is now very little behind the Land Revenue demand and it will shortly exceed it. At present Land Revenue is realized by the very summary

* See Bengal Act IV of 1907.

process known as the Revenue Sale Law (Act XI of 1859), while the only method of compulsion in force for the recovery of cesses is that known as the Certificate Procedure, which is extremely cumbrous and dilatory in comparison with the so-called "sunset law." With the rise in the cess demand, a simplified procedure will soon be called for, for the recovery of cesses.

Income-tax.

At present the annual demand on account of income-tax is about Rs. 1,02,000. In 1892 it was only Rs. 68,965. The difference is mainly due to an increase in the number of assessees and this indicates an increase in activities, commercial and otherwise. As already shown, the actual collections in 1908 were Rs. 93,050. In all there were 1,397 assessees, most of whom were traders. A small number of Government servants, pensioners and others pay income-tax directly. The minimum taxable income is now Rs. 1,000 per annum.

Registration.

The average number of documents of all sorts presented annually for registration under Act XVI of 1908 is about 23,000. This figure increases gradually but surely, every year, as the tendency is for verbal or implied agreements to be reduced to writing and thus made explicit. This is especially the case as regards documents relating to immovable property, registration being now obligatory to a far greater extent than heretofore.

Administration of Justice, Civil.

The District and Sessions Judge of Bhagalpur usually sits at Bhagalpur but he also holds sessions at Monghyr. A proposal to appoint a separate District and Sessions Judge for Monghyr is now under consideration. There are in addition two Subordinate Judges, one of whom sits always at Bhagalpur and one, occasionally at Monghyr and occasionally at Bhagalpur.

There are, in addition, Munsiffs who sit at Bhagalpur, and the outlying subdivisions of Supaul, Madhipura and Banka.

Criminal.

The District Magistrate is the chief magistrate of the district and is the head of the police as well. In addition to him there are usually 5 or 6 Deputy Magistrates with first and second class powers and 2 or 3 Sub-Deputy Magistrates with second or third class powers.

Honorary Magistrates.

There are, as well, Independent Benches of Honorary Magistrates at Bhagalpur (usually 18 Honorary Magistrates); at Banka (about 12 Honorary Magistrates); at Madhipura (6 Honorary Magistrates); at Colgong (8 Honorary Magistrates); at Supaul (12 Honorary Magistrates); at Sultanganj (5 Honorary Magistrates); at Bihpur (7 Honorary Magistrates); and at Bangaon (7 Honorary Magistrates). As a rule only petty cases that can be disposed of at a single hearing are made over to the

Independent Benches. Some of the Honorary Magistrates are empowered to sit singly and they often deal with more intricate cases which can be adjourned if necessary. This obviates the difficulty of assembling the same members of the Bench time after time to deal with adjourned cases.

Crimes. Bhagalpur compares favourably with other districts of the division from the point of view of criminality. Of course there always are a number of cases of theft and housebreaking and riots of an agrarian nature, but there are no purely criminal tribes resident in the district. In years gone by, river-pirates were an intolerable nuisance on the river Ganges near Colgong in particular, but their depredations have long ceased.

In 1903, owing to short rainfall, an outbreak of grain looting occurred in Banka subdivision and lasted for three days (30th and 31st July and 1st August) till a heavy fall of rain came and put a stop to it. The grain dealers had formed a combination to put up prices and the people of the locality would not endure it any longer. About 134 persons were convicted.

In 1903-04 a series of professional dacoities took place in the north of the district, headed by one Bhadda Jat. He was tried in July 1904 with eighteen of his gang, and sentenced to transportation for life.

In 1908 there was an increase of thefts and burglaries, due directly to the prevalent scarcity. These crimes are inevitable and are practically impossible of detection.

Criminal classes. Most of the criminals are to be found in the ranks of Dharhis, Musahars, Doms and Dusadhs in this district. No genuine criminal tribes are to be found in Bhagalpur. The Dharhis approach most nearly to a genuine criminal tribe. They nominally live by manual labour and the breeding of animals, but in reality they rely very largely on thieving for their livelihood. It is said that they look individually on specific localities as their own special preserve, and the exclusive right of thieving therein is so highly valued that if another Dharhi poaches in that special preserve, intermarriage between the two families becomes impossible. In the neighbouring district of Monghyr, these Dharhis are more numerous and more dangerous than here.

The Dusadhs are traditionally swine-keepers, village chaukidars or watchmen and thieves. They and Musahars live largely by manual labour.

Doms are basket-makers and bamboo-weavers; they also dispose of the dead bodies and act as common scavengers. They are undoubtedly looked on as the most degraded class in the social system.

At present there are twelve thanas or police-stations and ten independent outposts which are also investigating centres for cognizable offences, distributed as follows :— Police.

Subdivision.	Thana.	Area (sq. miles).	Independent outpost.
Sadar	Bhagalpur...	181	Nathnagar.
	Colgong	413	Gopalpur. Pirpainti.
	Sultanganj	165	Shahkand.
	Bihpur	175	*Nil.*
Banka	Banka	354	Dhurja.
	Katauria	534	Belhar.
	Amarpur	294	Rajaun.
Madhipura ...	Madhipura	547	*Nil.*
	Bangaon	268	*Nil.*
	Kishanganj	366	*Nil.*
Supaul	Supaul	593	Dagmara. Daparkha.
	Pratapganj	341	Bhimnagar.

The police force of the district consists of 1 District Superintendent, 4 Inspectors, 28 Sub-Inspectors, 42 Head-constables, 376 constables and 4,770 chowkidars. Each of the four subdivisions has its Police Inspector who is a gazetted officer. The subdivisions are divided up into smaller areas each of which is a police-station. There may or may not be outposts dependant on each police-station. Again, each police-station contains a number of dafadari circles, each circle is under the charge of a dafadar and contains about 20 village chowkidars.

The ordinary police force is divided into four classes—armed, civil, town and rural police. The armed police consist of the district police reserve, created by order of the Government of India to deal with organised disturbances, and always kept up to full strength. They are not employed except by order of the District Magistrate. The civil police perform all the ordinary duties of escorting prisoners, working at police-stations and outposts and attending the courts. The literate among them supply the police clerical staff, and one writer-constable is attached to each police-station and one literate constable to each outpost. Town police are employed only at night within the town or municipality in which they are enlisted.

There is a constables' training school at Nathnagar and a company of military police, 100 strong, is maintained at Bhagalpur.

A central jail with accommodation for about 1,960 prisoners is situated at Bhagalpur. In it blanket-making is the most important industry as already described in Chapter VIII, 33 power looms and 34 hand looms being used. Jails.

In addition, carpet-making, rope and mat making, oil pressing and grain grinding are carried on.

At Banka, Supaul and Madhipura there are subsidiary jails in which accused persons are kept while awaiting trial if they are not released on bail, and short term prisoners (sentenced to not more than fourteen days' imprisonment) are kept to serve out their sentences. Oil pressing and grain grinding are the industries carried on in the subsidiary jails.

CHAPTER XII.

LOCAL SELF-GOVERNMENT.

THIS exotic plant lives only by careful and constant supervision. There are two agencies through which activity in this direction is manifested—namely, the District Boards (including the Local Boards subordinate to it) and the Municipalities. General.

The District Board, constituted by the Local Self-Government Act, III of 1885 (Bengal Code), is the direct descendant of the old Road Cess Committee. It consists at present of thirty-one members of whom six are *ex-officio* members; in addition ten are nominated by Government and fifteen are elected. In the year ending March 31st, 1908, this Board held 17 meetings and the average attendance of members at each meeting was 16·5 or a little over 50 per cent. of the members. Origin.

The directions in which the activities of the District Board are exerted can best be judged from an enumeration of the main heads of expenditure to which its funds were applied in the year ending March 31st, 1908. The year opened with a balance in hand of Rs. 1,02,901 and the income that accrued during the year—exclusive of this balance—was Rs. 3,22,084. This income was expended as follows:—General administration, Rs. 8,358, Cattle pound maintenance, Rs. 1,491; Education, Rs. 37,235: under this the main sub-heads are "Grants-in-aid," Rs. 24,519; Scholarships, Rs. 1,004; Maintenance and management of training and special schools, Rs. 2,467; Maintenance and management of middle schools, Rs. 4,008; Inspection, Rs. 3,315; Medical (mainly contributions to the upkeep of Hospitals and Dispensaries), Rs. 13,684; Veterinary charges, Rs. 1,947; Famine (Charitable) relief, Rs. 5,879; Civil Works (including buildings, road construction and upkeep, water-supply, arboriculture, staging bungalows and miscellaneous), Rs. 2,36,682. The establishment charges and contingencies in connection with road construction and upkeep amounted to Rs. 34,259. The actual amount expended on roads (including bridges) was Rs. 1,71,855 of which Rs. 76,516 was on original works and Rs. 95,339 on Expenditure.

repairs. Thus the total expenditure chargeable to current income was Rs. 3,08,343.

Income. The main source of income is derived from the Road Cess fund, from which Rs. 1,43,229 was received in 1907-1908. The receipts under the Cattle Trespass Act amounted to Rs. 30,524. The pounds maintained under this Act are usually farmed out for a year by public auction. A few are kept under direct management when suitable farmers are not forthcoming.

Under the head "Medical" a sum of Rs. 5,121 was received by contributions from private individuals. The income under Civil Works (tolls on ferries and contributions) amounted to Rs 68,332. The Provincial Government contributed Rs. 13,413.

Incidence of taxation. The incidence of taxation per head of population was 1 anna 2 pies and the incidence of income per head of population, for the year, was 2 annas 4 pies. This is practically the same as that in the neighbouring districts of Monghyr and Purnea, in each of which the incidence of income was 2 annas 5 pies. The incidence of taxation was less in Purnea being only 1 anna per head, and greater in Monghyr in which it was 1 anna 3 pies per head. In considering these figures the population per square mile must also be borne in mind. It is in Bhagalpur, 494 persons: in Monghyr 527 persons and in Purnea 375 persons according to the census figures of 1901.

Local Boards. Subordinate to the District Boards are the Local Boards four in number, located one in each of the administrative subdivisions of the district. These Local Boards have charge of such local and village roads as are not directly under the District Engineer, and of the pounds in their respective jurisdictions. They also have the charge of primary schools. The duties of the Local Boards are virtually discharged by the subdivisional officers at each subdivision. Their duties and activities are rather restricted in scope. Their finances are derived practically entirely from doles made by the District Board. Their budget is framed on the basis of this allotment and is submitted for the approval of the District Board. It is generally considered inadvisable to extend to the Local Boards any of the powers now exercised by the District Board as the latter is a far more efficient agency.

The Sadar Local Board now maintains about 280 miles of roads. The Banka Local Board maintains about 130 miles: the Madhipura Local Board about 288 miles and the Supaul Local Board about 225 miles.

Union Committees, etc. The recent amendments to the Local Self-Government Act have imposed many new duties on District Boads. No Union

Committees under that Act have as yet been established in Bhagalpur district. So, too, the system of village government known as the panchayat President system has not as yet been tried in this district, mainly owing to the difficulty of getting in each local area a suitable man to fill the post of President.

There is of course a chaukidari panchayat in every chaukidar, circle, but the functions of the members of this panchayat are confined to assessing and realizing sufficient taxes to pay the village watch.

There are two municipalities in the district, one at Bhagalpur, constituted in 1864, and one at Colgong constituted in 1869. In the former the system of appointment of members is partly by election and partly by nominations by Government. In Colgong, all the members are appointed by Government. Municipalities.

The population of the municipal area is about 76,000. This includes several truly rural villages, the area which presents unmistakably urban characteristics being very small and practically restricted to the centre of the town. There are 22 members of the Municipal Committee of whom one is an *ex-officio* member, seven are nominated and 14 are elected. Out of the total number of members 19 are non-officials; 18 are natives, only four being Europeans. Bhagalpur Municipality.

During the year ending March 31st, 1908, the total income of this municipality was Rs. 1,93,562. This includes a special grant of Rs. 56,000 from Government for the improvement of the water-supply, to which further reference will be made below. In addition to this special grant, a loan of Rs. 85,500 was also given by Government for the same purpose.

The chief sources of municipal income, excluding the extraordinary grant and loan just specified, were as follows in that year :—Rates on holdings, Rs. 41,739 ; Taxes on animals and vehicles Rs. 11,032; Tolls on roads and ferries, Rs. 10,823 ; Water-rate, Rs. 27,278; Latrine-rate (for conservancy establishment), Rs. 14,687 ; Miscellaneous items of income, Rs. 13,266. Income.

The main heads of expenditure are as follows :—General and tax-collection establishment, Rs. 12,400; Improvement and maintenance of water-supply, Rs. 1,04,000; Conservancy (including road-cleaning and watering), Rs. 31,388; Hospitals, etc., Rs. 16,608; Plague charges, Rs. 4,710; Roads, Rs. 19,221 : Repayment of loans and interest on loans, Rs. 40,500. Expenditure.

Bhagalpur is one of the few towns in this province that has a filtered water-supply. For many years past the charges on account of it have been a serious drain on the municipal finances. Thus in 1904-05 the annual charges incurred were Water-works.

about Rs. 43,000, out of which the water-rate brought in only Rs. 25,000, leaving a heavy balance to be defrayed from general revenues. The daily average supply provided is about 7 gallons per head. The Ganges is the source of supply. The water is raised by pumps; it is passed through filter beds and settling tanks and distributed by gravity. The river has for many years been receding from the intake of the pumps and it has proved a very expensive thing to keep open a channel up to the pumps. The original pumping engines were expensive to work and were inefficient. They have now been replaced by four Diesel oil-engines and a marked improvement in the water-supply is confidently anticipated. But as long as the river recedes to the north, so long will it be extremely difficult to prevent the water channel from silting up in the dry weather when the water-level is lowest and the need for water sorest.

DRAINAGE CONSERVANCY. Bhagalpur is situated on a ridge with a good natural fall in all directions. Hence no elaborate drainage scheme is necessary. Surface drains of masonry work carry off the storm water quite rapidly: in fact, the rush at one outfall was alleged to have caused serious damage to private property by erosion and the Municipality had to pay damages after a civil suit.

The efforts of the Conservancy Department of the Municipality are directed mainly towards disposing of nightsoil by trenching grounds. There are four trenching grounds in regular use, situated fairly conveniently for the various quarters in which the population is dense. No attempt at a septic tank scheme has ever been adumbrated as yet though Bhagalpur, with its fairly regular water-supply, offers an excellent site for an experiment of this sort.

Colgong Municipality. Colgong Municipality was established in the year 1869. It is situated on the bank of the Ganges at about 20 miles from Bhagalpur. Its population was 5,860 in 1901. The Municipal Committee consists of 11 members, one of whom is an official All of them are natives of India and all are nominated by Government as the elective system has not been introduced as yet in this municipality.

Income. The total income from municipal rates and taxes in Colgong was Rs. 3,751 in the year ending March 31st, 1908, the greater portion of which is derived from a capitation tax: the tax on houses and lands brought in only Rs. 188 in that same year Various other items of income, of which the most important was he rent of Rs. 500 paid by the farmer of the municipal pound, throught the total income up to Rs. 5,639.

In that year the main heads of expenditure were (1) Hospitals and Dispensaries, Rs. 1,661; (2) Conservancy, Rs. 968; (3) General Administration and Establishment, Rs. 993. Expenditure.

The number of rate-payers amounts to 20 per cent. of the total population, whereas, in Bhagalpur itself, the percentage is only 14. The attendance at the monthly meetings averaged 62·8 per cent. of the Municipal Commissioners, which is a remarkably high average. Other details.

CHAPTER XIII.

EDUCATION.*

GENERAL. It must be recognized from the outset that education though making considerable progress is in a backward condition in this district. The test of literacy adopted at the last census was very easy, namely, ability to read and write any vernacular. The census enumerators generally interpret this test in a far from stringent manner, and classify as literate any one who can read and write his own name. Even this test was only passed by 69,260 persons in 1901. As regards literacy in English, only 2,591 persons were returned as able to read and write English.

This means that only 66 males per thousand and 1 female per thousand are literate. In 1891, 61 males and 1 female per thousand were returned as literate and learning. The subdivision into literate, learning and illiterate was maintained in the enumerations of 1881 and 1891, but has been dropped since as it gave rise to considerable anomalies without any compensating gain.

In 1881, 42 males only per thousand were learning and literate: no females were returned as learning or literate. As the learners in 1881 and 1891 are the literates in 1891 and 1901, it is clear that there has been steady progress made in the direction of literacy during the last twenty years. The figures of the 1911 census will probably show a further increase.

Another point of view from which this question may well be regarded is the consideration of the number of persons per thousand, over the age of 15, that are literate. In 1891 the figures were 86 males and 1 female per thousand; in 1901 the corresponding figures were 95 males and 2 females. This shows a very considerable increase and is a hopeful indication for the future.

Distribution of literates. The Sadar subdivision contained in 1901 30,675 literates out of the district total of 69,260. In Bhagalpur thana itself there were 17,033 literates and the majority of these no doubt were living in the town. So too in Colgong thana there were 5,867 literates, most of whom were living in the Municipality of Colgong.

*I am indebted to G. E. Fawcus, Esq., B.A., Inspector of Schools, Bhagalpur Division, for the revision of this chapter.

Banka subdivision had 13,117 literates out of a population of 433,499. Its standard of literacy was thus higher than that of Madhipura, with 12,791 literates out of 559,310 inhabitants; and higher also than that of Supaul which had 12,677 literate out of 510,900 inhabitants.

Numbers attending school.

In this district, the number of boys of school-going age is about 154,130. In 1907-08 only 15·4 per cent. of those were attending school and in 1908-09, only 19·9 per cent. In this respect this district is almost the worst in the Province, only two (Palamau and Champaran), and those notoriously backward districts, returning smaller percentages.

Collegiate education.

Collegiate education in Bhagalpur is identified with the Tej Narain Jubilee College, which was established in 1887 by Babu Tej Narain Sing, a local zamindar. It was at first a second grade College but in 1890 it was raised to its present status as a first grade Arts College. Law classes were opened then but they have recently been abandoned as "affiliation in law" was refused to this college.

No Government grant is taken by this college. It is maintained entirely by subscriptions and donations supplemented by the receipts from fees. The fees are rupees five and rupees six per month. In 1902 the college had 213 students on its roll and 28 in the Law Department. These figures have not been maintained. In 1904, there were 138 on the rolls: in 1906, 183; and in 1908, 178. In this last year, the average monthly roll number was 148, and the average daily attendance 102. The total expenditure in 1908 was Rs. 18,994, which sum was derived in practically equal proportions from fees and from endowments and other private sources. The cost per annum of each student was thus Rs. 128. Fifty-six students were presented for the First Arts examination of whom 24, or 30·3 per cent., were successful. Forty-two students were presented for the B. A. examination of whom 14, or 33·3 per cent., passed. The corresponding figures for the whole Province are 41 per cent. of successes in the First Arts examination and 37 per cent. in the B. A. degree examination, so this college is a little below the general average.

The following figures, taken from the Annual Administration Report of the Bhagalpur Division for 1908-09, give an idea of the number of educational institutions in the district and of the amount expended on education from various sources.

High Schools.

There were seven High schools with 1,454 pupils on the rolls. They received Rs. 9,257 from Provincial revenues; Rs. 26,221 from fees and Rs. 12,755 from other sources in the year 1908-09. The average cost per pupil was thus Rs. 33·17. As compared with the figures for 1894-95, there was a marked increase under every one of the heads just enumerated. No financial aid was given by the District Board or by the Municipalities in that year to High schools.

Middle Schools. Including English and Vernacular schools, there were in all 11 Middle schools with 907 pupils on roll in 1908-09. They received Rs. 600 from Provincial revenues; Rs. 2,961 from the District Board; Rs. 480 from Municipal Funds; Rs. 3,578 from fees, and Rs. 2,333 from other sources in that year. The average cost per pupil was Rs. 10·9.

Primary Schools. Including Upper and Lower, there were 984 Primary schools with 25,042 pupils on rolls in that year. Provincial revenues contributed Rs. 5,608 in that year; District Board funds contributed Rs. 23,062; Municipal funds contributed Rs. 1,398. The receipts from fees amounted to Rs. 38,070 and from other sources Rs. 22,771. The average cost per pupil was Rs. 3·6 only.

Other Schools. There were also nine training schools for teachers attended by 149 pupils. The total cost to Provincial Revenues was Rs. 7,610 and the sum realized from fees was Rs 455. The cost per pupil was thus Rs. 54·1.

In addition there are some Sanskrit *tols* of which the most important is the Vidyasagar Memorial Sanskrit Tol at Kanangarh. It is attended by about 75 pupils. A monthly sum of Rs. 25 is granted by Government to it and private donations and subscriptions help to maintain it. The subjects taught are Sanskrit grammar and literature, astronomy and *smriti*.

There are 52 Muhammadan *maktabs* as well, the cost of which to Provincial Revenues was Rs. 1,789. The sum realized from fees was Rs. 1,527 and from other sources, Rs. 680. The cost of each institution was thus Rs. 76·8 per annum. There are also some schools for aboriginals such as the Sonthals, Dhangars, etc., who are numerous on the eastern and southern borders of the district.

CHAPTER XIV.

GAZETTEER.

Alamnagar, situated in *pargana* Chhál, in N. lat. 25° 33′ 45″, and E. long. 86° 56′ 21″, about 7 miles south-west of Kisshanganj, was once the principal village of the Chandel chiefs, who possessed fifty-two adjacent townships, and a considerable revenue. These Rājās were highly esteemed in the district until the grandfather of the present holder of the estate wasted his property, ruining himself and his heirs. At present but two villages out of the fifty-two remain to the family. Traces of many fine tanks and the earthenwork ramparts of forts are still visible. These and a masonry manor-house, now in ruins, alone remain to show the former wealth of the owners. The prevailing castes of the village are Rājputs and Brāhmans.

Balua, situated in *parganā* Dhaphar in 26° 24′ 40″ N. lat., and 87° 3′ 1″ E. long., formerly an inland market, is now within two miles of the Kūsī, owing to recent changes in the course of that river. As a place of commercial activity, it holds a more prominent place than Khandaulī. Its trade consists almost entirely of oilseeds—mustard, rape, and linseed—which are brought from all parts of the Supaul subdivision, and also from Nepāl and the Alapur *parganā* of Darbhanga to be exported down the Kūsī to Calcutta. The imports are salt and piece-goods, which are sold to merchants from Nepāl. The leading traders are nearly all Bengālis from the metropolitan districts round Calcutta.

Banaili Raj estate includes Mahalat Kharakpur, Touzi No. 445 in the district of Bhagalpur, which is an extensive estate situate in the districts of Bhagalpur, Monghyr and Sonthal Parganas. It originally included the Lachmipur estate (officially called Chandwai Passai), consisting of properties in the Bhagalpur district, in that district and in the district of Sonthal Parganas; but before 1840 A. D. (in consequence of the recommendation of the Sader Dewani Adalat), the Lachmipur estate was severed from the parent estate of Mahalat Kharakpur and was formed into a separate estate paying revenue directly to the Government instead of paying the same through the zamīndār of Mahalat Kharakpur. Mahalat Kharakpur consists of many ghatwali and mokarari tenures and altogether is a very extensive property included in one Touzi number, and includes the following Parganas :—Sahroi, Lakhanpur, Kherhī, Sakharābādi, Parbatpārā (including Tappas Lodhwa, Sinroun, Dighi, etc.) Wasīlā, Goddā, Hāzar Takhi, Amlo-Motiā, Handwai (including a ghatwali held by the Rani of Handwai), Chandan Katoria, Jahangira and Masdi, Dhararha, Abhaipur, Singaul Dāoda Sakhwārā.

Mahalat Kharakpur, including those now held by the Lachmipur estate, and together with pargana Haveli, Kharakpur and Petghanna Kajra, formed the vast estate of the Muhammadan Rājā of Kharagpur. Sir William Hunter in his Statistical Accounts of Bengal (Volume XV., Monghyr and Purneah, page 177) gives some interesting account of the Muhammadan Rājās of Kharakpur. It appears that the original holders of this estate were of Kshetouri caste who held not only this estate and its dependencies but also the estates of Barkope and Manihari in the district of Sonthal Parganas and, in fact, according to traditions, there were fifty-two Kshetouri Chiefs in this part of the country. About the middle of the sixteenth century three brothers of the Rājput tribe of Khandwar named Dandu Rai, Basudeo and Mahadeo Rai took service under one of these Chiefs, Rājā Sesunk of Kheri (the ruins of whose fort is still to be seen on the Kheri Pahar included in Banaili (Rāj) gained great influence. With the help of their tribe-fellows they succeeded in murdering their master and his family and assumed his powers. They then subjugated all the neighbouring chiefs and, firmly establishing themselves, Danda Rai invested his eldest son Rup Sahai with the authority of Rājā, who was succeeded by his son Sangram Sahai in 1839. He incurred the displeasure of Emperor Jehangir, who directed the Subadar of Bengal, Jahangir Kuli Khan, to chastise him. For this purpose Baz Bahadur advanced on Kharakpur. It is stated that in consequence of the treachery of his servant Sangram Sahai was killed and his adherents were about to fly when his wife, Rani Chandrajote, encouraged them to stand their ground. She placed her own son Toral Mall at their head and resisted Baz Bahadur for several months. It was then proposed to her that it would be much better if she herself went to Delhi and endeavoured to obtain the Emperor's favour. She agreed to this and, when she arrived at Delhi, her son at first was thrown into prison, but was soon after released through the intercession of Baz Bahadur. Subsequently

Toral Mall was induced to change his religion and become a Musalman. He was given the title of Roz Afzan and married to a daughter of a noble, and subsequently to Boga Sultana, daughter of Murad Bux Khan, first cousin of the Emperor. Toral Mall, now Roz Afzan, advanced to the rank of Munsabdar of 300 horses and got a Farman creating him Rājā of Kharagpur. The tradition is that pargannah Haveli Kharagpur was given to his wife for residence, a pargannah for the expenses of applying *kajal* (a black stuff) to her eyes, a pargannah for the expense of applying *sindoor* (red stuff) to her forehead and lahaita for expenses of *lahthi* (worn on wrist). This family prospered greatly until the then ruling Chief of Kharagpur, Mozuffer Ali, fell under the displeasure of Nawab Kasim Ali and was put in prison. After the downfall of Kasim Ali Mozuffer Ali obtained his liberty but the estate was managed by Muhammad Asir Khan, an Afghan, till 1766, and afterwards by Mir Haider Ali, another Amil. During this period Faiz Ali, son of Mozuffer Ali, appealed to the British Agent at Patna and was put in possession, a new Amil, Abu Talib, being still left at Kharagpur to watch matters on behalf of the Company. This officer soon laid a charge against the Rājā alleging that he was a turbulent man. Thereupon he was deprived of all authority and the Rājā effected his escape to the jungle fastnesses of the rebel Ghatwal Jaggernath Deo (ancestor of the present holders of the Lachmipur estate). Subsequently, in 1781, Mr. Warren Hastings ordered the whole estate of Kharagpur to be restored to Kadir Ali, who was succeeded by his son Eqbal Ali Khan, who again was succeeded by his brother Rahmat Ali Khan. In 1839 he fell into arrears of revenue of October kist and the estate of Kharagpur, including the Ghatwali of Handwai, was sold in 1840, and purchased by Raja Bidyanand Singh, grandfather of the present proprietors of Banaili [Kumar Kalanand Singh and Kumar Krityanand Singh], and by Balnath Sahu of Bhagalpore, who subsequently, in 1841, transferred his share to Raja Bidyanand Singh Bahadur, on 24th September 1841 (the transfer fee receipt of the Collector bears date 28th July 1843). The *hukumnama* is dated the 5th of April 1781 A.D., and is granted by order of the Hon'ble Governor-General in Council on 1st May 1781 in the name of Raja Kadir Ali. The perpetual settlement pattah was granted on 25th January 1796. This included pargana Chandwai Passai and Sathiari now held by the Lachmipur estate.

The founder of the Banaili Raj family was Hazari Chou dhry, who acquired by purchase about 1780 A. D. pargana

Tirakbarda in the district of Purnea. His son, Dular Singh, was a Government Kanungo in Purnea about 1790 and acquired property in Monghyr, Bhagalpur and Purnea in about the year 1800 A. D. And on his death, after some litigation, the estates were divided equally between his two sons, Rājā Bidyanand Singh and Kumar Rudranand Singh, grandfather of the Srinagar Kumars.

There was litigation between them, which resulted in the division of the property into two equal parts—one part being given to Rājā Bidyanand Singh, and the other part to Kumar Rudranand Singh. Subsequent to the partition between Rājā Bidyananda Singh and his brother, the former purchased Mahalat Kharagpur, which is the extensive property of the Banaili proprietors.

Rājā Bidyanand Singh subsequently purchased Mahalat Kharagpur and, in 1851, was succeeded by his son Raja Lilanand Singh Bahadur, who also added to the estate by purchasing Chandpur Hossain and Taluq Khajuria. Rājā Lilanand Singh died in 1883, and was succeeded by his son Rājà Padmanand Singh Bahadur, leaving a minor son, Kumar Kalanand Singh, and a posthumous son, Kumar Krityanand Singh. In 1888 a suit was instituted by the Kumars Kalanand Singh and Kirtyanand Singh by the minors through their mother, Rani Sitabati, in the Court of the District Judge of Bhagalpore, which ended in a compromise decree, under which Kumar Kalanand Singh and Kumar Kirtyanand Singh were declared to be owners of nine annas of the Banaili Rāj and Rājā Padmanand Singh of the remaining seven annas. In 1903, Kumar Chandranand Singh, son of Rājā Padmanand Singh Bahadur, brought a suit against his father for partition and other reliefs, which also ended in a compromise decree, under which the son was declared to be owner of a 3½ annas share and Rājā Padmanand Singh owner of the remaining 3½ annas share of the Banaili Rāj. Subsequently, however, in September 1905, Rājā Padmanand Singh Bahadur transferred his rights and interests to his son Kumar Chandranand Singh, so that the present owners of the Rāj are Kumars Kalanand Singh and Kirtyanand Singh to the extent of nine annas and Kumar Chandranand Singh to the extent of seven annas. Kumars Kalanand Singh and Krityanand Singh are now in possession of the entire estate. The Collector of Bhagalpore was appointed Receiver under the orders of the District Judge of Bhagalpur, and he gave them a lease of the entire seven annas share for 12 years from 1311 to 1323 Fasli. The seven annas share is involved in debt to the extent of about 50 lakhs of rupees, the nine annas proprietors Kumar Kalanand Singh and Kumar Krityanand Singh being their principal creditors. The Court of Wards has recently taken charge of the seven annas share on behalf of Kumar Chandranand Singh, who has been declared a disqualified proprietor on his own application, but the actual management of the entire Banaili Rāj has been in the hands of the Kumars Kalanand Singh and Krityanand Singh since 1904.

Since the purchase of Mahalat Kharagpur by the Banaili Rāj there have been constant disputes and litigation in connection with this Mahal. The principal dispute was with the Maharaja of Darbhanga, who acquired by purchase in 1848 A. D. at the sale for arrears of Government revenue, Haveli Kharagpur, which is surrounded on all sides by Mahalat Kharagpur already purchased by Rājā Bidyanand Singh Bahadur of Banaili. Several times the litigation was carried to the Privy Council costing both the Darbhanga and the Banaili Rāj a great amount of money.

There was further litigation in connection with Mahalat Kharagpur regarding the Ghatwali tenures under it. Mahalat Kharagpur originally consisted of many Ghatwalis (Lachmipur was also a Ghatwali under it but subsequently formed into a separate tauzi number independent of Mahalat Kharagpur as shown above). The Ghatwali tenures of Kharagpur have a history of their own and have formed the subject of many High Court and Privy Council decisions. They were with a very few exceptions resumed by Government as Thanadari lands. Rājā Lilanand Singh Bahadur contested the resumption and although he was worsted in the Indian Courts, he ultimately succeeded in having the resumption set aside by the Privy Council. The Government entered into an agreement in or about the year 1863 with Rājā Lilanand Singh Bahadur by which it accepted Rs. 10,000 a year in lieu of these services, and this amount was added to the Government revenue fixed for Mahalat Kharagpur. Since then most of the Ghatwali tenures were converted into Mokarari Istamrari* tenures by Rājā Lilanand Singh Bahadur and only a few, including the big Ghatwali of Handwai in the Sonthal Perghannas and Kakwara in the Banka subdivision of Bhagalpore, still retain their Ghatwali character. It now appears to be settled law that though the Banaili Rāj cannot oust these Ghatwals or enhance their rent such tenures cannot be alienated without the consent of the

* *i.e.*, perpetual tenures at a fixed rent.

zamīndār (Banaili Rāj) and; if so alienated, the Banaili Rāj will be entitled to recover Khas possession of such Ghatwali. These Ghatwals are also, it is apprehended, liable to render police services if they be called upon to do so by the zamīndār. Those tenures that have been converted into Mokarari are regulated by the terms of the agreement entered into between the Rāj and such Mokararidars.

Bangaon, Mahessi and **Chainpur** are villages lying close together in parganas Kabkand and Uttarkand in Madhipura subdivision: these villages are very ancient and many celebrated Brahman *pundits* lived there.

Banka, a village situated on the Chandan river in 24° 53′ N., and 86° 56′ E, headquarters of the subdivision of the same name, in that part of Bhagalpur district that lies south of the Ganges. In 1901 the population of the village was 1,091. It contains the usual subdivisional offices and court, a munsifi and a subsidiary jail with accommodation for 12 prisoners.

Barantpur is in thana Kishanganj, and is about 15 miles from Madhipura to the south. It is situated on the Local Board road from Bangaon to Shahmora. There are ruins of a fort which is said to have been the residence of King Birat mentioned in Mahabharata. The Pandavas in disguise, the Mahabharata says, accepted service under him. Kichak, the brother-in-law of King Birat, wanted to take Draupadi, the wife of the Pandavas, and was killed by Bhim at this village. It is said that the party of Raja Durjodhan took away one lakh heads of cattle belonging to King Birat. Arjun, one of the Pandavas, fought with them and recovered the cattle. "Uttarago-griha" (or northern grazing fields) of the ancient time was situated in the vicinity of Barantpur. Population 1,024 souls.

Bausi.—A village in the south of the district situated near the base of Mandar hill in 24° 48′ N., and 87° 2′ E. The population in 1901 was 649. The numerous buildings, tanks, large wells and stone figures found for a mile or two round the base of the sacred hill show that a great city must once have stood here. The people of the neighbourhood say that it contained 52 markets, 53 streets and 88 tanks. According to local tradition on the night of the Dewāli festival a large building (the ruins of which still exist, and the walls of which contain an immense number of small holes, evidently intended to hold *chiraghs*, or small native lamps) was formerly illuminated by a hundred thousand of these lights, each householder being allowed to supply only one. How or when the city fell into ruin is not known though popular tradition ascribes its destruction to Kālapahār. A Sanskrit inscription on a stone triumphal arch seems to show that the city was in existence less than 300 years ago. After the destruction of the temple of Madhusudan on Mandar Hill, the image of the god was brought to Bausi where it now remains. Once a year, on the Pous Sankrānti day, the image is carried from Bausi to the foot of the hill, and is swung on the triumphal arch above referred to. About 50,000 pilgrims assemble at this festival from all parts of the country, to bathe in the sacred tank at the foot of the hill, and a fair is held which lasts for 15 days.

Bhāgalpur.—The chief town and administrative head-quarters of the district and division of this name; situated on the right bank of the Ganges in 25°15′N., and 87°0′E. Bhāgalpur, railway station on the East Indian Railway, is distant from Calcutta 265 miles by rail and 326 by river. Bhāgalpur figures more than once in Muhammadan chronicles of the 16th century. Akbar's troops marched through the town when invading Bengal in 1573 and 1575. In Akbar's second war against the Afghān King of Bengal, his general, Mān Singh, made Bhāgalpur the rendezvous of all the Bihar contingents which in 1592 were sent thence over Chota Nāgpur to Burdwan where they met the Bengal levies before the united army invaded Orissa. The town was subsequently made the seat of an imperial *fauzdār* or military governor. The town contains two monuments to the memory of Mr. Augustus Cleveland, sometime Collector of Bhagalpur district, one of brick, erected by the landholders of the district; the other of stone sent out by the Court of Directors of the East India Company from England Within the town and its neighbourhood (at Champānagar) are some interesting Muhammadan shrines, and two remarkable places of worship, belonging to the Jain sect of Oswals, one of them erected by the great banker of the last century, Jagat Seth. The Karnagarh plateau near the town formerly contained the lines of the Bhāgalpur Hill Rangers organized by Cleveland in 1780.

The population at the last four censuses was 1872, 65,377; 1881, 68,238; 1891, 69,106; 1901, 75,760. The growth is due mainly to a great development in the export trade in agricultural produce, which has led to the opening of a second railway station and to a great extension of the accommodation provided for goods. On the south, moreover, the municipal limits have been enlarged. Of the population in 1901, 70 per cent. were Hindus and 29 per cent. Musalmāns, while there were 333 Christians and 118 Jains. The town contains the usual public buildings consisting of the criminal, revenue and civil courts, central jail, arts college, dispensary with 70 beds, Lady Dufferin hospital and a new Victoria Memorial hospital, a hideously ugly building. The jail has accommodation for 1,964 prisoners and the chief industries carried on are the manufacture of blankets and carpets, cane work, furniture making, carving, oil pressing, grain grinding and rope making.

Cerebro-spinal fever has been practically endemic in the central jail since 1897: outbursts occur at varying intervals. The disease appears to be commonest among prisoners employed on dusty forms of labour, in the garden and on road making.

The Jubilee college, built by Babu Tez Nārāyan Singh, a zamīndār of the town in 1887, was raised to a first grade arts college in 1890. The college has a fine building and a strong staff of professors; a boarding house is attached to it. A fuller account of this college is given in Chapter XIII—Education.

Bhāgalpur was constituted a municipality in 1864, and the board now consists of 22 commissioners, of whom 14 are elected. The chairman is not an official for some years past. The area within municipal limits is 9 square miles. Details of the financial position of the municipality are given in Chapter XII—Local Self-Government. The town is a very healthy one with a natural system of drainage and a filtered water-supply, which was extended in 1896-97 to the suburbs of Nāthnagar and Champānagar, a loan of 3 lakhs being taken from Government for the purpose.

Birpur is a village in *parganā* Dhaphar in 26° 31′ 30″ N. lat. and 87° 2′ 36″ E. long., on the Nepāl frontier, with a population of about 3,630 souls. The trade here was formerly very brisk, but it is fast losing its importance owing to the village being abandoned by merchants, who fear that further inroads of the Kosi may carry away their store-houses.

Colgong (Kahalgaon).—A town situated on the south bank of the Ganges in 25°16′N., and 87°14′E. Population (1901) 5,738. Colgong is a station on the East Indian Railway 245 miles from Calcutta and of some commercial importance. Mahmud Shāh, the last independent King of Bengal, died here in 1539 after the sack of Gaur. There is a rock temple of peculiar style which formerly contained several fine specimens of sculpture, and the place appears to have been visited by the Chinese pilgrim Hiuen Tsiang. In later times it was notorious as the resort of thugs.

Colgong was constituted a municipality in 1869, and the municipal board consists of 11 commissioners nominated by Government. The area within municipal limits is 0·6 square mile.

Dumrāon lies a mile north of the village of Umarpur: the remains of an old fort of Debī Rājā exist there. It was about a mile or more in circumference, and consisted entirely of a wall of mud surrounded by a deep ditch. The only approaches to the fort were by seven large gates, some of which are still to be seen. The wall near these gates is tolerably high, but in most places it is scarcely more than two or three feet above the ground, while at some points it has entirely disappeared. It was within this fort that the last Kshetaurī Rājā fell fighting for independence against the Muhammadan invaders Tradition relates that, being besieged and finding himself unequal to the contest, he resolved to abandon his capital and fled at night with the little band of his remaining followers. A washerwoman who was with child could not run as fast as the soldiers wished. One of the latter, observing her condition, sneeringly enquired who told her to bring herself to that pass; she replied: "The Rājā told me to do so, but had I known he would, like a coward, desert his capital, I should not have been what I am." This speech was reported to the Rājā, who, ashamed of his cowardice, immediately returned with his troops and contested, at fearful odds, every inch of ground till every man was killed.

Ghazipita is in thana Kishangunge and is about 16 miles to the south of Madhipura town. It is situated on the Local Board road from Bangaon to Shahmora. It is contiguous to Basantpur, a little on the south of it. There is a Chandisthan here which is called "Barantpur temple." The idol of Chandi devi is inside the temple and the idol of Budhai, who is said to have been of Dosadh caste and a servant of Chandi, is outside the temple. The puja is first made to Budhai and then to Chandi. Goats and buffaloes are sacrificed as offerings to the goddess Chandi. The Pandas who are goalas by caste and are called "debhara" sometimes drink up the blood of the sacrificed animals. Every Tuesday and the 10 days of Dasahara are considered auspicious days for making these sacrifices. There is a legend that a Musulmān king, named Ali Khan, who had his fort about one mile north of the temple and ruins of which are still known as "Aligarh," wanted to marry Chandi Devi. The goddess consented to marry Ali Khan if he could sacrifice a goat at every step when coming to the temple and reach there before daybreak. Ali Khan accepted the condition and acted as told by the goddess. When he arrived close to the temple and it was before daybreak the goddess was alarmed for fear of being compelled to have to marry Ali Khan and ordered her servant Budhai to crow as a cock. Budhai did accordingly, and Ali Khan was deceived into thinking that the night had ended and so he returned to his fort disappointed. When on arrival there he discovered the trick, it was too late to return to the temple. For this meritorious act Budhai was made a god and is worshipped in priority of the goddess herself.

Jahangīrā.—Island in the Ganges situated in the Bhagalpur district in 25° 15′ N. and 86° 44′ E. It contains a lingam temple and several interesting rock sculptures fully described in Chapter II—History.

Kahalgāon —See COLGONG.

Karanāgarh.—Hill or more properly plateau near Bhagalpur town, Bhagalpur district, Bengal in 25° 15′ N. and 86° 56′ E., said to derive its name from Karna, a pious Hindu king of olden times, and the plateau, which is locally known as the kilā or fort is believed to be the site of one of the historical and famous pre-Buddhist forts in Bengal. Several bastions and the ditch in the west can still be made out. In modern times it formerly contained the lines of the Hill Rangers, a body of troops raised from among the hill people by Mr. Augustus Cleveland, Collector of the district, in 1780, for the pacification of the lawless jungle tribes. The corps was disbanded in 1863 on the reorganization of the native army. For some time afterwards it was held by a wing of a native regiment, but Bhagalpur has long since ceased to be a cantonment.

The only objects of interest are Sivāite temples of some celebrity. These consist of four buildings (maths), with square bases and the usual pointed pinnacles. One is several hundred years old, the others being modern buildings. Numbers of Hindus, though not usually worshippers of Siva, pay their devotions here on the last day of the month of Kārtik. The temples contain several of the so-called seats of Mahādev or Siva, one much prized being made of stone from the Nerbudda said to have come from the marble rocks near Jubbulpur. Two monuments are here erected to the memory of Mr. Cleveland—one by Government and the other by the landholders of the district. The Bidyāsāgar memorial Sanskrit tol occupies a fine building in the fort compound.

The following account of Karnāgarh is taken from Dr. Buchanan-Hamilton :—"The ruin is exactly in the same style with that in Purniah which is said to have been the house of Kichak, contemporary with the Karnā Rājā, to whom this work is attributed; that is, it consists of a square rampart, without works, but surrounded by a ditch. There is no cavity within the rampart; the ruins have been sufficient to fill up the whole space, which is still very high. The troops are now cantoned on the ruins, which are finely adapted for the purpose, as they are dry, level and of abundant extent, both for quarters and for a parade." The people in the vicinity pretend that this Karnā was the half-brother of Yudhishthirā by the mother's side, and the style of the ruin is rather favourable to their opinion. This opinion is also adopted by Major Wilford, in his account of the Kings of Magadhā; where he mentions that this person, taking part with Jarasandha, the opponent of his brother, was rewarded with a small kingdom, called after his own name Karnadesh, which long continued to be enjoyed by his descendants. In one place Major Wilford mentions this kingdom as coinciding with the present area of Bhagalpur district; but in others it is considered as the same with the Angā, or the western parts of Bīrbhum. "Perhaps the kingdom of Karnā may have included both territories. All the Brāhmans of the district, however, that I have consulted concerning this Karnā Rājā, disallow the idea of his being the contemporary of Yudhishthirā, and consider him as a prince who attempted to seize on the throne of Vikram. As, however, there have been many Vikrams and many Karnās, all usually confounded together by the Brāhmans, I shall not pretend to determine the discordant opinions. I need only remark that the princes of Champā named Karnā were, in all probability, of the Jain religion, as Vasupujyā, the twelfth great teacher of that school, was born at their capital, and as the monuments of that religion are the only ones of note in the vicinity. It must, however, be allowed that on the ruin at Karnāgarh there are two small temples, one of Siva and one of Parvatī—two deities of the Brāhmans—each of which is provided with a *pujāri* of the sacred tribe. Those in the vicinity, although still tolerably entire, are attributed to Karnā. Even allowing to this all due weight, the opinion of the heterodoxy of Karnā, which I have mentioned, need not be relinquished, as the Jains admit not only of the existence, but also of the worship of all the Hindu *debatās*."

Khandauli is a village in *parganá* Nārīdigar, situated in 26° 26′ 58″ N. lat. and 86° 49′ 6″ E. long., within a short distance of the Nepāl frontier. A large *hāt* or market is held there twice a week, and though the population is small, it is considered one of the most flourishing trading places in the north of Bhāgalpur. It largely exports rice, oilseeds and *maruá*, and in favourable seasons is a centre for imports from Nepāl.

Kishanganj.—It was formerly the headquarters of Thana Kishanganj, but owing to the encroachments of the river Kosi, the police station has been removed to a village Puraince about 6 miles to the south. It is situated on the District Board road from Lattipur to Madhipura. It is about 20 miles to the south of Madhipura. There is a small bazar at the village the trade of which is mainly of a retail character. There is a post office and a dispensary, the latter maintained by the District Board. Formerly there was a Munsif's court here, which has now been removed to Madhipura. There is also a dāk bungalow at Kishanganj. The overflow of the Kosi water into the village has been gradually ceasing during the last few years and it is now practically out of danger from inundation. The chief castes in the village are the Banias in the bazar and Brāhmans, Koeris and Goalas in the surrounding hamlets. Population 2,047. The exports and imports are not so large as those of Mūrlīganj, as the trade is mainly of a retail character. The bāzārs both of Mūrlīganj and Kishanganj were originated by merchants who formerly lived at the Nāthpur bāzār in the Supaul subdivision, which, owing to the encroachments of the Kūsī, has now been almost entirely abandoned.

Madheli.—In Thana Madhipurā, is about 10 miles from Madhipura, to the north-east. It is situated on the Local Board road from Chaora to Madheli. The river Daroswari flows a little off to the east of it. The village is situated on a piece of high land and is not liable to floods as are the surrounding tracts. There is a mart where some Marwari traders and Kalwars deal in grains, ghee, jute, etc., which they occasionally export to Sahebgunge and Calcutta both by country boat down the Dareswari and by rail through Raghopur, Bengal and North-Western Railway. The Marwaris import cloths, Liverpool salt, spices, sugar, iron, etc., from Calcutta. To the south-east of Madheli is Basantpur, which contains the ruins of a fort said to have belonged to the Rājās Shit and Basant. Population of Madheli 1,953 souls.

Madhipurā.—Headquarters village of the subdivision of the same name, Bhāgalpur district, Bengal, situated on the right bank of the Parwān river, about 52 miles from Bhagalpur town, in 25° 56′ N. and 86° 48′ E. Population (1901) 5,188. The neighbourhood is associated with the popular ballad of Lurik, the deified cowherd, given in Chapter III. The village contains the subdivisional offices, and a sub-jail with accommodation for 15 prisoners.

Maheshi.—Is in thana Bongaon, about 21 miles from Madhipurā to the west. It is situated on a District Board road. The river Dhimra flows to the east of it. The village appertains to the zamīndārī of the Maharaja of Darbhanga and is mostly inhabited by Brāhmins. It is said that Bashistho Mani used to perform his religious devotions at this village. There is a temple of Ugra Tara Devi where, during the ten days of Dasahara and in the Kali Puja time, buffaloes and goats are sacrificed as offerings to the goddess. The place is considered as one of the 24 " Upa pithas " of Devi Bhagabat. It is said that when Mahadeo was wandering about with the dead body of his wife Bhagabati on his shoulder, the god Vishnu, being afraid that the creation might be thereby destroyed, began to cut away the dead body of Bhagabati with his weapon "Shudershun Chakra." It is said that the pieces of the principal limbs of Bhagabati fell to earth in 52 places and became places of pilgirimage known as " Pitha Sthan" of Bhagabati, pieces of the minor limbs of Bhagabati fell down in 24 places, and these became sacred places as " Upa Pitha Sthan."

Mandār Giri Hill.—This hill is about 700 feet high and is situated about 30 miles south of the town of Bhagalpur, in 24° 50′ N. and 87° 4′ E. The hill, which consists of a huge mass of granite overgrown near the summit with low jungle, is very sacred in Hindu mythology; the sacred places are described in the Mandar Māhātma, a portion of the Skanda Purān. The oldest buildings are two temples now in a ruin near the top of the hill, approached by steps hewn out of the rock. These are attributed to Rājā Chhatra Sen of the Chol tribe, who lived before the time of the Muhammadans. There are two inscriptions and some rude carvings on the rock, and numerous small artificial tanks have been cut in the side of the hill. The largest of these, known as the Sītā Kund tank, is 100 feet long by 500 feet wide and is situated in front of the ruins of the oldest temple at a level of 500 feet above the surrounding plain. A detailed description is given in Chapter II—History.

Murliganj.—In Thana Madhipurā, is about 13 miles to the east of Madhipurā. It is the terminus of the District Board road from Madhipurā to Murliganj, and Murliganj is situated on the right bank of the river Daus which is now virtually the main Kosi. The place was once an important centre of trade; some Marwaris who have their headquarters at Azimgunge (Murshidabad) and in district Shahabad carry on brisk trade in paddy, linseed, oilseed, ghee, cotton, coarse saltpetre, etc., which they export to Calcutta, Sahebgunge, Murshidabad and other places, in country boats down the river Kosi and the Ganges. They import cloth, Liverpool salt, spices, sugar, iron and fine rice from Calcutta and other places. For the last few years the trade of the village has considerably declined owing to the flowing of a channel of the Kosi right into the village. The village appertains to the Sonbersa Ràj. Population 3,934 souls.

Panchgachia, from which the estate derives its name, is in Thana Bangaon and is situated on the District Board road from Bhaptiahi to Bulhi. It is about 18 miles to the west of Madhipurā. The Mansi-Bhaptiahi extension of the Bengal and North-Western Railway has got a station called Panchgachia, which is about 2 miles to the east of the village.

Babu Priabarat Narain Singh of Panchgachia is the principal proprietor of the estate, owning about 12½ annas share of it, while Babus Chummun Singh, Kedar Narain Singh and Bacha Singh of Panchgachia own the remaining 3½ annas in equal shares. The family traces its origin from Rājā Vikramaditta the Great, of Ujjaini, and belongs to the Gandhwaria clan of the Pramara branch of the Rajputs. It is said that one of Vikramaditta's descendants, Prithi Raj Singh, migrated from Dhar in Malwa and settled down at Garh Gandhwar in Tirhoot. From Garh Gandhwar his descendants are known as Gandhwaria Rajputs. Pakhesh Singh, one of the descendants of Prithi Raj Singh left Garh Gandhwar to his brother Lakhesh Singh and migrated to Kapranti in North Bhagalpur. The descendants of Lakhesh Singh acquired extensive territories in Tirhoot and North Bhagalpur. One of them, namely Keshri Singh, is said to have obtained the *sanad* and title of Rājā from the Emperor of Delhi. It is said that the Rājā of Mithila, a predecessor of the present Maharaja of Darbhanga, refused to recognize the Rajship conferred upon Keshri Singh and hence it is said there was a sanguinary battle between the parties. At last they came to terms and the Tiljuga river was fixed as the boundary between the dominions of the Gandhwarias and those of the Mithila Rāj.

These Gandhwarias are scattered over all Tirhoot and North Bhagalpur. The families of Sonbersa, Shahpur, Durgapur, Baraoari, Sukhpur, Barail, Parsarma, Judia, Maugunje, Kapsia, Dhabouli, etc., all belong to it.

Sardar Singh, one of the descendants of Lakhesh Singh, settled down in the vicinity of Panchgachia, and was the ancestor of the present owners of the Panchgachia estate. Ruder Narain Singh, father of the present zamīndār Babu Priobarat Narain Singh, obtained the title of Rai Bahadur for his good services at the famine of 1281 F. S. He incurred heavy debts for his large acts of charity and died leaving a minor son, namely Babu Priobarat Narain Singh. The management of his share in the estate was taken up by the Court of Wards.

The rent-roll of the entire estate is said to be about one lakh of rupees and Government revenue with cesses amounts to about Rs. 6,000. Its area is said to be about 75 square miles.

Pathargh̄ātā Hill.—Hill in the Bhāgalpur district, Bengal, situated on the banks of the Ganges in 25°17′ and 25°22′ N. and 87°12′ and 87°16′ E. On the northern side of the hill are some rock sculptures dating prior to the 7th or 8th century A. D. They are known as the chaurasi munni (84 sages) but are supposed to represent scenes from the adventures of Krishna and Rām. The hill also contains five caves, in the most important of which, the Bateswar cave, bronze and silver relics have been discovered.

Pīrpāintī.—Village in Bhagalpur district, Bengal, and a station on the East Indian Railway in 25° 18′ N., and 87° 25′ E. Population (1901) 2,741. There is a considerable export of country produce. Stone is quarried in the neighbourhood.

Pratapganj, a village in *parganā* Harāwat, is situated about six miles from the site of the old thānā of Nāthpur, which has long since been swept away by the westerly advance of the river Kūsī. It has a police station and a mart of considerable importance. The trade carried on is mostly in grain, cotton and oil-seeds.

Sarsendi.—A village in Madhipurā subdivision, about which many legends are current.

There is a mosque in ruins about a mile to the south-east of village Sarsendi, which is said to be more than 500 years old. The mosque was situated about the centre of a plot of land 400 feet or so square, raised above the level of the surrounding fields. The *Ajan*, or place for calling the "faithful," is still visible. About 50 years ago mango-trees were planted in lines on the raised plot of land which now afford an excellent shade. On special days Muhammadans from surrounding villages attend the place for their prayers. No inscription nor other indication of the age of the mosque has been found.

About half-a-mile to the north of the mosque is a mound about 120 square feet in area, said to have been the *garh* (fort) of Rājā Bairisal, who is said to have been the head of the Ganbharia Rajputs, who originally came and settled in this part of the country. The surface of the mound is about 12 feet above ground level and apparently the mound has gradually been cut away on three sides and levelled for cultivation. The tradition current in the neighbourhood is that Rājā Bairisal (*Bairi* means an enemy and *Sal*, a conqueror) was a very rich man and had a boat containing gold and silver coins embedded in the mound, and two old palm trees about 100 feet apart are pointed out as the transformed sentries who kept watch at the two ends of the boat. It is further believed that the coins come out in dark nights to get an airing and the chinking of the coins has often been heard by the villagers. It is not unlikely that the noise made by the quills of the porcupines that burrow in the mound was mistaken for chinking of coins.

About 75 feet to the east of the mound is a deep tank with a covering of vegetation thick enough to enable people to cross over the surface of the tank with little or no difficulty.

There is another mound $100' \times 60'$ to the south-west of the other mound, said to have been the prison house of the Rājā, whose powers were unlimited in those days.

A legend is current in the neighbourhood that two faquir-cultivators, Shah Sherul Mulk and Shah Sadul Mulk, brothers, came and settled in the time of the Rājā of Bairisal. They lived like other peaceful cultivators and occasionally did *begar* or compulsory service for the Rājā. They would often carry a greater quantity of sheaves of paddy from the fields to the Rāj *khalian* by night than a hundred men could do in a day. One day, while the brothers were busy with their prayers, a peon of the Rājā came to call them. They refused. The Rājā sent more men to exact obedience. The brothers took their *khurpis* and, attaching them to ropes, began to whirl them round. The heads of the peons began to fall about as soon as the extraordinary *khurpis* touched them, and the news was conveyed to the Rājā who sent all his available force to kill the brothers. The carnage was terrible, all sharing the fate of the first batch of the peons. The *khurpis* did their work wonderfully well, so much so that 12 punsaries (a punsari = 5 seers) or 1½ maund of *janow* (holy thread) were collected by the brothers from the slain Rajputs and sent to the Emperor at Delhi. Rājā Bairisal, to save himself from conversion to the Islam faith, gave his sister Dai Thakurani to Sadul Mulk in marriage. Subsequently years after, so the story goes, the brothers allowed themselves to be killed and the lady breathed her last on her dead husband's breast. It is alleged that Ganbharia Rajputs still sacrifice fowls in memory of Dai Thakurani before each marriage.

It is reported that silver coins, equivalent in weight to 6 annas of current silver coins, of Rājā Bairisal's hoard have been picked up by ploughmen in the neighbourhood.

The tomb of Dai Thakurani is still pointed out. The tomb is in ruins; on the surrounding walls many remnants of earthen horses and elephants are seen. Seven separate graves indicated by roughly set bricks were found in the enclosure. Beginning from west they were alleged to be of—

(1) Sherul Mulk.
(2) Sadul Mulk.
(3) Dewan Anwar, son of (1) or (2).
(4) Wife of (1).
(5) Wife of (2).
(6) Daughter of (1) or (2).
(7) Daí Thakurani.

It is not known whose Dewan No. 3 was. The allegations that the brothers allowed themselves to be killed subsequently and the graves of the whole family would lead one to believe a different version of the fight between Bairisal and the faquir brothers. Probably the so-called marriage of Dai Thakurani with Sadul Mulk had much to do with the fight and the graves of the whole family indicate the result.

Shahpurchaomukh.—In thana Kishangunge, is about 14 miles from Madhipurā to the south-east, and is situated on the District Board road from Madhipurā to Lattipur. Nothing of archæological interest could be found at Shahpur. At Lohund (Lohur), which is contiguous to Shahpur, a little to the south, there is a shrine of "Lachhmi Narayan" which consists of a block of black stone (one-half of the original block, which perhaps being too heavy for conveyance had been divided into two pieces) with carved statues of Mahadeo (with serpent), Kalika Devi (with 4 hands and a bead of human heads round her neck) and some other Hindu gods and goddesses. This shrine, which is under an ancient banian tree, is held in great reverence by the Hindus of the surrounding villages who resort there for prayers and offerings at the time of epidemics, drought and other calamities.

Singheswarthan, in *parganā* Nīsankpur Kūrhā, in N. lat. 25° 58′ 48″ and E. long. 86° 50′ 31″, four miles north of Madhipurā, is in itself a small and poor village, but is well known in Bihar for being the scene of the best elephant fair north of the Ganges with the possible exception of Sonpur Fair (Saran district). This fair is held in the month of January and is attended by people from Purnea, Bihar generally, and the neighbouring parts of Nepal. Elephants are brought from various parts of India. Native shoes, English cloth, horses and many of the usual articles seen at fairs are also exposed for sale. The Nepālīs bring their curved knives or *kukris*, and shoes made of undressed skin. There is a temple in the village containing a *linga*, which is believed to have the power of causing barren women, who pray and make offerings at the shrine, to conceive. The land on which it is built is said to have belonged at one time to the Bhars, who gave it to the Pāndes, on condition that they should receive a portion of the offerings annually; but on the decline of the Bhar power the Pāndes refused to carry out their engagement, and are now the sole proprietors of the temple and its lands.

Sonbursa, in North Bhagalpur, is about 14 miles west of Kishanganj Thana and 19 miles south of Madhipura subdivisional town. It is situated on a District Board road, and is at the extreme boundary of the Bhagalpur district, verging on the District of Monghyr on the other side of river Tilawe. The nearest railway station is Salkhua, a station on the Mansi-Bhaptiahi extension of the Bengal and North-Western Railway.

This family traces its descent from Rājā Bikramadatia and belongs to the Agni branch of Kshatriya. One of his descendants is said to have migrated from Malwa and settled at Mithila. This information, however, is, unlike what follows, more or less legendary. Maharaja Nil Deb, who is the 22nd predecessor of the late Maharaja Bahadur Sir Hurbullub Narain Singh, K.C.I.E., seems to have been the founder of the Rāj at Mithila. In 1654 A. D., the Emperor Aurungzeb bestowed the title of Rājā, as also the zamīndāri of Narsinghpur upon Rājā Kesri Singh who was a predecessor of the Sonbursa House. Rājā Amar Singh, the seventh predecessor of the late Maharaja, built a fort at Sihaul which is still known. Rājā Fateh Singh, the fourth predecessor, is said to have sided with the British Government against Mir Kasim in the battle of Udainala.

After the murder of the late Maharaja Bahadur Sir Hurbullub Narain Singh, K.C.I.E., in 1907 (he died from the effects of a gun-shot wound), his two widows, Maharanee Tarabati Kumari and Maharanee Naulakh Kumari, became the joint owners of the estate and the management of the estate was taken up by the Court of Wards.

The area of the estate is about 72,570 bighas or 23,990 acres. The rent-roll amounts to a little more than two lakhs and the revenue payable to Government including cesses is Rs. 24,324-11-3. The ancient Sonbursa palace was not a building of any note. The late Maharaja Sir Hurbullub Narain Singh, however, built a new palace which is of considerable architectural beauty.

Srinagar in thana Madhipurā, is about 10 miles to the north-west of Madhipurā town. The village is situated in the

Panchgachia Estate. There are remains of 2 forts at the village and of one "devali." It is said that Rājā Sri Deve used to live here. He had 2 brothers, Bijal Deve and Kup Deve. The former had his fort at Bijalgarh or Bijalpur and the latter at Kupgarh, both in Thana Bongaon. There are 2 large tanks on the west and south-west of the fort ruins at Srinagar. One of them is called "Harsar" and is said to have been excavated with ploughshares and the other is called "Gupa."

In the Devalai there is a Siva "linga" and stone pillars with faint signs of inscriptions which could not be deciphered. One broken stone door frame has the following inscription in Kaithi character "Magaradhaja" Jogi 100. The inscription is quite legible and it is doubtful whether it is so old as it purports to be, though it is not clear what era was meant by 100. Population 1,027 souls.

Sultānganj.—Village in Bhāgalpur district, Bengal, situated close to the Ganges, near a railway station of the same name, in 25° 15′ N. and 86° 45′ E. Population (1901) 4,410. Sultānganj is conspicuous for two great rocks of granite, one of which on the river bank is crowned by a Musalmān mosque. The second and larger one is occupied by a temple of Ghāibnāth Siva, and is a place of great holiness in the eyes of Hindus, and few persons of position pass the place without making offerings to the idol. The river here impinges on a stone cliff and this is believed to be the scene of the loves of the river nymph and the god Siva. Close to the railway station are extensive remains of Buddhist monasteries, where a number of figures have been exhumed, and near by is a fine old stupa. Served as it is by rail and river the town is a flourishing mart.

The tradition runs that a devotee or Sanyāsī named Hārīnāth, who had forsaken the pleasures of the world, dwelt here at one time. He used, at vast trouble, to make pilgrimages to the shrine of Baidyanāth, near Deogarh; until, at length, the god informed him in a dream that he would have no further occasion to go so far, as on his return to the island rock he would find an image there to which he might address his prayers. He found the promised idol awaiting him at Sultānganj, and, founding a convent of devotees, he became its first *mahant* or abbot. This could not have occurred at a very remote period, as Digambar, the *mahant* in Dr. Buchanan-Hamilton's time, stated that he was the thirteenth who had enjoyed that dignity, to which no young man can hope to aspire. The place does not seem to have risen into great reputation until lately as Ananta, the *mahant* at the beginning of the last century, is said to have erected most of the buildings that now exist. Almost everyone who comes to bathe at Sultānganj visits the temple, and carries up a vessel of water to pour over the image. In order to render the ceremony more efficacious, some of the worshippers carry the water to the summit of the spire and dash it from thence. The *mahant* acknowledges no *guru* or superior. In the rainy season the community have little communication with the mainland, the stream at that season rushing past with great violence ; but during the fair weather a large number of the neighbouring Hindus receive instruction there. Almost every Hindu of position who passes up or down the river in fair weather makes offering here.

Supaul.—Headquarters village of the subdivision of the same name, Bhagalpur district, Bengal, situated in 26° 6′ N. and 86° 36′ E. Population (1901) 3,101. The village, which is an important mart, contains the subdivisional offices and sub-jail with accommodation for 18 prisoners.

Umarpur, a village situated in 25° 2′ 23″ N. lat. and 86° 57′ 0″ E. long., in *parganā* Bhagalpur, is one of the chief collecting centres for the rice and Indian-corn trade in the south of the district, and exports much of these grains by way of Monghyr and Sultānganj. It contains a large *dighi* or tank with a mosque on its bank, which is generally ascribed to Prince Shāh Shujā. The tank is about 1,300 feet in length and 700 feet wide. The mosque, which, in the language of the peasantry, was as high as the tallest palm tree, was pulled down by a neighbouring zamīndār for the sake of some hidden treasure it concealed, but which no one dared to touch on account of a prophecy, that the offender, if a Hindu, would eat beef, and if a Muhammadan, was to partake of pork. For seven days and nights, so runs the legend, the treasure, consisting of gold and silver coin, was carried away in carts. The zamīndār was formerly one of the greatest and richest men in the subdivision, but the moment the hidden wealth was dug up in spite of the solemn injunction, the ghost of its original owner haunted him day and night. He prospered in nothing he undertook ; he became almost insane ; his wealth disappeared, no one knew how ; his estates were sold ; and at last he died a ruined man.

INDEX.

N

O.

P.

R.

S.

S

T.

U.

V.

W.

Z.

B. S. Press— 12-5-1911—2070J—541—G. A.